The Date of the Muratorian Fragment:
An Inference to the Best Explanation

The Date of the Muratorian Fragment: An Inference to the Best Explanation

John F. Lingelbach

An Imprint of the
Global Center for Religious Research
1312 17th Street • Suite 549
Denver, Colorado 80202

info@gcrr.org • gcrr.org

GCRR Press
An imprint of the Global Center for Religious Research
1312 17th Street Suite 549
Denver, CO 80202
www.gcrr.org

Copyright © 2020 by John F. Lingelbach

DOI: 10.33929/GCRRPress.JFL20201203

All rights reserved. No part of this publication may be reproduced, stored in a retrieval system, or transmitted in any form or by any means, electronic, mechanical, photocopying, recording, or otherwise, without the prior permission of GCRR Press. For permissions, contact: info@gcrr.org.

Typesetting: Erika Spong
Copyediting: Valerie Costa

Library of Congress Cataloging-in-Publication Data

The date of the muratorian fragment : an inference to the best explanation / John F. Lingelbach
p. cm.
Includes bibliographic references.
ISBN (Paperback): 978-1-7362739-9-9
ISBN (eBook): 978-1-7362739-8-2
1. Muratorian fragment.   2. Bible. N.T.—Canon.   I. Title.

BR 60-67   .L564   2020

For Cora

Contents

Abbreviations   viii

Acknowledgments   ix

Introduction   1

        A Problem   1
        Review of the Related Literature   6
        The Present Study   21
        Summary   25

1   The Muratorian Fragment   26

        Description   26
        Content   37
        Authorship   39
        Provenance   40
        Language   42
        Summary   44

2   A Date: The Evidence   45

        The Evidence   45
        Summary   72

3   A Date: The Hypotheses   73

        The Early Hypothesis   73
        The Late Hypothesis   84
        The Treatment of Texts   91
        Summary   95

4   Weighing the Hypotheses   97

        The Early Hypothesis   97
        The Late Hypothesis   109
        The Findings: A "Winner"   120

5   The Chronological Fiction Argument   122

        The Argument   122

Conclusion   139

        Recapitulation   139
        A Plausible Interpretive Scenario   141
        Implications for Historical Study
        of the New Testament Canon   142
        Further Research   145

Appendix A: The Original Latin Fragment   146

Appendix B: The Restored Latin Fragment   149

Appendix C: English Translation of the Fragment   152

Bibliography   155

Abbreviations

ANF   *Ante-Nicene Fathers*

EH   *Ecclesiastical History*

Epiph.   Epiphanius

Euseb.   Eusebius

Jer.   Jerome

Justin   Justin Martyr

NPNF   *Nicene and Post-Nicene Fathers*

PG   *Patrologia Graeca*

Tert.   Tertullian

Acknowledgments

No man is an island. This work originally took the form of my doctoral dissertation which was conducted under the expert and wise mentorship of my committee chairperson, Dr. Ken Cleaver at Liberty University. Ken, I deeply appreciate your love for God, your family, and your students. You made me see what really matters in Christianity. Thank you for helping me through the dissertation process and your patience when you did not think that I would actually ever send you the entire thing ... done. I am also profoundly grateful for the sage advice of my two doctoral readers, Drs. Doug Taylor and Ben Laird, who gave me many nuggets of wisdom through their suggestions that have only served to make my work all the better.

Furthermore, one of my PhD classmates was Dr. Darren Slade, who in short order became my friend during those days at Liberty. Darren always had a knack for asking the tough questions of the professors and of me. His questions have served as a driving force pushing me to reasonably articulate my faith. Whereas 2 Peter commands Christians to give a reason for their hope, Darren compelled me to do so through his questions. This work would not have seen the light of day if it had not been for his unwavering encouragement. I appreciate him, his professionalism, and especially his loyal friendship.

Finally, I have to thank my wife for the joy she finds in having a husband who is an author. Her excitement at the prospect was at times the only thing that kept me going through what can be on some days an onerous yet highly worthy process. She often tells me that the best things in life cost.

Introduction

A Problem

Statement of the Problem

Three hundred years after its discovery, scholars find themselves unable to identify the more likely of the two hypotheses regarding the date of the Muratorian Fragment, whether it is a late second- to early third-century composition or a fourth-century composition.

Background of the Problem

In the year 1700, in the Bibliotheca Ambrosiana of Milan, philologist and historian Ludovico Antonio Muratori (1672–1750) discovered a manuscript fragment of eighty-five lines identifying and describing several Christian texts.[1] During the two and one-quarter centuries following the publication of this "Muratorian" Fragment, most scholars believed that the author's reference to these texts constitutes the oldest orthodox catalog of New Testament texts, or canon, in existence, dating it to the late second or early third centuries.[2] In general, they inferred these dates from the Fragmentist's references to two data:

---

[1] In 1740, Muratori published the fragment in the third volume of a six-volume compilation of works entitled *Antiquitates italicæ mediiævi*, in *Dissertatio XLIII*. Ludovico Antonio Muratori, ed., *Antiquitates italicæ mediiævi: sive dissertations de moribus, ritibus, religione, regimine, magistratibus, legibus, studiis literarum, artibus, lingua, militia, nummis, principibus, libertate, servitute, foederibus, aliisque faciem & mores italici populi referentibus post declinationem Rom. imp. ad annum usque MD.* (Mediolanum, IT: Ex typographia Societatis palatinæ, 1740), cols. 3:853–54. The document is considered a "fragment" because it appears to be a copy of a text which begins mid-sentence.

[2] Eckhard J. Schnabel, "The Muratorian Fragment: The State of Research," *Journal of the Evangelical Theological Society* 57, no. 2 (2014): 231, 238–40. Though Marcion's list may predate the Muratorian Fragment's list, the church catholic did not consider him to be orthodox. See Tertullian, *Against Marcion* and Eusebius, *Ecclesiastical History* 4.

First, the Fragmentist states that the *Shepherd of Hermas* was written during his own lifetime and during the bishopric of Pius (ca. 140– ca. 154).[3] This suggests that the Fragmentist lived and wrote during or after this period.[4]

Second, the two heresies mentioned, Marcionism and Montanism (lines 65, 81–5), prevailed during the second century, so their mention indicates a possible composition date in the late second or early third century.[5] While initially only one scholar, Friedrich Zimmermann, disagreed with this hypothesis of a late second- or early third-century date, canon scholar B. F. Westcott, in his *General Survey of the History of the Canon of the New Testament*, dismissed Zimmermann's protest as unworthy of serious consideration.[6]

However, in the late 1960s and again in the early 1990s, two scholars argued extensively that the Fragment was a composition of the fourth century. First, New Testament scholar Albert C. Sundberg, Jr. cast doubt on the hypothesis of a second-century date by questioning the traditional interpretation of the evidence that led to that conclusion.[7] Instead, he looked to other evidence which he believed pointed less ambiguously toward the fourth century, and he argued for an eastern origin. Though the majority of canon scholars summarily dismissed Sundberg's conclusion, distinguished patristics scholar, Everett Ferguson, furnished a reasoned, extensive response to Sundberg, maintaining that the Fragment's evidence was better explained by the hypothesis that it was a second-century composition.[8] Later, Episcopalian priest, Geoffrey M. Hahneman, joined Sundberg in arguing that the Fragment was a composition of the fourth

---

[3] Muratorian Fragment, lines 73–76. From here throughout the paper, references to portions of the Muratorian Fragment will be noted parenthetically in-text. For the chronology of the bishops of Rome and the time of Pius's bishopric see Euseb., *Ecclesiastical History* 4.11; 5.6, 24.

[4] Schnabel, "The Muratorian Fragment," 240.

[5] Ibid.

[6] Friedrich Gottlieb Zimmermann, *Dissertatio historico-critica scriptoris incerti de canone librorum sacrorum fragmentum a Muratorio repertum exhibens* (Jena: Göpferdt, 1805), 33–39; Brooke Foss Westcott, *A General Survey of the History of the Canon of the New Testament*, 7th ed. (London: Macmillan, 1896), 216.

[7] Albert C. Sundberg, "Towards a Revised History of the NT Canon," in *Studia Evangelica*, vol. 3, *Papers Presented to the Third International Congress on NT Studies held at Christ Church, Oxford, 1965, Part 1, The NT Scriptures*, ed. Frank Leslie Cross (Berlin: Akademie-Verlag, 1968), 452–61; idem, "Canon Muratori: A Fourth-Century List," *Harvard Theological Review* 66, no. 1 (1973): 1–41.

[8] Everett Ferguson, "Canon Muratori: Date and Provenance," in *Studia Patristica*, vol. 19, ed. Elizabeth A. Livingstone (Oxford, UK: Pergamon, Press, 1982), 677–83.

century, and he also brought several new reasons to the debate.[9] Again, Ferguson weighed in on the issue by reviewing Hahneman's book and questioning several of the latter's assumptions.[10] Professor of New Testament, Joseph Verheyden, responded to Hahneman by highlighting the similarities between the Fragment and other known second-century texts, concluding that the Fragment could not be a fourth-century composition.[11]

Therefore, as the twentieth century closed, the question of the Fragment's date, which previously appeared to be settled since its discovery, hung in the balance. Sundberg and Hahneman had challenged the *status quo*, and Ferguson and Verheyden had questioned their assumptions. Both sides agreed on one thing: the debate appeared to be at a standstill. For example, Ferguson acknowledged the real complexity of what appeared to be an otherwise simple problem by highlighting the significant roles the evidence, coupled with one's presuppositions, plays. According to him, "The issue . . . is not clear cut, and the evidence is finely balanced. There needs to be caution exercised, moreover, about the framework in which this material is put."[12] In the wake of Sundberg's and Hahneman's work, canon scholar and fourth-century adherent Lee Martin McDonald conceded that "we cannot insist on" a fourth-century date.[13] It is for this reason that, while on one hand, professor of New Testament and early Christianity, Charles E. Hill believes "the stage is set for important work to be done in this area," on the other hand, professor of religious studies, Harry Y. Gamble, acknowledges that "it is hard to imagine what more could be said on either side."[14]

---

[9] Geoffrey M. Hahneman, "The Muratorian Fragment and the Development of the Canon," (D.Phil. thesis, University of Oxford, 1987); idem, "More on Redating the Muratorian Fragment," in *Studia Patristica*, vol. 19, ed. Elizabeth A. Livingstone (Leuven, BE: Peeters Press, 1989), 359–65; idem, *The Muratorian Fragment and the Development of the Canon* (Oxford, UK: Clarendon Press, 1992); idem, "The Muratorian Fragment and the Origins of the New Testament Canon," in *The Canon Debate*, eds. Lee M. McDonald and James A. Sanders (Grand Rapids: Baker Academic, 2002), 668–86.

[10] Everett Ferguson, review of *The Muratorian Fragment and the Development of the Canon*, Geoffrey M. Hahneman, *Journal of Theological Studies* 44, no. 2 (October 1993): 691–97.

[11] Joseph Verheyden, "The Canon Muratori: A Matter of Dispute," in *The Biblical Canons*, edited by J.-M. Auwers and H. J. De Jonge (Leuven: Leuven University Press, 2003), 487–556. For example, Verheyden notes that Clement of Alexandria and Origen, like the Fragmentist, knew of a Fourfold Gospel canon.

[12] Ferguson, review of *The Muratorian Fragment*, 697.

[13] Lee Martin McDonald, *The Biblical Canon: Its Origin, Transmission, and Authority* (Grand Rapids: Baker Academic, 2007), 693.

[14] Charles E. Hill, "The Debate Over the Muratorian Fragment and the Development of the Canon," *Westminster Theological Journal* 57, no. 2 (Fall 1995): 452; Harry Y. Gamble, "The New Testament Canon: Recent Research and the Status Quaestionis," in *The Canon Debate*, eds. Lee M. McDonald and James A. Sanders (Grand Rapids: Baker Academic, 2002), 442.

Nevertheless, in the twenty-first century another argument for a fourth-century date surfaced. In an article entitled "The Muratorian Fragment as Roman Fake," biblical scholar Clare K. Rothschild argued that the Fragment is a fictional piece, written in the fourth century in an attempt to link the standards of canonicity back to the second century by pretending to have been written then.[15] According to her, this forgery "betrays itself through anachronisms . . . clichés, and mistakes."[16] Like Sundberg and Hahneman, Rothschild favored the fourth-century theory but for altogether different reasons. Rothschild also cited several earlier scholars who seem to have come close to drawing similar conclusions.[17] First, in 1845, around the one hundredth anniversary of Muratori's publication of the Fragment, philologist and theologian H. W. J. Thiersch insinuated that the Fragment was a hoax; a production of the eighteenth century.[18] In addition, Westcott noticed that the Fragment appeared to constitute a compendium of several different sections, possibly written by more than one unknown person and edited together by the Fragmentist, yet Westcott still favored a second-century date.[19] Also, Rothschild cited Robert M. Grant in his review of Hahneman's book, acknowledging that, though the Fragment dates itself to the second century, it can only be a work of the fourth.[20] Thus, with two separate conclusions having been reached about the Fragment's date, each apparently carrying arguably equal weight, yet stemming from a variety of presuppositions, disparate evidence, and dissimilar reasons, Rothschild acknowledges that "today scholarship has reached an impasse."[21]

Significance of the Problem

The problem of whether the Muratorian Fragment is a late second- to early third-century or fourth-century composition warrants consideration because the elimination of one of the hypotheses will contribute to the resolution of other critical problems surrounding the document. For example, scholars still have not reached a consensus on who authored the Fragment. The list of possibilities manifests remarkable diversity, including the names of Papias,

---

[15] Clare K. Rothschild, "The Muratorian Fragment and Roman Fake," *Novum Testamentum* 60, no. 1 (2018): 55–82.

[16] Ibid., 59.

[17] Ibid., 60n13, 62, 79n122.

[18] H. W. J. Thiersch, *Versuch zur Herstellung des historischen Standpuncts für die Kritik der neutestamentlichen Schriften* (Erlangen, DE: Carl Heyder, 1845), 384–87, which contain endnote 7 for Ch. 16.

[19] Westcott, *A General Survey*, 223.

[20] Rothschild, "The Muratorian Fragment," 79n122; Robert M. Grant, review of *The Muratorian Fragment and the Development of the Canon*, Geoffrey M. Hahneman, *Church History* 64, no. 4 (December 1995): 639.

[21] Rothschild, "The Muratorian Fragment," 58.

Irenæus, Tertullian, Hippolytus, and Clement of Alexandria among others.[22] Furthermore, because of the recently suggested possibility that the Fragment is a fourth-century composition, the list of possible authors has now expanded to include the Cappadocian Fathers, Athanasius, Eusebius, Lactantius, and Hilary. Solving the problem of the Fragment's date would establish a *terminus a quo* and a *terminus ad quem*.

In other words, for example, if the Fragment proved to be a fourth-century composition, no author who died prior to ca. 300 could possibly have written it. The finding with regard to date thus narrows the pool of authors to a more manageable number of "more-likely" names. Scholars could then further narrow the list by comparing the possible authors with the Fragment's internal evidence to determine which authors are more likely to have written it. If, on the other hand, for example, the Fragment proved to be a second-century composition, Tertullian, while a possible author, might prove to be an unlikely author given the Fragment's apparent censure of Montanism.

Moreover, knowing the likely author leads to the resolutions of other questions, such as: in what language was the Fragment probably originally written, Latin or Greek? What is its provenance? What was its destination (if any)? What was the situation the author sought to address? The possible answers to each of these questions could be further narrowed by filtering them through the Fragment's internal evidence. While this process does not necessarily lead to certainty based on indisputable evidence, it does result in higher likelihood based on a preponderance of circumstantial evidence.

Furthermore, and finally, the answers to these questions lead to the solutions of problems of arguably greater import. If one could reasonably determine the most likely author, original language, provenance, destination, and situation, one might also be able to infer conclusions regarding the author's theology, including his theological method (theological sources, epistemology). In turn, understanding the theology driving the Fragment's composition leads to a greater comprehension of the factors driving the development of other supposed New Testament canonical lists (or *not* driving them, as the case may be). Also, the theology driving and controlling the compilation of these lists has remarkable implications for the historical development of ancient Christian theology as well as for the more momentous issue of what most scholars consider to be orthodox theology's interaction with heterodoxy.[23]

---

[22] For a list of some of the possible authors and the scholars who suggest them see Schnabel, "The Muratorian Fragment," 240.

[23] The traditional view of the very nature of early Christian theology has at times been challenged and reaffirmed by scholars. For examples see Walter Bauer, *Rechtgläubigkeit und Ketzerei im ältesten Christentum* (Tübingen, 1934) and Andreas J.

In the final analysis, answering the question of the Fragment's date may ultimately shed light on the residual effects of ancient orthodox theology's interaction with heterodoxy upon the twenty-first century, effects possibly having a direct correlation with the authority that Christianity ascribes to the texts which it currently includes in the New Testament. Coming to an understanding of which of these texts are the "right" ones is critical, for it is primarily from the New Testament that Christianity claims to derive its theology. As D. F. Strauss recognized, the problem of the New Testament canon may very well be Christian theology's Achilles's heel.[24]
This significance is not lost on scholars. For example, McDonald acknowledges that knowing whether or not the Fragment is a second- or fourth-century composition has a direct bearing on our understanding of "the concerns and criteria of the church . . . in establishing its canon of Scriptures."[25] For this reason, an understandably substantial corpus of literature related to this problem of the Fragment's date has emerged.

Review of the Related Literature

Muratori's hypothesis that the Fragment was written in 196 initially encountered some disagreement, but the vast majority of these disputations revolved around the late second or early third centuries as the period of composition. Every scholar seemed to have his particular year of preference, whether it be 170, or 196, or 220, or others. Nevertheless, for the most part, Muratori's hypothesis offered a good explanation for the evidence. That being said, the question is: how did the issue of the Fragment's date become such a controversy, expanding the possibilities from a sixty-year period (from ca. 160–220) to a 215-year period (from ca. 160–392)?[26] The following review of the related literature answers this question by tracing the manner in which scholars have tried to explain the available evidence.[27]

Köstenberger and Michael J. Kruger, *The Heresy of Orthodoxy: How Contemporary Culture's Fascination with Diversity Has Reshaped Our Understanding of Early Christianity* (Wheaton, IL: Crossway, 2010).

[24] D. F. Strauss, *Die christliche Glaubenslehre in ihrer geschichtlichen Entwicklung und im Kampfe mit der modernen Wissenschaft* (Tübingen: Osiander, 1840), 1:136.

[25] McDonald, *The Biblical Canon*, 694.

[26] Samuel Prideaux Tregelles, *Canon Muratorianus: The Earliest Catalogue of the Books of the New Testament* (Oxford: Cambridge, 1867), 64; Schnabel, "The Muratorian Fragment," 240; Hahneman, *The Muratorian Fragment*, 216.

[27] In addition to the literature treated in this review, other secondary literature on the Fragment's date which may be of interest to the reader includes Adolf von Harnack, "Das Muratorische Fragment," *Zeitschrift für Kirchengeschichte* 3 (1878): 595–99; J. B. Dunelm, "The Muratorian Fragment," *The Academy* 36, no. 907 (September 21, 1889): 186–88; Johannes Leipoldt, *Geschichte des neutestamentlichen Kanons: Erster Teil, Die Entstehung* (Leipzig: Hinrichs, 1907), 1.34–35n3; Johann Peter

Muratori, as its discoverer, was the first to suggest a date for his Fragment, and he argued that it was a second-century work. He did this by linking the Fragment's reference to the Cataphrygians with a controversy in which Roman priest Caius played a role by debating one Proclus, "who contended for the Phrygian heresy."[28] According to Photios of Constantinople, a Caius flourished around 196, and Muratori credited this Caius as the Fragment's author, supposing that he had written it that year.[29] In addition, Muratori reinforced his hypothesis with what he called "a stronger argument," namely the Fragmentist's claims that the *Shepherd of Hermas* was written "very recently in our time" and that Hermas was a

---

Kirsch, "Muratorian Canon," in *The Catholic Encyclopedia*, ed. C. G. Herbermann et al. (London: Caxton, 1911), 10:642; Carl Erbes, "Die Zeit des Muratorischen Fragments," *Zeitschrift für Kirchengeschichte* 35 (1914): 331–62; B. H. Streeter, *The Primitive Church* (London: Macmillan, 1929), 205; Nils Dahl, "Welche Ordnung der Paulusbriefe wird vom muratorischen Kanon vorausgesetzt?," *Zeitschrift für die neutestamentliche Wissenschaft* 52 (1961): 39–53; Hans von Campenhausen, *The Formation of the Christian Bible* (Philadelphia: Fortress Press, 1972), 242–62; Jerome D. Quinn, "P46, The Pauline Canon?," *The Catholic Biblical Quarterly* 36, no. 3 (July 1974): 379–85; Werner Georg Kümmel, *Einleitung in das Neue Testament*, 17th ed. (Heidelberg: Quelle und Meyer, 1975), 434–35; Raymond E. Brown, *The Epistles of John* (Garden City, NY: Doubleday, 1982), 10n14; William F. Farmer and Denis M. Farkasfalvy, *The Formation of the NT Canon: An Ecumenical Approach* (New York: Paulist, 1983), 60; Brevard S. Childs, *The NT as Canon: An Introduction* (Philadelphia: Fortress, 1984), 238; Denis M. Farkasfalvy, "The Ecclesial Setting of Pseudepigraphy in Second Peter and its Role in the Formation of the Canon," *The Second Century* 5, no. 1 (Spring, 1985–1986): 29n50; Bruce M. Metzger, *The Canon of the New Testament: Its Origin, Development, and Significance* (Oxford, UK: Clarendon Press, 1987), 191n3; Helmut Koester, *Ancient Christian Gospels: Their History and Development* (London: SCM, 1990), 243; Wilhelm Schneemelcher, "General Introduction," in *New Testament Apocrypha*, vol. 1, *Gospels and Related Writings*, ed. Wilhelm Schneemelcher, trans. R. McL. Wilson, rev. ed. (Louisville, KY: Westminster John Knox Press, 1991), 28, 72; Gregory A. Robbins, "Muratorian Fragment," in *Anchor Bible Dictionary* (New York: Doubleday, 1992), 4:929; Lee M. McDonald, *The Formation of the Christian Bible*, 2nd ed. (Peabody, MA: Hendrickson, 1995), 213–20; John Barton, *The Spirit and the Letter: Studies in the Biblical Canon* (London: SPCK, 1997) 10; John Barton, "Marcion Revisited," in *The Canon Debate*, 559–84; Theo K. Heckel, *Vom Evangelium des Markus zum viergestaltigen Evangelium* (Tübingen: Mohr Siebeck, 1999), 339–45; and Charles F. D. Moule, *The Birth of the NT* (London: Continuum, 2002), 260n; Edmon Gallagher and John Meade, *The Biblical Canon Lists from Early Christianity: Texts and Analysis* (New York: Oxford University Press, 2017), 175–83.

[28] Muratori, *Antiquitates italicæ mediiævi*, col. 3:851; Euseb., *Ecclesiastical History*. 6.20.3, in Philip Schaff and Henry Wace, eds., *The Nicene and Post-Nicene Fathers (NPNF)*, 14 vols., (1890–1900; repr., Peabody, MA: Hendrickson, 1995), 2:1:268.

[29] Muratori, *Antiquitates italicæ mediiævi*, col. 3:851.

contemporary of Pius.[30] These statements appear to establish a date in the second century.

However, in his *Dissertatio historico-critica scriptoris*, theologian Friedrich Gottlieb Zimmermann declared that he was not convinced that the Fragmentist's statement about Hermas and Pius was best explained by a second-century date because he doubted the veracity of the Fragmentist's claim that Hermas and Pius were brothers; a claim that he posited had never been verified. In addition, while Zimmermann agreed that Caius flourished around 196, he was not so quick to form a connection between the Fragmentist's Cataphrygian heresy and Caius's debate with Proclus. The link is not necessary as it is likely, in Zimmermann's opinion, that many would have agreed with Caius against the Cataphrygians, and the Fragmentist may simply have been one of them. Furthermore, and contrary to Muratori's hypothesis, Zimmermann concluded that the Fragmentist did not live before the fourth century because the Fragmentist's treatment of Christian texts (i.e. his approval of some and his rejection of others) betrayed, in his opinion, a fourth-century theological context.[31]

Other scholars' positions did not fall so neatly on one side of the line or the other. In *Einleitung in die Schriften des Neuen Testaments*, Johann Leonhard Hug disagreed with both Muratori and Zimmermann. He believed the Fragment to be an early third-century work, though he made no mention of the supposed relationship between Hermas and Pius, nor did he point back to Zimmermann's doubts about it.[32] Siding with Muratori, Karl August Credner (*Zur Geschichte des Kanons*) believed both Zimmermann's fourth-century date and Hug's third-century date to be impossibilities due to the evidence which, in his view, betrayed a Fragmentist who clearly placed himself in the second century. Credner maintained that the document was composed around 170, or "possibly a few decades later."[33] He cited the Fragmentist's mention of Hermas and Pius as evidence of this.[34]

Because of these disagreements, in his *Critical History of Christian Literature and Doctrine*, classics scholar James Donaldson understood that "we must content ourselves with an approximation to a date."[35] He

---

[30] Muratori, *Antiquitates italicæ mediiævi*, col. 3:852; the Latin for "very recently in our times" in the Latin is "nuperrime temporibus nostris."

[31] Zimmermann, *Dissertatio historico-critica scriptoris*, 33–34, 36–39.

[32] Johann Leonhard Hug, *Einleitung in die Schriften des Neuen Testaments*, 4th ed. (Stuttgart: Cotta, 1847), 1:105–8.

[33] Karl August Credner, *Zur Geschichte des Kanons* (Halle: Verlag der Buchhandlung des Waisenhauses, 1847), 84.

[34] Ibid.

[35] James Donaldson, *A Critical History of Christian Literature and Doctrine: From the Death of the Apostles to the Nicene Council*, vol. 3, *The Apologists (Continued)* (London, Macmillan, 1866), 212.

contented himself with the early third century. He preferred an approximation because he, like Zimmermann, did not believe the Fragmentist's reference to Hermas and Pius was well explained by the second-century hypothesis. The Fragment's mutilated condition, apparent omissions, the author's poor use of Latin, and the possibility of interpolations all detracted from any confidence one may have in establishing a date based on internal evidence. In addition, *nuperrime temporibus nostris* may not mean during the author's lifetime, but instead may have been the author's way of drawing a distinction between the times of the apostles and his own. Also, the expression "sitting in the seat of the church of the city of Rome" indicated a context more in line with that of Cyprian of Carthage (ca. 200–258) than with Tertullian (ca. 155–220), leading Donaldson to date the Fragment in the early third century.[36] Moreover, Donaldson denied the historicity of the person of Hermas, but he cited no reason for this departure from the hitherto held consensus that the putative author of *Shepherd* existed.

However, biblical scholar, textual critic, and theologian, Samuel Prideaux Tregelles (*Canon Muratorianus*), like Muratori and Credner, argued that the Fragment is as early as 160 due to the author's statement that Hermas had written his *Shepherd* "very recently in our time" while Pius was "sitting."[37] Tregelles did not believe that more than twenty years passed between the composition of *Shepherd* and the Fragment.[38]

On the other hand, though theologian George Salmon ("Muratorian Fragment" in *A Dictionary of Christian Biography, Literature, Sects and Doctrines*) did not consider the statement about Hermas and Pius to be conclusive, he determined that the Fragment was a late second- or early third-century composition. He argued that the Fragment was written during the bishopric of Zephyrinus (ca. 199–ca. 217). First, and in accord with Donaldson, Salmon believed the expression *temporibus nostris* did not necessitate a date within the speaker's lifetime, and Salmon cited Irenæus and Eusebius as having used similar expressions regarding events which clearly took place before their lifetimes. This possibility would allow for a case in which the Fragmentist may have been contrasting "our time" against the time of the apostles and not referring literally to a point in time during his own life. Against Tregelles, Salmon maintained that even if the Fragmentist wrote fifty or sixty years after the death of Pius, he could conceivably have used such an expression. Also against Tregelles, but in agreement with Donaldson, Salmon believed the Fragmentist's language, in

---

[36] Donaldson believes the Fragment to be of a North African provenance thus his reference to these two particular Fathers. The Latin for "sitting in the seat of the church of the city of Rome" is "sedente cathe tra urbis romae aeclesiae."

[37] "Sitting" is "sedente" in the Latin here.

[38] Tregelles, *Canon Muratorianus*, 64.

his assertion that the *Shepherd of Hermas* was written with Pius "sitting on the seat of the church of the city Rome," indicated a date after the time of Pius and Hermas. According to Salmon, the date of composition was so removed from their time that the writer probably had no recollection of the struggle for the bishopric of Rome that had taken place during the second century.[39] However, Salmon provided no evidence for such a contested See of Rome. Regardless, Salmon concluded that the Fragment was written at some time between Tertullian's *Prayer* and his *Modesty* due to Tertullian's change in position on the authority of *Shepherd*.[40] While at one point, Tertullian cited *Shepherd* as normative, at another he called it "that apocryphal '*Shepherd*' of adulterers."[41] Between these writings, said Salmon, apparently both the Catholic church and the Montanists came to look askance at *Shepherd*, and Salmon believed this was why the Fragmentist was against its public reading with the prophets and the apostles (lines 73–80). Salmon believed that the Fragment possibly represented the church's official step in censuring *Shepherd*.[42]

Salmon was the last of the nineteenth-century scholars to cast a skeptical eye on a literal interpretation of the internal evidence offered by the Fragmentist regarding the date of the work. Until Sundberg in the 1960s, the rest considered the statement regarding Hermas and Pius in a literal sense and as best explained by either a second or third century Fragment. For example, the New Testament canon scholar Theodor Zahn, in *Geschichte des neutestamentlichen Kanons* and his article "Muratorian Canon" in *The New Schaff-Herzog Encyclopedia of Religious Knowledge*, did not doubt that the Fragmentist lived during the time of Pius as claimed. However, Zahn thought it likely that he had only been a child during the bishop's reign and that he penned the Fragment after Pius; the work being "a writing of about 200–210."[43] In addition, Zahn shunned the notion of a fifth-century, or even a fourth-century Fragment because it was his opinion that the question regarding the public reading of the *Shepherd of Hermas* was

---

[39] George Salmon, "Muratorian Fragment," in *A Dictionary of Christian Biography, Literature, Sects and Doctrines: Being a Continuation of "The Dictionary of the Bible, Volume 1,"* vol. 3., ed. William Smith and Henry Wace (London: Murray, 1882), 1002.

[40] Salmon, "Muratorian Fragment," 1002–3.

[41] Tert., *Prayer* 16; idem, *Modesty* 19, in Alexander Roberts and James Donaldson, eds., *The Ante-Nicene Fathers (ANF)*, 10 vols., (1885–1887; repr., Peabody, MA: Hendrickson, 1995), 4:97.

[42] George Salmon, "Muratorian Fragment," 1003.

[43] Theodor Zahn, *Geschichte des neutestamentlichen Kanons*, vol. 1, *Das Neue Testament vor Origenes* (Erlangen, DE: Deichert, 1888–1889), 340, 438; idem, *The New Schaff-Herzog Encyclopedia of Religious Knowledge*, s.v. "Muratorian Canon," (New York: Funk & Wagnalls, 1908–1914).

Introduction 11

limited to the time around 200.[44] Also, Westcott was under the impression that the mention of Hermas and Pius in the Fragment offered support for a second-century date, and he corroborated this internal evidence by citing a Latin, anti-Marcionite poem which made the same statement and was attributed to Pius himself.[45] Thus, Westcott had no doubt that the Fragment came from the second century, and he considered the author's statement regarding *Shepherd's* having been written during his and Pius's time as "perfectly clear, definite, and consistent with its contents, and there can be no reason either to question its accuracy or to interpret it loosely."[46] Likewise, patrologist Johannes Quasten took the Fragmentist's statement about Hermas and Pius at face value and concluded that it was written sometime between the death of Pius (ca. 155) and the end of the second century.[47]

However, in the middle of the twentieth century, the hypothesis that the Fragment is a second- or third-century composition faced perhaps its greatest challenge. In 1957, at Harvard University, Albert Sundberg authored his dissertation arguing that the Old Testament canon was not fixed until the fourth century and that the church, prior to that time, had received and recognized only a loose list of putatively authoritative Jewish scriptures.[48] For this reason, Sundberg believed that the history of the New Testament canon stranded in need of revision and that the Muratorian Fragment represented the work of a fourth-century author, thus resurrecting the Zimmermann thesis. Sundberg initially presented this theory about the New Testament canon in 1965, at the Third International Congress of New Testament Studies held at Oxford, in the form of an essay entitled "Towards a Revised History of the New Testament Canon." Later, Sundberg turned this essay into his landmark article "Canon Muratori: A Fourth-Century List."

In making his case for a fourth-century Fragment, Sundberg first dismantled scholars' confidence that the statement regarding Hermas and Pius was necessarily explained by the second-century hypothesis by casting doubt on their translation of the phrase *nuperrime temporibus nostris*. While, as some claimed, the term *nuperrime* should be translated "very recently," Sundberg showed that it could just as viably mean "most recently."[49] Sundberg contended that, in this way, the Fragmentist was comparing the

---

[44] Zahn, "Muratorian Canon," 54.
[45] Westcott, *A General Survey*, 199.
[46] Ibid., 215n1.
[47] Johannes Quasten, *Patrology*, vol. 2, *The Ante-Nicene Literature after Irenæus* (Westminster, MD: Christian Classics, 1950), 208.
[48] Albert Carl Sundberg Jr., "The Old Testament of the Early Church (A Study in Canon)" (PhD diss., Harvard University, 1957).
[49] Sundberg, "Canon Muratori," 8.

Shepherd of Hermas's composition with the previously mentioned texts. In other words, the Fragmentist was stating that, of all these texts, *Shepherd* was written last or most recently, not necessarily that it was written during his own lifetime.

Moreover, inasmuch as some scholars had translated the expression *temporibus nostris* to mean "in our lifetime," Sundberg insisted that it may also indicate a broader period of time after the apostles, and therefore could be more general in nature and include any time, both within or subsequent to the second and third centuries.[50] The church fathers made a sharp distinction between themselves and the apostles.[51] For example, church historian Hegesippus (ca. 110–180) contrasted the time of the apostles with his own by declaring that during the apostles' time the church "was not yet corrupted by vain discourses."[52] Later, in the fourth century, Eusebius also drew a line between the "apostolic age" and subsequent times.[53] More significantly, Irenæus (ca. 115–202) used language almost identical to that of the Fragmentist (except in Greek) when characterizing the Apocalypse as having been written "almost in our day, towards the end of Domitian's reign."[54] For Irenæus to have considered Domitian's time (ca. 81–96) as his own, when about nineteen years had passed between Domitian's death and his own birth, he had to have been "utilizing the tradition which differentiates between apostolic and subsequent time."[55]

In short, Sundberg did not find a solution to the problem of the Fragment's date in the reference to Hermas and Pius due to a perceived ambiguity in the language. Given this doubt, yet acknowledging the *possibility* that the expression *nuperrime temporibus nostris* may *still* mean what it had traditionally come to mean to most scholars, Sundberg next set out to offer a positive conclusion for the date. Sundberg transitioned from this negative argument to his positive one by making it clear that the language of Canon Muratori could be understood as making its case against the *Shepherd of Hermas* without any reference to the lifetime of the author of the list. The translation that states "but Hermas wrote the *Shepherd* most recently, in our time (i.e., in post-apostolic times), in the city of Rome, while his brother Pius was the bishop occupying the episcopal chair of the church of the city of Rome," is not the only possible translation of the text, though it is a viable alternative to the traditional dogmatic interpretation of the

---

[50] Sundberg, "Canon Muratori," 8.
[51] Ignatius, *To the Ephesians* 13; Polycarp, *To the Philippians* 3.9.
[52] Euseb., *Ecclesiastical History* 4.22.4 (*NPNF* 2:1:199).
[53] Ibid., 3.31.6 (*NPNF* 2:1:163).
[54] Sundberg, "Canon Muratori," 9–10; Euseb., *Ecclesiastical History* 5.8.6 (*NPNF* 2:1:222; *PG* 20:449), "ἄλλα σχεδὸν ἐπί τῆς ἡμετέρας γενεάς, προς τῷ τέλει τῆς Αομετίανον ἀρχῆς."
[55] Sundberg, "Canon Muratori," 10.

passage. Thus, the argument that the author of the fragment must have been born before the death of Pius is inconclusive, and the phrase "*nuperrime temporibus nostris*" understood as contrasted with the times of the prophets and of the apostles is another viable meaning of the passage.[56]

In seeking a date, Sundberg found what he believed to be stronger evidence for a date elsewhere in the Fragment. According to him, the Fragmentist's treatment of several of the texts listed betray a fourth-century context in the East rather than any context in the West. First, Sundberg considered the Fragmentist's treatment of the *Shepherd of Hermas* to be more consistent with Eusebius's (303) and Athanasius's (367) than with the Fathers of the second and third centuries.[57] Second, no parallels to the way the Fragmentist handled the *Wisdom of Solomon* explicitly presented themselves prior to Eusebius, Epiphanius (ca. 310–403), and Athanasius.[58] *Wisdom*'s usefulness in the church did not become an issue until the fourth century, which is consistent with the Fragmentist's inclusion thereof. Finally, the Fragment's apparent equivocal treatment of the Apocalypse (i.e. John's) and the *Apocalypse of Peter*, by placing them last in the list, appears to match the way Eusebius treated the same; a development which did not manifest until late, and then only in the East. Based on these observations, Sundberg concluded that "it has become increasingly clear that there are several salient features of Canon Muratori that have no place in the early western church but find their earliest parallels in the eastern church during the late third and fourth centuries."[59] Therefore, if the Fragment is a second-century composition, it constitutes an "anomaly."[60] Based on this conclusion, Sundberg later went on to downplay the Fragment's role in the overall history of the New Testament canon.[61] Sundberg's theory initially faced mixed reception during the 1970s. Yale New Testament professor Nils A. Dahl thought Sundberg "proved" his case, but New Testament scholar John A. T. Robinson believed Sundberg's argument to be "questionable at

---

[56] Sundberg, "Canon Muratori," 11.

[57] Ibid., 12–15; Euseb., *Ecclesiastical History* 3.25.4; Athanasius, *Festal Letter* 39.

[58] Euseb., *Ecclesiastical History* 5.8.1–8; Epiphanius, *Refutation of All Heresies* 1.1.8.6.4. Sundberg maintains that Melito's Old Testament does not contain the *Wisdom of Solomon*, and that after him, no eastern Father included it in the Old Testament but tended to place it in the New Testament, a practice which is apparently consistent with that of the Fragmentist. Sundberg, "The Old Testament," 220n69.

[59] Sundberg, "Canon Muratori," 34.

[60] Ibid., 35.

[61] Albert C. Sundberg, Jr., "The Bible Canon and the Christian Doctrine of Inspiration," *Interpretation* 29, no. 4 (October 1975): 362.

many points."[62] Almost a decade after Sundberg published his findings in his "Canon Muratori: Date and Provenance," Everett Ferguson responded to Sundberg point-by-point.

Regardless of Sundberg's minimizing of the traditional view of *nuperrime temporibus nostris*, Ferguson asserted that interpreting it as "in our lifetime" is "the most natural meaning of the author's statement."[63] Also, contra Sundberg, Ferguson argued that Irenæus's expression ἄλλα σχεδόν ἐπί τῆς ἡμετέρας γενεάς means "*almost* to the present *generation*" [emphases added].[64] Irenæus was illustrating how close to his time the Apocalypse was written, not distinguishing between apostolic times and post-apostolic times. If, as Sundberg claimed, Irenæus was using the same type of language as the Fragmentist, then the former's ἡμετέρας γενεάς is equivalent to the latter's *temporibus nostris*, and this argues against Sundberg; it puts the *Shepherd of Hermas* within the lifetime (or generation) of the Fragmentist. Ferguson agreed with Sundberg that the Fathers had made a distinction between their own times and those of the apostles, but he held that this was not the way they did it. Moreover, Ferguson found that the Fragmentist's highlighting the lateness of a text to demonstrate its lack of authority finds a parallel in Tertullian.[65] To Ferguson, it seemed that not all in the Fragment was post-second-century.

Ferguson further charged Sundberg with the need to show that features in the Fragment could *only* have existed during the fourth century and not before. Because it is unlikely the text was originally written in Latin, linguistic analysis can only reliably determine the context of its translation. Ferguson did not believe the original was Latin but highlighted the fact that, if it was, it could only have a western provenance. However, if it was originally written in Greek, as Sundberg and most scholars held, it could have an early provenance in either the East *or* the West. Notwithstanding this possibility, for the sake of argument Ferguson cited two lexical features in the Fragment which had affinities in the second century. The Fragmentist's use of *disciplina* (line 63) sounds like Tertullian's "rules" and "discipline" for the church, and the Fragmentist's reference to the bishop's chair found a parallel in Irenæus's mention of the "chair" as the "symbol of teaching."[66]

---

[62] Nils A. Dahl, "The Origin of the Earliest Prologues to the Pauline Letters," *Semeia* 12 (1978): 237; John A. T. Robinson, *Redating the New Testament* (London: SCM, 1976), 319n41.

[63] Ferguson, "Canon Muratori," 678.

[64] Ibid. Ferguson supports this use by citing others: *1 Clement* 5, Euseb., *Ecclesiastical History* 3.32.8, 5.8.6, 5.26.22.

[65] Tert., *Prescription against Heretics* 30; idem, *Against Marcion* 4.5

[66] Ferguson, "Canon Muratori," 678; Tert., *Prescription against Heretics* 36, 44 (*ANF* 3:261, 265) and idem, *The Veiling of Virgins* 16 (*ANF* 4:36–37); Irenæus, *Demonstration of the Apostolic Preaching* 2.

Ferguson also rejected Sundberg's notion that the Fragmentist's attitude toward the *Shepherd of Hermas* was a uniquely fourth-century one. According to Ferguson, the Fragmentist may have been attempting to counter a second- or third-century wholesale approval for *Shepherd* similar to the perceived approval found in Irenæus and Clement of Alexandria.[67] In addition, he saw Tertullian's eventual reluctance toward *Shepherd* as a parallel to the Fragment's proscription against its being authoritatively and publicly read.[68] It is not impossible that both the Montanist Tertullian and the church catholic found fault with *Shepherd,* though for different reasons and to varying extents. Unlike Sundberg, Ferguson did not see a turning point regarding *Shepherd* in Eusebius, but rather a report of a condition that had existed since around the time of Tertullian, a text which "has been disputed by some, and on their account cannot be placed among the acknowledged books; while by others it is considered quite indispensable, especially to those who need instruction in the elements of the faith. Hence, as we know, it has been publicly read in churches."[69]

Though Sundberg claimed that the *Wisdom of Solomon* was not explicitly listed among the New Testament texts until Eusebius, Ferguson highlighted the fact that Eusebius's mention was in the context of describing Irenaeus's New Testament; Sundberg seemed to brush over this fact.[70] According to Eusebius, Irenaeus quoted *Wisdom* as Scripture.[71] Thus, as Ferguson noticed, "the New Testament canon of the Muratorian fragment has a parallel . . . before 200."[72]

Finally, Ferguson deemed Sundberg's statements regarding the Apocalypse and the *Apocalypse of Peter* uncertain. First, the Fragmentist's placement of the Apocalypse toward the end of the list did not necessarily mean it was on the "fringe" of acceptance, as Sundberg asserted.[73] Something had to come last, and since the *Apocalypse of Peter* was not permitted to be publically read by some, and the fact that both books were eschatological in character, placing them together at the end seems only natural. Also, not all in the East had doubts about the Apocalypse, and as Sundberg himself conceded, the Fragmentist's attitude toward it was more positive than that of Eusebius.[74] In addition, Ferguson did not see a

---

[67] Ferguson, "Canon Muratori," 679; Sundberg, "Canon Muratori," 12–13; Irenæus, *Against Heresies* 4.20.2; Euseb., *Ecclesiastical History* 5.8.7; Clement of Alexandria, *Miscellanies* 1.17, 29; 2.1, 9, 12.

[68] Tert., *Modesty.* 10, 20.

[69] Ferguson, "Canon Muratori," 679; Euseb., *Ecclesiastical History* 3.3.6 (*NPNF* 2.1.135).

[70] Ferguson, "Canon Muratori," 679.

[71] Euseb., *Ecclesiastical History* 5.8.1, 8 (*NPNF* 2.1.222, 223).

[72] Ferguson, "Canon Muratori," 679.

[73] Ibid., 680.

[74] Sundberg, "Canon Muratori," 26.

convincing argument in Sundberg's understanding that *Apocalypse of Peter* was only known in the East and that the Fragmentist's treatment of it found a parallel in Eusebius; Eusebius was more negative while the Fragmentist more positive.[75] This positivity may also account for why Clement of Alexandria offered "in the *Hypotyposes* [now lost] abridged accounts of all canonical Scripture, not omitting the disputed books, — I [i.e. Eusebius] refer to Jude and the other Catholic Epistles, and Barnabas and the so-called *Apocalypse of Peter*," a fact known to Sundberg.[76]

To summarize the Sundberg/Ferguson debate at this point, Sundberg cast doubt on scholars' interpretation of the author's statement that Pius lived during his lifetime. Sundberg sought to replace this doubt with confidence in another indication of the Fragment's date by arguing that evidence for a fourth-century date could be found in the Fragmentist's attitude toward the *Shepherd of Hermas*, the *Wisdom of Solomon*, the Apocalypse, and the *Apocalypse of Peter*. However, Ferguson, in turn, cast doubt on Sundberg's interpretation of these statements. Ferguson went on to argue for the second century in the West. He cited the Fragmentist's silence on the epistle to the Hebrews (a likelihood greater in the West rather than in the East); his treatment of the heresies; his emphasis on the "rule of faith;" his language when referring to the two advents of Christ; his description of the Fourth Gospel; and his classification of the "prophets and the apostles" as all proving consistent with a second-century milieu.[77] While the Fragment furnished evidence of its date, Sundberg and Ferguson interpreted that evidence differently, and the two hypotheses persisted.

Nevertheless, for the remainder of the 1980s most scholars dismissed Sundberg's arguments as unpersuasive. The exception to this trend was New Testament exegete Raymond Collins, who opined that Sundberg's consisted of a "careful analysis" and that Sundberg succeeded at showing the Fragment to be of the fourth century.[78] While Harry T. Gamble initially found Sundberg's argument "interesting" but "not convincing," he later changed his view and stated his belief in a fourth-century Fragment.[79] Had the Fragmentist written "nuper" instead of "nuperrime," or even simply "temporibus nostris," F. F. Bruce would have inclined towards Sundberg, yet Bruce held to a second-century date, though he credited Sundberg with

---

[75] Ferguson, "Canon Muratori," 680.

[76] Euseb., *Ecclesiastical History* 6.14.1 (*NPNF* 2.1.261); Sundberg, "Canon Muratori," 28.

[77] Ferguson, "Canon Muratori," 681.

[78] Raymond F. Collins, *Introduction to the New Testament* (Garden City, NY: Doubleday, 1983), 35.

[79] Harry T. Gamble, *The New Testament Canon: Its Making and Meaning* (Philadelphia: Fortress, 1985), 32n25; idem, "Canon. NT," in *Anchor Bible Dictionary* (New York: Doubleday, 1992), 1:856.

making an impressive case.[80] However, from the late 1980s into the early 1990s, Sundberg's hypothesis would garner support and expansion through the work of Geoffrey M. Hahneman.

In 1987, Hahneman presented a paper to the Tenth International Conference on Patristic Studies at Oxford in which he expressed his agreement with Sundberg that the Fragment is a fourth-century composition.[81] Hahneman cast doubt on the interpretations of the evidence pointing to a second-century date by questioning the veracity of statements by the Fragmentist regarding Hermas, Pius, and the *Shepherd of Hermas*. In 1992, Hahneman published his 1989 D.Phil. thesis, *The Muratorian Fragment and the Development of the Canon*, in which, like Sundberg, he dismissed the likelihood that the Fragment is a second-century work and made an argument that any dependence on *nuperrime temporibus nostris* should be set aside as featuring too many difficulties to lead to a reliable conclusion.[82] He then proceeded to argue for a fourth-century date via three avenues. First, he attempted to demonstrate that the Fragmentist's mention of "Miltiades" betrays a dependence on Eusebius; thus the earliest possible date for the Fragment would be 303. Second, he sought to show that Jerome looked to the Fragment as a source, putting its latest possible date at 392. Third, Hahneman saw three similarities between the Fragment and the *Refutation of All Heresies* of Epiphanius of Salamis (ca. 377): Epiphanius's inclusion of the *Wisdom of Solomon*, his mention of the supposed Marcionite *Epistle to the Laodiceans*, and the presence of the Apocalypse.

Hahneman's summation of and supplement to Sundberg's work met with credence from several scholars. For example, while conceding that Hahneman's monograph had "weak spots and some special pleading," J. K. Elliott believed it made a "creditable case," and Lee McDonald believed both Sundberg and Hahneman "carry the day."[83] So convinced by Hahneman was Robert M. Grant that he declared "the Sundberg-Hahneman theory is eminently convincing, and the Muratorian fragment . . . should be permanently removed from the second century."[84]

---

[80] F. F. Bruce, "Some Thoughts on the Beginning of the New Testament Canon," *Bulletin of the John Rylands Library* 65, no. 2 (1983): 56–57; idem, *The Canon of Scripture* (Downers Grover, IL: InterVarsity, 1988), 158, 158n2.

[81] Hahneman, "More on Redating," 359–65.

[82] Hahneman, *The Muratorian Fragment*, 35–73.

[83] John K. Elliott, review of *The Muratorian Fragment and the Development of the Canon*, Geoffrey M. Hahneman, *Novum Testamentum* 36, no. 3 (July 1994): 299; McDonald, *The Biblical Canon*, 694.

[84] Robert M. Grant, review of *The Muratorian Fragment and the Development of the Canon*, Geoffrey M. Hahneman, *Church History* 64, no. 4 (December 1995): 639.

However, other scholars did not find Hahneman persuasive and launched arguments against his case.[85] First, Ferguson contended that Hahneman failed to show proof that the evidence can only be explained by a fourth-century date, and he highlighted inconsistencies in the way Hahneman treats portions of the Fragment. Much of Ferguson's contention with Hahneman centers on the way the latter defines "canon" and other notions. For example, whereas Hahneman views parallels in the fourth century as "canon forming," Ferguson considers them to be "canon settling."[86] Indeed, Ferguson questioned many of Hahneman's presuppositions regarding the idea of "canon," as these presuppositions appear to steer his interpretation of the evidence and his reasoning. Also, whereas Sundberg found his primary dissenter in Ferguson, professor of New Testament Joseph Verheyden offered his rebuttal of Hahneman's argument in an essay presented in July, 2001, to the Fiftieth Colloquium Biblicum Lovaniense, which was published two years later in *The Biblical Canons*. Verheyden opined that, though there was "no 'hard' evidence for the traditional dating . . . there is an abundance of 'circumstantial evidence.'"[87] He flatly rejected the suggestion that the Fragment was from the fourth century. He still considered the information given regarding Hermas and Pius to be integral to the question of date, and he believed the similarities between the Fragment and other second-century works could not be ignored. For him, a second-century date best explained the apparent problems.

In addition to Ferguson's and Verheyden's responses in the wake of Hahnemann, other scholars disagreed with Hahneman's argument.[88] In his review of Hahnemann's book, professor of New Testament and early Christianity Charles E. Hill acknowledged that whereas Hahneman

---

[85] In 1993 Philippe Henne published an article reviewing both Sundberg's and Ferguson's arguments (not Hahneman's) and sided with Ferguson due to what he considers to be the "new" arguments of the latter. Philippe Henne, "La Datation du 'Canon' de Muratori," *Revue Biblique* 100, no. 1 (1993): 54–75.

[86] Everett Ferguson, review of *The Muratorian Fragment and the Development of the Canon*, Geoffrey M. Hahneman, *Journal of Theological Studies* 44, no. 2 (October 1993): 695.

[87] Verheyden, "The Canon Muratori," 556.

[88] Beside those elaborated on here, these "others" include the following: Bruce M. Metzger, review of *The Muratorian Fragment and the Development of the Canon*, Geoffrey M. Hahneman, *Critical Review of Books in Religion* 7 (1994): 192–94; Lionel R. Wickham, review of *The Muratorian Fragment and the Development of the Canon*, Geoffrey M. Hahneman, *Scottish Journal of Theology* 47 (1994): 418–19; J. Neville Birdsall, review of *The Muratorian Fragment and the Development of the Canon*, Geoffrey M. Hahneman, *Journal of Ecclesiastical History* 46 (1995): 128–30; Martin Parmentier, review of *The Muratorian Fragment and the Development of the Canon*, Geoffrey M. Hahneman, *Bijdragon* 56 (1995): 82–83; Graham N. Stanton, "The Fourfold Gospel," *New Testament Studies* 43, no. 3 (July 1997): 317–46.

supported Sundberg's case with further examples of parallels of the Fragment in the fourth century, he expressed reservation for a wholesale two-century displacement of the Fragment's date.[89] As promised, a year later, Hill published a longer article detailing his reasons for siding against Hahneman's case. Hill believed Hahneman's agenda (i.e. a reconsideration of the date of the formalization of the Old Testament canon) drove his analysis and that the traditional, early explanation did the most justice to the evidence.[90] In their consideration of Hahneman's case, New Testament scholars Michael W. Holmes and Robert F. Hull questioned the manner in which Hahneman handled the evidence. Holmes believed that Hahneman tended to push the ambivalent evidence in his direction and that he could have been more convincing had he treated the evidence more "evenhandedly."[91] Hull perceived a weakness in the way that, in his view, so much was dependent upon Sundberg's and Hahneman's view of "canon" as a concept. This pre-conception informed the dating to the extent that Hahneman too greatly minimized the opposing position.[92]

At the time of this writing, in the first two decades of the twenty-first century, scholarship seems to favor a nuanced early date. Theologian Peter Balla proposes that a second-century date "can be maintained" despite the respected efforts of both Sundberg and Hahneman.[93] Jonathan J. Armstrong contends that the author is Victorinus of Pettau (ca. 250–303) due to parallels in Victorinus's work and in the Fragment, thus he places it in the late third-century, though he still agrees with Hahneman regarding the unlikelihood of the Hermas-Pius connection.[94] Finally, theologian Christophe Guignard believes that Verheyden has soundly refuted

---

[89] Charles E. Hill, review of *The Muratorian Fragment and the Development of the Canon*, Geoffrey M. Hahneman, *Westminster Theological Journal* 56, no. 2 (Fall 1994): 438.

[90] Hill, "The Debate Over the Muratorian Fragment and the Development of the Canon," 437, 452.

[91] Michael W. Holmes, review of *The Muratorian Fragment and the Development of the Canon*, Geoffrey M. Hahneman, *Catholic Biblical Quarterly* 56, no. 3 (July 1994): 595.

[92] Robert F. Hull, review of *The Muratorian Fragment and the Development of the Canon*, Geoffrey M. Hahneman, Journal of Early Christian Studies 3, no. 1 (Spring 1995): 90–91.

[93] Peter Balla, "Evidence for an Early Christian Canon (Second and Third Century)," in *The Canon Debate*, ed. Lee M. McDonald and James A. Sanders (Grand Rapids: Baker Academic, 2002), 627.

[94] Jonathan J. Armstrong, "Victorinus of Pettau as the Author of Canon Muratori," *Vigiliae Christianae* 62, no. 1 (2008): 1, 18, 19n56; Hahneman, *The Muratorian Fragment*, 52.

Hahneman, and "one can therefore consider that the older consensus (i.e. on an earlier date) has now been widely restored."[95]

Nevertheless, since Schnabel's 2014 "State of Research" on the Muratorian Fragment, a new voice has emerged, or perhaps the echo of some old voices. In her "The Muratorian Fragment as Roman Fake," Clare K. Rothschild has resurrected the nineteenth-century theory that the Fragment is a hoax. Rothschild argues that the Fragmentist intentionally misrepresented himself as a second-century author.[96] She seeks to reconcile features of both the second- and fourth-century arguments. Rothschild looks to both external and internal evidence, concluding that the Fragment is indeed a fourth-century composition. In this way, her position falls in line with that of Sundberg and Hahneman. In short, with Rothschild, yet another fourth-century conclusion has been reached, simply by incorporating different evidence and approaching the problem with new presuppositions.

In any case, Rothschild's hopes of offering a "conciliating position" notwithstanding, the problem of the impasse remains.[97] The very nature of her argument means that the Fragmentist essentially "planted" evidence. Therefore, any evidence in the Fragment is suspect, yet Rothschild must show two things: First, she must show evidence that the Fragmentist did this. Second, she must show that the Fragment is from the fourth century. Unless she does these two things, exhaustively considering all the other arguments to date, the evidence points away from any conclusive interpretation of the text to an even greater degree.

In summary, the history of Fragment research is a history of scholars' attempts to explain why the evidence points either to a late second- to early third-century composition, on one hand, or to a fourth-century composition, on the other. Upon examination of this history, several methodological issues manifest themselves. First, the scholars bring different presuppositions to the inquiry. For example, Sundberg comes espousing a differentiation between "scripture" and "canon," while others may not necessarily make this distinction.[98] Second, different evidence is considered to greater or lesser degrees over the years. For example, none seem to consider the issue of idiolect until Donaldson's link between the Fragmentist's expression regarding the Roman See and a particular ecclesiastical milieu (for Donaldson this milieu shares similarities with that

---

[95] Christophe Guignard, "The Original Language of the Muratorian Fragment," *Journal of Theological Studies* 66, no. 2 (October 2015): 598.

[96] Rothschild, "The Muratorian Fragment," 55–82.

[97] Ibid., 58–59, 59n9. Christophe Guignard has recently responded to Rothschild in an article where he disagrees with Rothschild's conclusion. See Christophe Guignard, "The Muratorian Fragment as a Late Antique Fake? An Answer to C. K. Rothschild," *Revue Des Sciences Religieuses* 93, no. 1/2 (2019): 73–90.

[98] Sundberg, "Canon Muratori," 35.

of Cyprian). However, more recently, this tendency to favor some evidence over other evidence has been identified; for example, Holmes observes that Hahneman seems to "cherry pick," preferring evidence which supports his position over evidence which does not.[99] Moreover, the scholars interpret the evidence differently. For example, whereas adherents to the second-century hypothesis translate *nuperrime* as "very recently," Sundberg argues that a possible translation may be "most recently."[100] Again, for some *temporibus nostris* is understood as "during our lifetime," yet for others, "during the post-apostolic age."[101] Given, these various approaches and interpretations, it is no wonder that neither hypothesis has yet to manifest itself as the best explanation of the evidence for the Fragment's date.

The Present Study

Purpose of the Study

In light of the lingering problem of the Muratorian Fragment's date and significance, this present study seeks to break the impasse. What makes this study unique in its contribution to both theology and apologetics is the fact that it marks the first time the rigorous application of an objective methodology, known as "inference to the best explanation" (or IBE), has been applied to the problem of the Fragment's date. Significantly, the study's findings may have remarkable implications for Bibliology, and the demonstration of its methodology may serve as a template for the resolution of apologetic problems.

The Research Question

The study strives to answer the following question: Which of the two hypotheses regarding the date of the Muratorian Fragment is more likely—that it is a late second- to early third-century composition or that it is a fourth-century composition?

Delimitations

This study limited its inquiry to the consideration of evidence that has bearing on the date of the Fragment's composition. It treats questions of authorship, provenance, and language to the extent that these issues have bearing on the primary problem under consideration, that of date.

---

[99] Holmes, review of *The Muratorian Fragment*, 595.
[100] Sundberg, "Canon Muratori," 8.
[101] Salmon, "Muratorian Fragment," 1002.

Definitions

For the sake of brevity, when referring to the hypothesis that the Fragment is a late second- to early third-century composition and to the hypothesis that it is a fourth-century composition, the study uses the terms "Early Hypothesis" and "Late Hypothesis" respectively.

Methodology

The Nexus: Problem, Purpose, and Plan

Inasmuch as Muratorian Fragment scholars formulated hypotheses (e.g. that the Fragment is a second-century composition) which explained the evidence (e.g. the statement that the *Shepherd of Hermas* was written "very recently in our times"), they engaged in abductive reasoning; that is, they exhibited "a preference for . . . one hypothesis over others which would equally explain the facts."[102] This process has come to be known as drawing an "inference to the best explanation," hereafter referred to as IBE.[103] According to epistemologist Gilbert Harman, this type of inference takes place every time a person infers the veracity of a hypothesis from that hypothesis's ability to explain the evidence.[104] Scholars interested in determining the Fragment's date have been engaged in this type of reasoning for almost three hundred years, and they have formulated two possible hypotheses, or explanations, but which one is the *best*?

Harman understood that, at times, while applying IBE, multiple hypotheses manifest, and these naturally compete for preference. For this reason, Professor of History and Philosophy of Science, Peter Lipton sees IBE as a two stage process: The first stage consists of hypothesis generation. From 1740 to 2018, Fragment scholars have been in this stage. Stage Two

---

[102] Douglas Walton, *Abductive Reasoning* (Tuscaloosa: University of Alabama Press, 2005), xiii; Justus Buchler, ed., *The Philosophy of Peirce: Selected Writings* (London: Routledge, 2014), 151. Logician Charles Sanders Peirce coined the term "abductive reasoning," or "retroduction."

[103] "'The inference to the best explanation' corresponds approximately to what others have called 'abduction,' 'the method of hypothesis,' 'hypothetic inference,' 'the method of elimination,' 'eliminative induction,' and 'theoretical inference.'" Gilbert Harman, "The Inference to the Best Explanation," *Philosophical Review* 74, no. 1 (January 1965): 88–89. Others who have further developed IBE include P. Thagard, "The Best Explanation: Criteria for Theory Choice," *Journal of Philosophy* 75, no. 2 (February 1978): 76–92; T. Day and H. Kincaid, "Putting Inference to the Best Explanation in its Place," *Synthese* 98, no. 2 (February 1994): 271–95; E. Barnes, "Inference to the Loveliest Explanation," *Synthese* 103, no. 2 (May 1995): 251–77; and S. Psillos, "Simply the Best: A Case for Abduction," in *Computational Logic: Logic Programming and Beyond*, ed. A. C. Kakas and F. Sadri (Berlin: Springer-Verlag, 2002), 605–26.

[104] Harman, "The Inference to the Best Explanation," 89.

"is the process of selection from among those live candidates."[105] Harman laid the groundwork for this selection process by alluding to several criteria that scholars could bring to bear in choosing one hypothesis over the others. Thus, according to him, "there is, of course, a problem about how one is to judge that one hypothesis is sufficiently better than another hypothesis. Presumably such a judgment will be based on considerations such as which hypothesis is simpler, which is more plausible, which explains more, which is less ad hoc, and so forth."[106]

The Harman-McCullagh Criteria

Where Harman and Lipton left off, history philosopher C. Behan McCullagh took over. In justifying descriptions of the past, which is the task of history, McCullagh saw a use for IBE in cases where there is no evidence to provide strong direct support for a particular hypothesis about the kind of information an historian wants to discover, and so the historian has to draw upon very general knowledge to arrive at plausible hypotheses about its origin. As the name of this form of inference suggests, it proceeds by judging which of the plausible hypotheses provides the best explanation of what is known about the creation of the evidence in question.[107]

Moreover, like Harman, McCullagh knew that, at times, two hypotheses manifest. He suggested that in cases where scholars are "unable to exclude all but one of the possible explanations of their evidence, . . . they have to weigh up the comparative merits of each."[108]

At this point, McCullagh built upon Harmon's criteria and described the process by which one weighs the merits of competing hypotheses. Among competing hypotheses, the one that meets these criteria to a greater degree than the others possesses a greater likelihood of being the correct hypothesis. The criteria which preferred hypotheses more satisfactorily meet are the standards of *plausibility*, *explanatory scope*, *explanatory power*, *credibility*, and *simplicity*.[109] First, hypotheses that demonstrate *plausibility* are those which are implied by the evidence, such that, in McCullagh's words, "it [the hypothesis in question] could well have been."[110] Second, the amount of evidence explained by a hypothesis constitutes the hypothesis' *explanatory scope*; the greater the amount of

---

[105] Peter Lipton, *Inference to the Best Explanation*, 2nd ed. (London: Routledge, 2004), 149.
[106] Harman, "The Inference to the Best Explanation," 89.
[107] C. Behan McCullagh, *The Logic of History: Putting Postmodernism in Perspective* (London: Routledge, 2004), 49.
[108] Ibid., 51.
[109] McCullagh, *The Logic of History*, 51–52.
[110] Ibid., 52.

evidence explained, the greater the hypothesis' explanatory scope. Third, hypotheses that explain the evidence to a greater degree of likelihood possess *explanatory power*. Fourth, there should not exist any evidence which implies the hypothesis to be unlikely, nor should there be any existing evidence which a hypothesis cannot explain; hypotheses which meet this standard exhibit *credibility*.[111] Fifth and finally, superior hypotheses demonstrate *simplicity*. They require no unsubstantiated assumptions in order to stand, and when challenged, they do not resort to such assumptions. If a hypothesis does, it makes itself susceptible to Ockham's razor.[112] McCullagh explains simplicity best when he observes that a preferred hypothesis does "not include ad hoc components, designed simply to accommodate data which appear to disconfirm it."[113] To date, no scholar has weighed the merits of the two hypotheses regarding the Fragment's date in a deliberately and rigorously conducted "Lipton Stage Two scenario." This suggests that scholarship may profit from this present study, one which weighs the hypotheses through the application of the Harman-McCullagh criteria.

The question of the date of the Muratorian Fragment's composition is historical in nature, and scholars have employed historical methods to gather evidence, form hypotheses, and challenge one another. This present study, also historical in nature, supplements their work and builds upon it because it implements IBE Stage Two by considering the evidence they have gathered and by evaluating the hypotheses they have formed through the application of the Harman-McCullagh criteria. In this way it identifies the more likely of the two hypotheses regarding the date of the Fragment. Because they describe events that cannot be repeated, historical descriptions lack certainty. They can only be said to be *likely* true, *possibly* true, or *impossible*. These are what McCullagh calls the "degrees of credibility," and this study makes use of this concept when evaluating the likelihood of the veracity of the descriptions treated within.[114]

---

[111] McCullagh, *The Logic of History*, 52. This is McCullagh's insistence that acceptable theories are "not disconfirmed by other reasonable beliefs," this author has labeled it "credibility" as it is a type of implementation of the law of non-contradiction in probabilistic statements.

[112] The principle of Ockham's razor "says that a theory that postulates fewer entities, processes, or causes is better than a theory that postulates more, so long as the simpler theory is compatible with what we observe." Elliot Sober, *Ockham's Razors: A User's Manual* (Cambridge: Cambridge University Press, 2015), 2.

[113] McCullagh, *The Logic of History*, 52.

[114] Ibid., 12.

Preview of the Findings

The study found that, by making an inference to the best explanation, the Early Hypothesis is preferred. This methodology consisted of weighing the two hypotheses against the five criteria: *plausibility, explanatory scope, explanatory power, credibility, and simplicity*. The Early Hypothesis surpasses the Late Hypothesis in every category. Through implementing the methodology of inference to the best explanation, it appears more likely the Muratorian Fragment was written during the second or third centuries than that it was written during the fourth century.

Summary

The problem of the Muratorian Fragment's date has vexed scholars since its discovery in 1700. While the majority of scholars believe the Fragment was composed in the late second or early third century, some have recently made the case that it represents a work of the fourth century and reflects a more evolved understanding of which texts should make up the Christian New Testament canon. Resolving the problem of the Fragment's date is important because of the implications for understanding the theology of ancient Christianity, which ultimately drives contemporary theology. This present study, in seeking to determine the more likely date of the Fragment, implements an epistemological methodology known as "Inference to the Best Explanation" (IBE), a methodology often used to resolve historical problems. The hypothesis which best meets these criteria is the preferred hypothesis. To that end, the next chapter offers a description of the Fragment's background.

The Muratorian Fragment

Perhaps one of the reasons scholars have found it so difficult to date the Fragment is because it is so singular. No other known ancient sources explicitly cite it, and it was not discovered until the very end of the seventeenth century.[1] Until that time, the earliest extant listing of widely accepted New Testament texts was that of Origen, of which we have an account from Eusebius in the fourth century.[2] Also, the discovery of the Fragment is essentially a relatively recent and modern development. In order to conduct the type of evaluation for which this present study calls, it is critical to have a basic understanding of some of the facts concerning the Fragment itself.

First, this chapter describes the Fragment's discovery and its contents. For the reader's reference, it also includes two Latin transcriptions of the Fragment (original and revised) as well as an English translation; these can also be found in the appendices. Second, and of primary interest to the question of date, the chapter discusses the Fragment's authorship, provenance, and language, particularly as reflected by the determinations of scholars. Much of the debate about when the Fragment was composed depends in part on the solutions to these three special problems. Finally, the chapter offers a brief summary of how scholars may eventually use the answer to the date question in conjunction with the issues of provenance and language to resolve the authorship question by narrowing the list of possible authors.

Description

On September 7, 1607, Cardinal Federico Borromeo, Archbishop of Milan, founded the Bibliotheca Ambrosiana in that city "as a college of writers, a seminary of savants, a school of fine arts."[3] It was the second public library in Europe, the first being the Bodleian at Oxford. Scholar and

---

[1] Hahneman, *The Muratorian Fragment*, 217. Hahneman sees possible allusions in some fourth-century works, but none of these exhibit a clear dependence on the Fragment.
[2] Euseb., *Ecclesiastical History* 6.25.3–14.
[3] *The Catholic Encyclopedia*, s.v. "Federico Borromeo."

historiographer Ludovico Antonio Muratori (1672–1750) began working at the library in 1694.[4] In 1700, Duke Rinaldo I asked Muratori to serve as his librarian in Modena, but not before Muratori had discovered the Fragment in the Ambrosiana.[5] Forty years later, in Modena, he published the Fragment in Volume 3 of his six-volume collection of essays, *Antiquitates italicæ mediiævi, in Dissertatio* XLIII (cols. 807–880), "De Literarum Statu, neglectu, & cultura in Italia post Barbaros in eam invectos usque ad Annum Christi Millesimum Centesimum," which deals with the topic of religion in Italy as well as with other subjects such as institutionalism, economics, and social customs. According to Tregelles, Muratori's design in publishing the Fragment was to present it as an example of the poor Latin of the medieval Italian scribes, illustrative of a period during which learning suffered remarkable neglect.[6] It is likely due the Fragment's corrupted condition that Tregelles, along with several other scholars, made some corrections and revisions to the Latin found in the Fragment, an otherwise "blundering and illiterate transcript of a rough and rustic translation of a Greek original."[7] However, notwithstanding the poor orthography in the Fragment, Tregelles felt that "the peculiarity of its transmission in this form gives, if anything, a farther weight to its testimony as being something the genuineness of which is self-evident."[8]

Muratori discovered his Fragment within a 27 x 17 centimeter, 76-leaf, coarse parchment manuscript codex (Cod. Ambr. I 101 sup.). An inscription inside the codex identifies it as belonging to the Bobbio monastery, which is located on the Trebbia River southwest of Piacenza in northern Italy. Scholars believe the codex is from the eighth century. It contains theological treatises of Ambrose of Milan, Eucherius of Lyon, and John Chrysostom. The first three chapters are defective, but the fourth features a writing of Eucherius. Next, the Muratorian Fragment follows, and after this begins an extract from Ambrose. In addition to these, the codex includes five early Christian creeds. All of the datable works in the codex appear to be from the fourth and fifth centuries, but Hahneman concedes, it is possible that a second century work could be included in a codex of later texts.[9] In other words, for Hahneman, if the Fragment was a fourth-century composition, its presence in the Bobbio codex would merely be

---

[4] *Encyclopedia Britannica*, s.v. "Lodovico Antonio Muratori."
[5] Ibid.
[6] Tregelles, *Canon Muratorianus*, 2, 9. Tregelles viewed the Fragment toward the end of August, 1857 and made a facsimile tracing.
[7] Tregelles, *Canon Muratorianus*, 10.
[8] Ibid., 10.
[9] Hahneman, *The Muratorian Fragment*, 21.

corroborative. The codex is currently housed in the Bibliotheca Ambrosiana.[10]

As for the Fragment itself, it consists of 85 lines of relatively poorly composed Latin and inconsistent orthography.[11] At the top of folio 10 of the codex, the text of the Fragment begins mid-sentence with a portion of what is supposed by scholars to be a description of the Gospel of Mark (. . . *quibus tamen interfuit et ita posuit*). The Fragment takes up both sides of folio 10 and twenty-three lines of folio 11, the rest of which contains the beginning of Ambrose's extract. The copyist used red ink when referring to the Gospels of Luke and John (folio 10r, lines 2, 9).[12]

The original reading of the Muratorian Fragment follows. Words in bold are rubricated in the manuscript. The letters depicted in parentheses had been erased by correctors, and the letters in italics were added by correctors, either by means of substitution or superscription.[13]

> [folio 10r] quibus tamen Interfuit et ita posuit ·
> **tertio euangelii librum sec(a)*u* ndo Lucan**
> Lucas Iste medicus post ascensum ^{xpi}.
> Cum eo Paulus quasi ut iuris studiosum.
> 5 Secundum adsumsisset numeni suo
> ex opinione concri*b*set dñm tamen nee Ipse
> (d)uidit in carne et idó pro*ut* asequi potuit ·
> Ita et ad natiuitate Iohannis incipet dicere.
> **quarti euangeliorum Iohannis ex decipolis**
> 10 cohortantibus condescipulis et ^{eps} suis
> dixit conieiunate mihi · odie triduo et quid
> cuique fuerit reuelatum alterutrum
> nobis ennarremus eadem nocte reue
> latum andreae ex apostolis ut recognis
> 15 centibus cuntis Iohannis suo nomine
> cun*c*ta discri*b*eret et ideo licit uaria sin
> culis euangeliorum libris principia
> doceantur Nihil tamen differt creden
> tium f(e)*i*dei cum uno ac principali ^{spu} de

---

[10] For the library catalog entry, see "Manuscript Publication: 676–750," Venerable Ambrosian Library, accessed January 30, 2020, http://ambrosiana.comperio.it/opac/detail/view/ambro:catalog:76502.

[11] Muratori, *Antiquitates italicæ mediiævi*, col. 3:855.

[12] For a virtual examination of the codex in which the Fragment is situation, see the following website: http://213.21.172.25/0b02da82800c3ea6. The Fragment can be found on Frames 29–31; it ends about three-quarters of the way down the page on Frame 31.

[13] This particular transcription of the Fragment was copied from Hahneman, *The Muratorian Fragment*, 6–7.

20 clarata sint in omnibus omnia de natiui
tate de passione de resurrectione
de conue*r*satione cum decipulis suis
ac de gemino eius aduentu
Primo In humilitate dispectus quod (fo
25 tu) secundum potentate regali pre
clarum quod foturum est. quid ergo
mirum si Iohannes tarn constanter
sincula etiã In epistulis suis proferat
dicens In semeipsu Quae uidimus oculis
30 nostris et auribus audiuimus et manus
nostrae palpauerunt haec scripsimus (uobis)
[folio10v] Sic enim non solum uisurem sed (&)
auditorem
sed et scriptorṍ omnium mirabiliũ dñi per ordi
nem profetetur Acta autṍ omniu apostolorum
35 sub uno libro scribta sunt Lucas obtime theofi
le conprindit quia sub praesentia eius singula
gerebantur sicut(e) et semote passionṍ Petri
euidenter declarat Sed (&) profectionṍ pauli
a(d)*b* ur
be(s) ad spaniã proficescentis Epistulae autem
40 Pauli quae a quo loco uel qua ex causa directe
sint uolen(ta)tibus intellegere Ipse declarant
Primũ omnium corintheis scysmae heresis In
terdicens deIncepsb callae*c*tis circumcisione
Romanis autẽ or(ni)dine scripturarum sed
(et)
45 principium earum (osd) esse $^{x\bar{p}m}$ Intimans
prolexius scripsit de quibus sincolis Neces
se est ad nobis desputari Cum ipse beatus
apostolus paulus sequens prodecessoris sui
Iohannis ordinṍ nonnisi (c)*n*omenatĩ semptaṍ
50 eccles(e)*ii*s scribat ordine tali a corenthios
prima.ad efesios seconda ad philippinses ter
tia ad colosensis quarta ad calatas quin
ta ad tensaolenecinsis sexta. ad romanos
septima Uerum cor(e)*i*ntheis et *t*hesaolecen
55 sibus licet pro correbtione Itereetur una
tamen per omnem orbem terrae ecclesia
deffusa esse denoscitur Et Iohannis eñi In a
pocalebsy licet septṍ eccleseis scribat
tamen omnibus dicit ueru̅ ad filemonem una ·

60 et at titũ una et ad tymotheũ duas pro affec
to et dilectione In honore tamen eclesiae ca
tholice In ordinatione eclesiastice
[folio 11r] d(e)*i*scepline ˢᶜⁱᶠⁱᶜᵃᵗᵉ sunt Fertur etiam ad
Laudecenses alia ad alexandrinos Pauli no
65 mine fincte ad he*r*esem marcionis et alia plu
ra quae In c(h)atholicam eclesiam recepi non
potest Fel enim cum melle misceri non con
cruit epistola sane Iude et superscrictio
Iohannis duas In catholica habentur Et sapi
70 entia ab amicis salomonis in honoŕ ipsius
scripta apocalapse etiam Iohanis et Pe
tri tantum recip(e)*i*mus quam quidam ex nos
tris legi In eclesia nolunt Pastorem uero
nuperrim e(t) temporibus nostris In urbe
75 roma herma conscripsit sedente cathe
tra urbis romae aeclesiae Pio ᵉᵖˢ frat*r*e(r)
eius et ideo legi eum quidó Oportet se pu
plicare uero In eclesia populo Neque inter
profe(*)tas conpletum numero Neque Inter
80 apostolos In finó temporum potest.
Arsinoi autem seu ualentini. uel mitiad(ei)*i*s
nihil In totum recipemus. Qui etiam nouũ
psalmorum librum marcioni conscripse
runt una cum basilide assianum catafry
85 cum con*s*itutorem . . .

Next is David J. Theron's "restored" reading with more precise Latin spellings.[14]

[folio10r] quibus tamen interfuit et ita posuit
tertium euangelii librum secundum Lucam
Lucas iste medicus post ascensum Christi
cum eum Paulus quasi itineris sui socium
5 secum adsumsisset nomine suo
ex opinione conscripsit — Dominum tamen nec ipse
uidit in carne — et idem prout assequi potuit
ita et a natiuitate Iohannis incepit dicere
quarti euangeliorum Iohannis ex discipulis

---

[14] Daniel J. Theron, *Evidence of Tradition: Selected Source Material for the Study of the History of the Early Church, Introduction and Canon of the New Testament* (Grand Rapids: Baker Book House, 1957), 106–13.

10 cohortantibus condiscipulis et episcopis suis
dixit conieiunate mihi hodie triduum et quid
cuique fuerit reuelatum alteratrum
nobis enarremus eadem nocte reuelatum Andreae ex apostolis ut recognis-
15 centibus cunctis Iohannes suo nomine
cuncta discriberet et ideo licet varia sin-

gulis euangeliorum libris principia
doceantur nihil tamen differt creden-
tium fidei cum uno ac principali spiritu de-
20 clarata sint in omnibus omnia de natiuitate de passione de resurrectione
de conuersatione cum discipulis suis
et de gemino eius aduentu
primum in humilitate despectus quod fu-
25 it secundum potestate regali prae-
clarum quod futurum est quid ergo

mirum si Iohannes tam constanter
singula etiam in epistolis suis proferat
dicens in semetipso quae uidimus oculis
30 nostris et auribus audiuimus et manus
nostrae palpauerunt haec scripsimus uobis
[folio10v] Sic enim non solum uisorem sed et auditorem
sed et scriptorem omnium mirabilium Domini per ordinem profitetur Acta autem omnium apostolorum
35 sub uno libro scripta sunt Lucas optimo Theophi-
lo comprehendit, quae sub praesentia eius singula
gerebantur sicut et remote passionem Petri
evidenter declarat sed et profectionem Pauli
ab ur-
be ad Spaniam proficiscentis epistolae autem
40 Pauli quae a quo loco uel qua ex causa directae
sint uolentibus intelligere ipsae declarant
primum omnium Corinthiis schisma haeresis interdicens deinceps Galatis circumcisionem
Romanis autem ordine scripturarum sed
et
45 principium earum esse Christum intimans
prolixius scripsit de quibus singulis neces-

se est a nobis desputari cum ipse beatus
apostolus Paulus sequens prodecessoris sui

Iohannis ordinem nonnisi nominatim septem
50 ecclesiis scribat ordine tali ad Corinthios
prima ad Ephesios secunda ad Philippenses ter-
tia ad Colossenses quarta ad Galatas quin-
ta ad Thessalonicensibus sexta ad Romanos
septima uerum Corinthiis et Thessalonicen-

55 sibus licet pro correptione iteretur una
tamen per omnem orbem terrae ecclesia
diffusa esse denoscitur et Iohannes enim in A-
pocalypsi licet septem ecclesiis scribat
tamen omnibus dicit uerum ad Philemonem unam

60 et ad Titum unam et ad Timotheum duas pro affec-
tu et dilectione in honore tamen ecclesiae ca-
tholicae in ordinatione ecclesiasticae
[folio 11r] disciplinae sanctificatae sunt fertur etiam ad

Laodicenses alia ad Alexandrinos Pauli no-
65 mine fictae ad haeresem Marcionis et alia plura quae in catholicam ecclesiam recipi non
potest fel enim cum melle misceri non congruit epistola san Iudae et superscriptio

Iohannis duas in catholica habentur et Sapi-
70 entia ab amicis Salomonis in honorem ipsius
scripta apocalypses etiam Iohannis et Petri tantum recipimus quam quidam ex nostris legi in ecclesia nolunt pastorem uero

nuperrime temporibus nostris in urbe
 75 Roma Hermas conscripsit sedente cathe-
dra urbis Romae ecclesiae Pio Episcopo fratre
eius et ideo legi eum quidem oportet se pu-
blicare uero in ecclesia populo neque inter
prophetas completum numero neque inter
80 apostolos in finem temporum potest

Arsinoi autem seu Ualentini uel Mitiadis
nihil in totum recipimus qui etiam nouum
psalmorum librum Marcioni conscripserunt una cum Basilide Assianum Catafrygum
85 constitutorem. . . .

Finally, Bruce M. Metzger's English translation follows:[15]

[folio 10r] ... at which nevertheless he was present, and so he placed [them in his narrative].

The third book of the Gospel is that according to Luke.
Luke, the well-known physician, after the ascension of Christ,
when Paul had taken with him as one zealous for the law,
5 composed it in his own name,
according to [the general] belief. Yet he himself had not
seen the Lord in the flesh; and therefore, as he was able to ascertain events,
so indeed he begins to tell the story from the birth of John.
The fourth of the Gospels is that of John, [one] of the disciples.
10 To his fellow disciples and bishops, who had been urging him [to write],
he said, 'Fast with me from today for three days, and what
will be revealed to each one
let us tell it to one another.' In the same night it was revealed
to Andrew, [one] of the apostles,
15 that John should write down all things in his own name
while all of them should review it. And so, though various
elements may be taught in the individual books of the Gospels,
nevertheless this makes no difference to the faith
of believers, since by the one sovereign Spirit all things
20 have been declared in all [the Gospels]: concerning the
nativity, concerning the passion, concerning the resurrection,
concerning life with his disciples,
and concerning his twofold coming;
the first in lowliness when he was despised, which has taken place,
25 the second glorious in royal power,
which is still in the future. What
marvel is it then, if John so consistently
mentions these particular points also in his Epistles,
saying about himself, "What we have seen with our eyes
30 and heard with our ears and our hands
have handled, these things we have written to you"?
[folio 10v] For in this way he professes [himself] to be not only an eye-witness and hearer,
but also a writer of all the marvelous deeds of the Lord, in their order.

---

[15] Metzger, *The Canon of the New Testament*, 305–7.

Moreover, the acts of all the apostles
35 were written in one book. For "most excellent Theophilus" Luke compiled
the individual events that took place in his presence—
as he plainly shows by omitting the martyrdom of Peter
as well as the departure of Paul from the city [of Rome]
when he journeyed to Spain. As for the Epistles of
40 Paul, they themselves make clear to those desiring to understand, which ones [they are],
from what place, or for what reason they were sent.
First of all, to the Corinthians, prohibiting their heretical schisms;
next, to the Galatians, against circumcision;
then to the Romans he wrote at length, explaining
45 the order (or, plan) of the Scriptures, and also that Christ is their principle
(or main theme). It is necessary
for us to discuss these one by one, since the blessed
apostle Paul himself, following the example of his predecessor
John, writes by name to only seven
50 churches in the following sequence: to the Corinthians
first, to the Ephesians second, to the Philippians third,
to the Colossians fourth, to the Galatians fifth,
to the Thessalonians sixth, to the Romans
seventh. It is true that he writes once more to the Corinthians and to
55 the Thessalonians for the sake of admonition,
yet it is clearly recognizable that there is one Church
spread throughout the whole extent of the earth. For John also in the
Apocalypse, though he writes to seven churches,
nevertheless speaks to all. [Paul also wrote] out of affection and love one to Philemon,
60 one to Titus, and two to Timothy; and these are held sacred
in the esteem of the Church catholic
for the regulation of ecclesiastical
[folio 11r] discipline. There is current also [an epistle] to
the Laodiceans, [and] another to the Alexandrians, [both] forged in Paul's
65 name to [further] the heresy of Marcion, and several others
which cannot be received into the catholic Church
—for it is not fitting that gall be mixed with honey.
Moreover, the epistle of Jude and two of the above-mentioned (or, bearing the name of)
John are counted (or, used) in the catholic [Church]; and [the book of] Wisdom,

70 written by the friends of Solomon in his honor.
We receive only the apocalypses of John and Peter,
though some of us are not willing that the latter be read in church.
But Hermas wrote the Shepherd
very recently, in our times, in the city of Rome,
75 while bishop Pius, his brother, was occupying the [episcopal] chair
of the church of the city of Rome.
And therefore it ought indeed to be read; but
it cannot be read publicly to the people in church either among
the prophets, whose number is complete, or among
80 the apostles, for it is after [their] time.
But we accept nothing whatever of Arsinous or Valentinus or Miltiades,
who also composed
a new book of psalms for Marcion,
together with Basilides, the Asian
85 founder of the Cataphrygians…

After Muratori's discovery of the Bobbio codex in Milan, four additional manuscripts containing excerpts of the text of the Fragment surfaced. These belonged to the Benedictine monastery at Monte Cassino, three of which date to the eleventh century and one from the twelfth, all of which contain the *Corpus Paulinum*. Because the Latin in these is comparatively better than that in the Bobbio copy, scholars believe that they are not dependent on it, but upon another source.[16] These Benedictine manuscripts feature lines 42–50, 54–7, 63–8, and 81–5 of the Milan Fragment.[17] These were first published in *Miscellanea Cassinese* in 1897.[18] The text follows; the bolded text is that which is found in the Fragment, as well.[19]

1 Primo omnium Corinthis scisma heresis
interdicens. deinde Galathis circumcisionem,
Romanis autem, ordinem scripturarum sed et
praecipuum earum esse Christum intimans, pro-
5 lixius scripsit. de quibus singulis necesse est

---

[16] Metzger, *The Canon of the New Testament*, 192–93; Schnabel, "The Muratorian Fragment," 234.

[17] Schnabel, "The Muratorian Fragment," 234.

[18] "Fragmentum Muratorianum. Iuxta Codices Casinenses," 1–5, *Miscellanea Cassinese, ossia nuovi contributi alia storia, alle scienze e arti religiose, raccolti e illustrati per cura dei PP, Benedettini di Montecassino*, Anno I, Parte I, Fasc. I: Memorie e Notizie (Nova); Parte II, Fasc. I: Documenti (Vetera) (Tipografia di Montecassino, 1897).

[19] Hahneman, *The Muratorian Fragment*, 9–10.

nobis disputare, cum ipse beatus apostolus Paulus sequens precessoris sui Johannis ordinem, nonnisi nominatim, septem aecclesiis scripsit ordine tali (nam) cum Romanis ita agit apostolus
10 Paulus quasi cum incipientibus, qui post gentilitatem et initia fidei sortiantur et perveniant ad spem vitae aeternae, multa de phisicis rationibus insinuat, multa de scripturis divinis; ad Corinthios prima consecutos iam fidem non recte conversantes obiurgat; ad Corinthios
15 secunda contristatos quidem sed emendatos ostendit; Galatas in fide ipsa peccantes et ad Iudaismum declinantes exponit; Ephesios quia incipiunt et custodiunt laudat, quod ea quae acceperunt servaverunt; Philippenses quod in quo crediderunt servantes ad fructum
20 pervenerunt; Colosenses collaudat quia velud ignotis scribit et accepto nuntio ab Epafra custodisse evangelium gratulatur; Thesalonicenses prima in opere et fide crevisse gloriatur; in secunda praeterea quod et persecutionem passi in fide perseveraverint, quos et sanctos ap-
25 pellat, ut illos qui in Iudaeam Christum confessi persecutiones fortiter tolerarunt; (ad) Hebraeos, ad quorum similitudinem passi sunt Thesalonicenses, ut in mandatis perseveratnes persecutiones promptissime patiantur. **fertur etiam ad Laudicenses, aliam ad Alexan-
30 drinos, Pauli nomine ficte, ad heresim Marcionis, et alia plura quae in aecclesia catholica recipi non oportet. fel enim cum melle miscui non congruit, Arsinofa autem seu Valentini, vel Mitiadis, nihil in totum recipimus, qui etiam
35 novum psalmorum librum Marcionis conscripserunt, una cum Basilide (sive) Asyano Catafrigum consitutorem, verum Corinthis, et Thesalonicensibus licet procorreptione uteretur, una tamen per omnem orbem terrae aecclesia catho-
40 lica diffusa esse dinoscitur.** Triplex igitur Hebraeorum esse dinoscitur lingua. Heber unde Hebrei dicti sunt. Hanc linguam Moyses a domino legem accepit et tradidit, nam et Chaldeorum est alia, quam imperiti Iudaei vel Syri hebraeam fingunt, et ideo in multis
45 male interpretes apud illos dissonat multa, apud nos autem auctor est beatus apostolus Paulus dicens, se Hebraeum ex Hebraeis, hoc est, de tribu Beniamin.

Content

Due to its content, some have dubbed the Fragment "the Muratorian *Canon*."[20] It mentions several texts, most of which comprise the currently recognized canonical New Testament. It omits Matthew and Mark (probably within the supposed missing piece at the beginning), Hebrews, James, and 1 and 2 Peter. Beginning with the Gospels and Acts, the Fragmentist appears primarily interested in demonstrating their *historical value*. The Fragment begins mid-sentence with what is probably Mark, by noting that whoever reported the events recording therein was present when they occurred (line 1). In the same manner with Luke, the Fragmentist supports that Gospel's historicity by observing that Luke was able to "ascertain" what had happened (line 7). Additionally, for the Fourth Gospel, he believes John to be the author and that John was both an "eyewitness and hearer" (line 32). Finally, he notes that the events in the book of Acts "took place in his [Luke's] presence" (line 36).

Moving on to the epistles, the Fragmentist goes to lengths to emphasize their *universal applicability*. Though Paul writes to a discreet number of churches, "it is clearly recognizable that there is one Church spread throughout the whole extent of the earth" (lines 55–7). He also does this with the letters that open the Apocalypse by stating that "John also in the Apocalypse, though he writes to seven churches, nevertheless speaks to all" (lines 58–60). For the Fragmentist even Paul's personal epistles have universal application; though Paul wrote "one to Philemon, one to Titus, and two to Timothy; and these are held sacred in the esteem of the Church catholic" (lines 59–62). The Fragmentist states that the letters to the Alexandrians and the Laodiceans, allegedly under the name of Paul, are rejected (lines 64–7). These letters are likely the result of the revision of genuine Pauline epistles which Marcion had undertaken to fit his theology. They are therefore not to be included for consideration, as the Fragmentist considers them fictitious.

In addition to Paul's epistles, three other texts meet the Fragmentist's standard of universal applicability. These are Jude, two Johannine epistles, and the *Wisdom of Solomon*, which "are counted (or, used) in the catholic [Church]" (lines 68–70). Because the Fragmentist does not mention Hebrews, James, or the Petrine epistles within the extant portion of his work, it is impossible to draw any conclusions about how he viewed them. However, it is possible that he did not consider them applicable on a universal (i.e., catholic) level. All four of these texts are likely to have been written to Jewish audiences, and the Fragmentist may have seen these as thus limited in their application to the church as a whole. Also, because the

---

[20] Schnabel, "The Muratorian Fragment," 238–39.

Fragmentist only seems to mention two of John's epistles, it may be that he viewed 3 John as limited in its scope insofar as it is addressed to one "Gaius," and he may have deemed it too personal for inclusion in his description. While Philemon and the Pastorals are also personal, the Fragmentist includes them explicitly because they are suitable "regulation of ecclesiastical discipline" (lines 62–3); he may not have viewed 3 John in this light.

Next, the Fragmentist briefly addresses the specific issue of public ecclesiastical reading. Neither the *Apocalypse of Peter* nor the *Shepherd of Hermas* are acceptable for this purpose; *Shepherd* because it was written too late and is therefore non-historical, unlike the Gospels. The Fragmentist does not state the reason why the *Apocalypse of Peter* cannot be read publicly, but it may also be due to its date (ca. mid-second century), or it may be because it lacks universal applicability. Nevertheless, despite this liturgical restriction, the Fragmentist declares that the *Apocalypse of Peter* is received and that *Shepherd* "ought indeed to be read." In the last remaining portion of the manuscript the Fragmentist states the rejection of Gnostic, Marcionite, and Montanist texts.

Based on the content of the Fragment, it appears that the Fragmentist, at least within the extant portion of the work, favors texts which are historically valuable and universally applicable for public reading in the entire church worldwide. Virtually nothing can be concluded about the Fragmentist's notion of canon based on the omission of Hebrews, James, and the Petrine epistles due to the likelihood that we do not possess the entire manuscript. To develop theories based on these texts' not being mentioned here would be to construct interpretations upon evidence that simply does not exist, and it remains critical that modern scholars not interpret the Fragment by reading modern notions of canon back into the manuscript. It is also unclear from the Fragment whether its author considered the Gospels in the same way he did the epistles; that is, as universally applicable for use in the church catholic. It seems that he did consider them historically significant, having been written by eyewitnesses or direct recipients of their testimony. In addition, it can be said that he "received" certain texts as authoritative enough for the edification of the public church including the Pauline epistles, several of the general epistles, the Apocalypse, and the *Wisdom of Solomon*. Thus, it may be too much to infer that the Fragmentist even understood the "Old and New Testaments" the way they eventually came to be viewed by Christianity. Again, his interest was two-fold, what was historically valuable and universally applicable.

It may be that the Fragmentist did not set out to answer the question of the New Testament canon in the same manner that Eusebius and Athanasius did. Therefore, to reach conclusions about his mention of the

Wisdom of Solomon and its relationship with the Old or New Testaments, as Sundberg and Horbury do, is probably to assume too much.[21]

Nevertheless, the information the Fragmentist offers is of value for understanding how these texts came to be understood by the early church. While scholars cannot be certain if the Fragmentist was directly addressing the problem of canon, he still provides information which lends itself to understanding why the early church accepted some texts, rejected others, and disagreed on still others.

Authorship

Knowledge of the author of the Fragment would lead to a greater understanding of the theological foundations undergirding its content with regard to its methodological, as well as its substantive, underpinnings. This understanding, in turn, would shed light on the development of the New Testament as well as on the greater question of the historical development of ancient Christian theology. This is why grappling with the Fragment's date is so important; knowing the date narrows the list of possible authors and thus lends to the ultimate desired outcome: that of understanding the early church's New Testament canon and theological authority. Once the list of authors is narrowed, addressing the problem of the Fragment's provenance, based on internal and relevant external evidence, would lead to a further narrowing of the author list. Coupling a study of the Fragment's provenance with a similar study of its likely original language would serve to both narrow the list of authors and corroborate tentative conclusions regarding those potential authors. For example, if the date is late, the list of authors is narrowed to only those who lived and worked during the fourth century. If the evidence points to a western provenance, one can conclude that the original language was probably Latin. Understanding who wrote it, from where, and in what language would help in determining who composed the Fragment, and this may also assist scholars in grasping some of the possible factors which drove its composition as well as an understanding of what the Fragmentist may have hoped to accomplish.

Over the years, scholars have proposed a number of different possible authors of the Fragment. Early Hypothesis adherents have suggested Caius, Papias, Hegesippus, Clement of Alexandria, Rhodon, Victor I, Zephyrinus, Hippolytus, Melito of Sardis, Apollinaris of Hierapolis, Polycrates of Ephesus, and Victorinus of Pettau.[22] Other possible

---

[21] Sundberg, "Canon Muratori," 15–18; Horbury, "The Wisdom of Solomon," 152–56.

[22] Muratori, *Antiquitates italicæ mediiævi*, col. 3:851; Simon de Magistris, *Daniel secundum septuaginta ex tetraplis Origenis nunc primum editus* (Rome: Typis Propagandae Fidei, 1772), 467–69; C. Bunsen, *Analecta Ante-Nicaena* (London:

early authors include Cyprian, Polycarp, Justin Martyr, and Irenæus. Westcott did not bother suggesting an author, as he believed "there is no sufficient evidence to determine" who wrote it, and that "such guesses" as those listed above "are barely ingenious."[23]

Perhaps for this reason, also, Late Hypothesis adherents are reluctant to venture any guesses, though they would probably not count Lactantius, Hilary, Ambrose, Jerome, or Augustine as likely candidates due to these Fathers having written in Latin (most Late Hypothesis proponents hold to a Greek original of the Fragment). Both Sundberg and Hahneman quoted Westcott on the author question and share the latter's opinion that there is not enough evidence to make an educated guess.[24] Rothschild stands out as an exception due to her hypothesis that the Fragment is pseudepigraphic. She suggests that it was written in the wake of the First Council of Constantinople (381) by Chromatius of Aquileia, Jerome, and Isidore of Seville, "whose writings are often considered dependent on the Fragment," in conjunction with Ambrose, in his role as a bishop, as supposed early evidence against heresy.[25]

Provenance

The traditional view of the Fragment's provenance is that it comes from the West.[26] Muratori believed this mostly due to his supposition that it was a work of Caius.[27] Because Donaldson saw parallels between the Fragment and the writings of Cyprian, he also believed it to have been written in the

---

Longman, Brown, Green, and Longmans, 1854), 1:142; J. Chapman, "Clement d'Alexandrie sur les Évangiles, et encore le Fragment de Muratori," *RBén* 21 (1904): 369–74; Adolf von Harnack, "Über den Verfasser und den literarischen Charakter des Muratorischen Fragments," *Zeitschrift für die Neutestamentliche Wissenschaft* (1925), 15; Vernon Bartlet, "Melito the Author of the Muratorian Canon," *The Expositor* 2 (1906): 214–24; Gottfried Kuhn, *Das muratorische Fragment über die Bücher des Neuen Testaments: Mit Einleitung und Erklärung* (Zurich: Höhr, 1892), 33; Armstrong, "Victorinus of Pettau," 1, 18.

[23] Westcott, *A General Survey*, 216.

[24] Sundberg, "Canon Muratori," 2–3; Hahneman, *The Muratorian Fragment*, 31.

[25] Rothschild, "The Muratorian Fragment," 81.

[26] Encouraged in part by the extensive research conducted by Harnack. Harnack, "Über den Verfasser," 5–7. However, Hugo Koch disputed Harnack's belief that the Fragment was an official church document in Hugo Koch, "Zu A.v.Harnacks Beweis für den amtlichen römischen Ursprung des Muratorischen Fragments," *Zeitschrift für die Neutestamentliche Wissenschaft* 24 (1925): 154–63. Quasten agrees with Koch that "there are too many reasons against such an opinion." Quasten, *Patrology*, vol. 2, 208.

[27] Muratori, *Antiquitates italicæ mediiævi*, col. 3:851.

West.[28] In addition, because the Fragmentist expresses familiarity with Pius's family and refers to Rome as "urbs" (lines 38–9), Salmon thought it likely that the work hinted at a Roman situation.[29] For Zahn, the absence of James and Hebrews in the Fragment, as well as the manner in which the Fragmentist writes of Pius's office, indicate to him that its provenance is the West.[30] While Ferguson did not insist on a Roman provenance, he did see a western situation, "a place where Rome was important."[31] In addition, with Zahn, Ferguson considered the omission of Hebrews and the Fragmentist's treatment of the Apocalypse as more consistent with a western attitude than with an eastern.[32] Likewise, Rothschild believes it to be of a Roman origin, albeit a fraudulent one.[33] With the exception of Rothschild, scholars who believe in a western provenance for the Fragment tend to be adherents to the Early Hypothesis.

Simon de Magistris placed the Fragment in the East, as did Kuhn and Lightfoot.[34] Sundberg did not take an explicit position on the Fragment's provenance but concludes that any "linguistic argument for the designation of place of writing as Rome is lost."[35] Like Sundberg, Hahneman did not reach a conclusion regarding the Fragment's provenance. For him its favorable mention of the Apocalypse is not remarkable unless the Fragment is post-fourth century.[36] Also, Hahneman maintains that, due to the extant copy's defective writing, conclusions based on the omission of any New Testament books are "inconclusive," rendering the Fragment's provenance "uncertain," this in spite of Hahneman extensive work on the Fragment's date based in part on these "defective" contents.[37] To summarize, a Greek and western Fragment is most likely to be early, and most scholars have concluded as much to be the actual case. A Greek and eastern Fragment could be early or late. On the other hand, a Latin and western Fragment would more likely be late, though this does not completely rule out the possibility of a third-century Fragment, as Donaldson and Armstrong (the minority) have concluded.

---

[28] Donaldson, *A Critical History*, 212.
[29] Salmon, "Muratorian Fragment," 1000.
[30] Zahn, "Muratorian Fragment," 54.
[31] Ferguson, "Canon Muratori," 677.
[32] Ibid., 681, 680.
[33] Rothschild, "The Muratorian Fragment," 82.
[34] de Magistris, *Daniel secundum septuaginta ex*, 467–69; Kuhn, *Das muratorische Fragment*, 33; Joseph Barber Lightfoot, *The Apostolic Fathers: A Revised Text with Introduction, Notes, Dissertations, and Translations* (London: MacMillan, 1885), 378–413.
[35] Sundberg, "Canon Muratori," 7.
[36] Hahneman, *The Muratorian Fragment*, 26.
[37] Ibid., 27.

Language

Though the Fragment's discoverer, Muratori, believed it to have originally been composed in Greek, several scholars over the years have argued that it has always been in Latin. Donaldson maintained that the Fragment was written in Latin in North Africa sometime between about 225 and 250.[38] Furthermore, Friedrich Hermann Hesse believed it unlikely that the original was Greek due to the difficulty in re-translating it back into that language from Latin.[39] Armstrong thought the Fragment to have originally been composed in Latin and that its poor quality is not due to an inept copyist but rather the result of its having been "penned by a notably poor Latinist," in other words, by Victorinus of Pettau, who was bilingual.[40] According to Jerome, Victorinus "was not equally familiar with Latin and Greek. On this account his works, though noble in thought, are inferior in style."[41]

The notion that the Fragment was originally composed in Latin has some, albeit limited, implications toward a likely hypothesis for its date. The church had begun to make the transition from Greek to Latin in Rome as early as the middle of the second century, the transition complete by the third century.[42] The church did not use Latin in the East. Therefore, it is unlikely that a Latin Fragment would have made its appearance prior to 150 in the West, and highly unlikely in the East at any point in time. However, if it were to be incontrovertibly ascertained that the Fragment was originally of Latin, this knowledge would still not necessarily lead to a greater understanding of a date, whether second, third, or fourth century, due to the beginning of the western transition from Greek in the second.[43] Nevertheless, if the Fragment was originally written in Latin, it seems *more likely* that it would have been composed late.

Muratori assumed the Fragment first appeared in Greek as he makes his case for Caius's authorship. De Magistris, the first to write on the Fragment following Muratori's description, agreed.[44] In the nineteenth

---

[38] Donaldson, *A Critical History*, 212.

[39] Friedrich Hermann Hesse, *Das Muratorische Fragment* (Giessen: J. Ricker'sche, 1873), 25–39.

[40] Armstrong, "Victorinus of Pettau," 4.

[41] Jerome, *On Illustrious Men* 74.

[42] Christine Mohrmann, "Les Origines de La Latinite Chretienne À Rome," *Vigiliae Christianae* 3, no. 2 (April 1949): 67–106; Hahneman, *The Muratorian Fragment*, 17.

[43] Other scholars who believe the Fragment to be based on an original Latin include Harnack, "Über den Verfasser," 1–16; and A. A. T. Ehrhardt, "The Gospels in the Muratorian Fragment," *Ostkirchliche Studien* 2 (1953): 121–38.

[44] Muratori, *Antiquitates italicæ mediiævi*, col. 3:851. Hahneman states that Muratori "suggested" a Greek original, but Schnabel more accurately observes that Muratori "assumed" one, as Muratori never explicitly argued for it. Hahneman, *The*

century, both Tregelles and Westcott held to a Greek original.⁴⁵ Salmon argued for a Greek original based on his supposition that were the Fragment's transcriptional errors corrected, no original Latin written by an "educated man" could accommodate a corrected copy; only a Greek *Vorlage* can explain the idiomatic expressions found in the Fragment.⁴⁶ Further, Salmon also favored a Greek original because he understood that Greek was the language of Rome in the second century. Sundberg thought the Fragment was originally written in Greek and he looked to Julio Campos for support. Campos's research of the Fragment's Latin found that it could have come no earlier than the early part of the fifth century.⁴⁷ Sundberg held that putting the Fragment's Latin at such a late date precluded the possibility of an early Latin original since the Fragment "contains elements that must be dated earlier than the Latin of the text."⁴⁸ Ferguson agreed on a Greek original, and noted that, if this was the case, any conclusions based on the Latin of the Fragment only bespoke the context during the time of translation.⁴⁹

In 2015, Christophe Guignard reopened the question of the Fragment's original language. Assuming an early date for the Fragment, he concluded that the gap in time from the original to the extant Latin manuscript, as well as the features of the Latin therein, demonstrate a greater likelihood that the Fragmentist wrote in Greek rather than in Latin.⁵⁰

If, as most scholars suppose, the Fragment was originally written in Greek, it could have been written at any time from the late second through the fourth centuries. However, in this case, it would have more likely come from the East than from the West. Nevertheless, as the West did not complete the full transition from Greek to Latin until the fourth century, a Greek original could still have obtained in the West as late as the third century.⁵¹ In short, if the Fragment was originally written in Latin, it only could have originated in the West, but it could have been composed either early or late, but more likely late. If it was originally composed in Greek, again it could have been written early in the East or West, but if late, only in

---

Muratorian Fragment, 13; Schnabel, "The Muratorian Fragment," 233n19; de Magistris, *Daniel secundum septuaginta*, 467–69.

⁴⁵ Tregelles, *Canon Muratorianus*, 4–5; Westcott, *A General Survey*, 214.
⁴⁶ Salmon, "Muratorian Fragment," 1000–1.
⁴⁷ Julio Campos, "Epoca del Fragmento Muratoriano," *Helmántica* 11, no. 34–36 (1960): 485–96.
⁴⁸ Sundberg, "Canon Muratori," 2n8.
⁴⁹ Ferguson, "Canon Muratori," 678.
⁵⁰ Guignard, "The Original Language of the Muratorian Fragment," 596–624.
⁵¹ Other scholars who believe the Fragment to be based on an original Greek include Kuhn, *Das muratorische Fragment*, 3–16; Zahn, "Muratorian Canon," 54; Lightfoot, *The Apostolic Fathers*, 405–13; Hahneman, *The Muratorian Fragment*, 13–17. Rothschild is ambivalent. Rothschild, "The Muratorian Fragment," 79.

the East. In other words, an original Greek Fragment yields an equal likelihood of being early or late.

Summary

Muratori discovered the Fragment in Milan in 1700, and published it in 1740. Several other manuscripts of the same texts were discovered in the Monte Cassino abbey and published in 1897. Most scholars believe the Fragment to be a corrupt Latin translation of a Greek original. The considerations of date, provenance, and language together lead toward a reduction of the possible authors by means of a process of elimination, so an early (i.e., second through third century) Fragment originally written in Greek in the West means that, of the suggested authors, only Caius, Victor I, Zephyrinus, and Hippolytus remain.

On the other hand, if the Fragment was early, and always in Latin, Donaldson's suggestion of Cyprian may warrant consideration. However, because most of the suggested authors are early, eastern, and Greek, the possibilities still remain daunting to scholars as that list allows for authorship by Papias, Hegesippus, Melito, Apollinaris, Polycrates, Clement of Alexandria, and Victorinus of Pettau.

Also, a late, western, and Latin Fragment could have been written by Ambrose, Chromatius of Aquileia, Jerome, and Isidore of Seville. While scholars have not suggested possible authors in the case that the Fragment is late, eastern, and Greek, possibilities range from the Cappadocian Fathers, to John Chrysostom, to the Antiochian Fathers (i.e., Diodore of Tarsus and Theodore of Mopsuestia), to Cyril of Alexandria. Athanasius would not be included as he published his own New Testament canon which is remarkably different from that of the Fragment. Once a list of possible authors is determined, other evidence, both internal and external to the Fragment, can play a role in further narrowing the lists of possibilities.

In order to apply the six criteria for which this study calls, it is crucial to have an exhaustive familiarity with the evidence compiled by scholars from 1740 to the present and cited in support of their claims regarding the Fragment's date. Only once this knowledge is attained can one begin to determine the degree to which the evidence implies the two hypotheses under investigation. Therefore, the following chapter offers a catalog of that evidence along with scholars' interpretations.

2

A Date: The Evidence

The previous chapter provides the reader with a basic description of the Fragment along with a discussion of several of the primary problems which vex scholars. Questions surrounding the document's authorship, provenance, and language are considered due to their relationships to the issue of the Fragment's date. All of these questions, and their potential answers, play a contributing role in understanding each other more fully. While this particular study concerns itself primarily with the Fragment's date, this cannot be done in a "vacuum"; an understanding of each background element works in synthesis to lead to the most likely answers. Having surveyed a relevant portion of the debate regarding the Fragment's content and background, the study now turns to consider the evidence proffered by scholars in their quest to determine its date.

With this in mind, the present chapter features a collection of that evidence compiled by scholars from 1740 to the present. In support of their positions, they cite evidence from the Fragment regarding its references to the Gospels and the Acts of the Apostles, the Johannine Corpus, the non-Johannine general epistles, disputed texts, pseudo-Pauline epistles, a catalogue of heresies, and the likely ecclesiastical context in which the Fragmentist finds himself. Along with each item of evidence, this chapter includes brief discussions of scholars' interpretations. The study considered this evidence in its weighing of the two hypotheses.

The Evidence

The Gospels and the Acts of the Apostles

The Fourfold Gospel

The Fragmentist subscribed to the notion that there were four Gospels, and he explicitly mentioned two of what are now considered the canonical Gospels, Luke and John. He listed these two Gospels, that of Luke, which he called the "third book of the Gospel" (*tertium euangelii librum*) and that of John, which he called the "fourth of the Gospels" (*quarti euangeliorum*) (lines 2–9). The condition of the Fragment precludes knowing what the

Fragmentist listed as the first and second Gospels, though they were likely Matthew and Mark. In this way, the Fragmentist exhibited an acquaintance with four Gospels.

Hahneman believed these mentions to be evidence for a fourth-century date. For him, not until that time did an exclusive Fourfold Gospel canon achieve recognition; therefore, it would prove surprising for a list of this type to appear in a second-century manuscript. He maintained that while it is not impossible for the Fragment to witness to a Fourfold Gospel in the way that Irenæus, Tertullian, and Clement of Alexandria do, it "is unlikely because the Fragment bears none of the marks of recent development for the Fourfold Gospel."[1] Hahneman concluded this because, according to him, lists of biblical texts prior to the fourth century typically show canonical development but not canonical finality. For Hahneman, canonical finality is characterized by the identification of rejected works, something which according to him we only see in the fourth century, and the Fragment includes this feature.

On the other hand, and against Hahneman's view of the Fragment's treatment of the Gospels, Verheyden argued that Clement of Alexandria and Origen knew of *only* four canonical Gospels, and thus did demonstrate a sense of exclusivity in the texts they selected.[2] While Clement cited the *Gospel of the Egyptians*, he made a distinction between it and the four Gospels, noting that the four were "handed down to us."[3] Thus, it appears that Clement was conceding more authority to the four than to *Egyptians*. Origen was more explicit; he declared that, "You should know that not only four Gospels, but very many, were composed. The Gospels we have were chosen from among these gospels and passed on to the churches."[4] In addition, Schnabel highlights Tertullian's belief in four Gospels and Irenæus's explicit assertion that "it is not possible that the Gospels can be either more or fewer in number than they are."[5] In this way, contra Hahneman, Early Hypothesis proponents show that features of "canonical finality" manifested themselves prior to the fourth century.

The Order of the Gospels

In ordering the Gospels, the Fragmentist placed Luke before John. He listed Luke as the third *(tertium)*, and explicitly identified John's as the *quarti*

---

[1] Hahneman, *The Muratorian Fragment*, 109.
[2] Verheyden, "The Canon Muratori," 516.
[3] Clement of Alexandria, *Miscellanies* 3.13, "Primum quidera, in nobis traditis quatuor Evangeliis non habemus hoc dictum, sed in eo, quod est secundum Ægyptios."
[4] Origen, *Homilies in Luke*, Homily 1.
[5] Schnabel, "The Muratorian Fragment," 248; Irenæus, *Against Heresies* 3.11.8; Tert., *Against Marcion* 4.2.

euangeliorum (i.e., fourth of the Gospels) (lines 2, 9). Whether his list included Matthew and Mark, and in what order, cannot now be known with certainty due to the Fragment's damaged beginning. However, that two other Gospels preceded those listed is deemed certain.

According to Hahneman, this sequence betrays a fourth-century context. An order such as that in the Fragment found in the second century would be "remarkable," but it "would not be in the least extraordinary" two hundred years later.[6] If the Fragment was a second-century work, this order of the Gospels would constitute an exception. However, there appears to be no "hard-and-fast" rule for ordering the Gospels. Irenæus listed them in this order on one occasion, though it is true that on four other occasions he lists them in different orders.[7] In addition, two fourth-century canons list the Gospels in a different order than that found in the Fragment and in Irenæus's "exception." The stichometric list in the Codex Claromontanus (dated around 300 by Zahn and Adolf von Harnack) has Matthew, John, Mark, and Luke.[8] The Cheltenham Canon (ca. 360) has Matthew, Mark, John, and Luke.[9] The Gospel orders in Irenæus and later in Claromontanus and Cheltenham suggest that the order of the Gospels was not unique to a particular era within early Christianity.

Gospel Identification

The Fragmentist identified Luke's Gospel as the "book of the Gospel according to Luke" (*euangelii librum secundum Lucam*) (line 2), and he referred to John's Gospel as "fourth of the Gospels" (*quarti euangeliorum Iohannis*) (line 9). Balla noted significance in these expressions insofar as, when referring to Luke's Gospel, the Fragment used a "title-like" nomenclature: "Gospel According to Luke," but with John's, he used a different type of designator, a "plural phrase": "Fourth of the Gospels."[10] Graham N. Stanton saw these types of reference as evidence that the Fragment fits "much more readily" in a second-century context than in a fourth, because the manner in which the Fragment identified the Gospels is similar to that of Irenæus.[11] For example, the Fragmentist's reference to Luke's Gospel (line 2) is a verbatim match to the Latin translation of Irenæus's "secundum Lucam."[12]

---

[6] Hahneman, *The Muratorian Fragment*, 187.
[7] Irenæus, *Against Heresies* 3.1.1; 3.9.1–11.6; 3.11.8; 3.11.7; 4.6.1.
[8] Metzger, *The Canon of the New Testament*, 310.
[9] Ibid., 311.
[10] Balla, "Evidence for an Early Christian Canon," 628.
[11] Stanton, "The Fourfold Gospel," 323.
[12] Irenæus, *Against Heresies* 3.11.7. This Latin rendering is a "very literal" translation of the now missing Greek original as seen when compared to extant Greek fragments of Irenæus's work, according to Quasten; Johannes Quasten, *Patrology*, vol. 1,

The Pauline-Lucan Association

The Fragmentist linked Luke with the apostle Paul, so it appears the author knew them to be associates ("[Luke] cum eo Paulus quasi ut iuris studiosum") (line 4).[13] Ferguson noted that over time this association became an issue of authority, particularly that of apostolic authority backing Luke's Gospel.[14] Even as early as the late second century, this authoritative link had been noted by Irenæus.[15] Later, Tertullian, Jerome, John Chrysostom, and the Monarchian Prologues would acknowledge the Pauline-Lucan relationship was more than a mere companionship.[16] Ferguson's point is that, were the Fragment later than the second century, the author likely would have mentioned Luke's Pauline authority to write, particularly given the Ferguson's perception of the Fragmentist's objective. Instead, the Fragmentist mentions how Luke wrote "as he was able" (lines 5–7). A statement of this type would be more likely prior to Irenæus who declared that Luke wrote what Paul preached.[17]

The Acts of the Apostles

The Fragmentist was careful to highlight Luke's eyewitness-status to the events which he recorded in the Acts of the Apostles. Of Luke's second work, he wrote:

> The Acts of all the Apostles are comprised by Luke in one book, and addressed to the most excellent Theophilus, because these different events took place when he was present himself; and he shows this clearly—i.e., that the principle on which he wrote was, to give only what fell under his own notice—by the omission of the passion of Peter, and also of the journey of Paul, when he went from the city-Rome-to Spain. (lines 34–39)

The Beginnings of the Patristic Literature (Westminster, MD: Christian Classics, 1950), 288, 290–91.

[13] Muratori, *Antiquitates italicæ mediiævi*, col. 3:853. Muratori transcribed the Fragment here as "cum eo Paulus quasi ut juris studiosum," which means "Paul was with [Luke] as a student of the law." Theron, *Evidence of Tradition*," 106–13. Theron offers a "restored" reading with spelling corrections and renders the text as "cum eum Paulus quasi itineris sui socium," which means "Paul was with [Luke] as a travel companion." Either way, the Fragmentist understood and communicated an association of Paul with Luke.

[14] Ferguson, "Canon Muratori," 681.

[15] Irenæus, *Against Heresies* 3.1.1, 3.14.1.

[16] Tert., *Against Marcion* 4.5; Jer., *On Illustrious Men* 7; John Chrysostom, *Homilies in 2 Timothy*, Homily 10; *The Monarchian Prologues*, The Argument of Luke.

[17] Irenæus, *Against Heresies* 3.1.1.

The Fragmentist emphasized that Luke was an authoritative witness to the events he recorded by noting the conspicuous absence of events such as Peter's martyrdom and Paul's travel to Spain. In this way he drew a comparison between Luke and John, who was a witness to the events he recorded regarding the life of Jesus.

Hahneman and Rothschild consider the manner in which the Fragmentist refers to Acts as an indication of a fourth-century date. Irenæus also referenced Luke's text but simply as "the Acts of the Apostles" rather than as "the Acts of all the Apostles."[18] Tertullian referred to the book as "the Acts of the Apostles" on five occasions but as simply "Acts" on four occasions.[19] However, the Fragmentist seems to have gone out of his way to emphasize the fact that the "Acts of *all* the Apostles are comprised…in *one* book" [emphases added] (lines 34–35). Both Hahneman and Rothschild agree that this type of "amplification" is seen only in texts of the fourth century.[20] For example, Gregory of Nazianzus called it the "catholic Acts of the wise apostles."[21] Hahneman suggested that such amplifications were needed in the fourth century, for the purpose of disambiguation, due to the proliferation of apocryphal "Acts," in particular the Manichaean compendium of the *Acts of Paul, of Peter, of Andrew, of Thomas,* and *of John*.[22] However, each of these were in circulation as early as both the second and third centuries. Tertullian spoke of the *Acts of Paul* when he mentioned "the writings which wrongly go under Paul's name," and which made certain claims regarding a woman Thecla.[23] The *Acts of Peter* was probably composed around 190 and the *Acts of John* between 150 and 180.[24] The third century likely saw the writing of the *Acts of Thomas* and those of Andrew.[25] It is neither more nor less likely that during the second- or third-century the Fragmentist was disambiguating the "one book" of the "Acts of all the Apostles" from these multiple, second- and third-century apocryphal *Acts* than that he was doing so during the fourth-century, as Hahneman proposed. Moreover, there are two other third-century apocryphal *Acts*, that

---

[18] Irenæus, *Against Heresies* 3.13.3.

[19] Tert., *Baptism* 10; idem, *The Flesh of Christ* 15; idem, *The Resurrection of the Flesh* 39; idem, *Against Praxeas* 28; idem, *Appendix: Prescription Against Heretics* 1. Cf. Tert., *Baptism.* 7; idem, *The Flesh of Christ* 23; idem, *Antidote for the Scorpion's Sting* 15; idem, *Against Praxeas.* 17.

[20] Hahneman, *The Muratorian Fragment*, 192–96; Rothschild, "The Muratorian Fragment," 78.

[21] Gregory of Nazianzus, *Lamentation for the Soul* 12.13. For other examples of this type of fourth-century amplification see Hahneman, *The Muratorian Fragment*, 193.

[22] Hahneman, *The Muratorian Fragment*, 193–94.

[23] Tert., *Baptism* 17.

[24] Quasten, *Patrology*, vol. 1, 133, 135.

[25] Ibid., 137, 139.

of Peter and Paul, and that of Thaddeus. Perhaps the Fragmentist was disambiguating from these as well. Regardless, proponents for an early date making nothing of the Fragment's inclusion of Acts of the Apostles nor of the Fragmentist's title for it.

The Johannine Corpus

The Fourth Gospel

Regarding the Fourth Gospel, the Fragmentist writes:

> *The fourth of the Gospels is that of John, [one] of the disciples. To his fellow disciples and bishops, who had been urging him [to write], he said, "Fast with me from today for three days, and what will be revealed to each one let us tell it to one another." In the same night it was revealed to Andrew, [one] of the apostles, that John should write down all things in his own name while all of them should review it.* (lines 9–16)[26]

Just as with Luke (and presumably Matthew as well as Mark), the Fragmentist identified the Gospel and furnished some background material as if to justify its status. In this case, he offered an explanation as to what prompted John to write it.

Proponents for an early date see the Fragmentist's explanation of the Fourth Gospel's origin as reason to hold their position. Zahn believed the Fragmentist's apologetic tone about John's Gospel means that he was probably aware of the Alogi attacks.[27] Ferguson recognized this tone as common during the second century, and he also thought that an anti-Alogi polemic may have prompted the Fragmentist here.[28] Stanton noted this as well, and added that during the fourth century such a defense of the Fourth Gospel as John's was not necessary but that it would have been necessary earlier.[29] In addition to the Alogi, the second century also featured Caius, who apparently may not have favored Johannine authorship for the Gospel in his contention with the Montanists, particularly in light of his disdain for the Apocalypse.[30] All of this means that the Fragmentist may have felt it necessary to describe the occasion which prompted the Gospel's

---

[26] Translation from Metzger, *The Canon of the New Testament*, 306.
[27] Zahn, "Muratorian Canon," 54; Epiph., *Refutation of All Heresies,* Proem 1.4.5, 1.5.6. According to Epiphanius, the Alogi did not accept John's Gospel.
[28] Ferguson, "Canon Muratori," 681, 681n19.
[29] Stanton, "The Fourfold Gospel," 324.
[30] Euseb., *Ecclesiastical History* 3.28.

composition as a way to justify its authority, an action which, according to some, would make the most sense in the second- or early third-centuries.

On the other hand, some interpret the Fragmentist's comments on the Fourth Gospel as evidence for a fourth-century context. Hahneman argued for a late date based on the details in the account of the Gospel's origin, particularly with regard to certain participants in the Fragmentist's narrative about it. This explanation in the Fragment is similar to other accounts about the Fourth Gospel which scholars have come to term the "Johannine Legend." First, Hahneman highlighted the fact that the Fragmentist referred to John's instigators as his "fellow-disciples and bishops" (line 10).[31] Hahneman argued that this inclusion of *bishops* betrays a later development. Clement of Alexandria did not mention bishops in his account of the Fourth Gospel, but stated that John was "urged by his friends."[32] Hahneman believed the vagueness of Clement's reference prompted the "later elaboration," seen in Victorinus of Pettau and Jerome, where they both declare that bishops also encouraged John to write.[33] Second, because the Fragmentist recounted that John's having participated in a fast led to the Fourth Gospel's inspiration (line 11), Hahneman concluded that this also indicates a fourth-century context. Clement made no mention of a fast, and like the reference to bishops, this too was possibly seen as a requisite elaboration and "as such represents a later development."[34]

However, Armstrong showed a possible third-century connection by highlighting the manner in which the account of the Fourth Gospel in the Fragment is followed up with a statement of the *regula fidei*.[35] Victorinus did something similar. According to Victorinus,

the Apocalypse is a measure rod, and the measure of God's temple is the command of God to confess the Father Almighty, and that His Son Christ was begotten by the Father before the beginning of the world, and was made man in very soul and flesh, both of them having overcome misery and death; and that, when received with His body into heaven by the Father, He shed forth the Holy Spirit.[36]

---

[31] Hahneman, *The Muratorian Fragment*, 188.
[32] Euseb. *Ecclesiastical History* 6.14.7.
[33] Hahneman, *The Muratorian Fragment*, 189–90; Victorinus of Pettau, *Commentary on the Apocalypse of the Blessed John* 11.1; Jer., *On Illustrious Men.* 9; Jer., *Commentaries in Matthew*, Preface.
[34] Hahneman, *The Muratorian Fragment*, 190.
[35] Armstrong, "Victorinus of Pettau," 8.
[36] Victorinus of Pettau, *Commentary on the Apocalypse of the Blessed John* 11.1.

This confession follows Victorinus's assertion that "the bishops...compelled him [John] himself also to draw up his testimony."[37] Therefore, scholars who disagree with the second-century view conclude that these parallels point to a later context (third or fourth centuries); a context in which the Fragmentist would have been a contemporary of Victorinus or Jerome, or as in Armstrong's case, Victorinus himself.

The Epistles

Regarding John's epistles, the Fragmentist stated the following: "John brings forward these several things so constantly in his epistles also, saying in his own person, 'What we have seen with our eyes, and heard with our ears, and our hands have handled, that have we written'." (lines 26–31). Later, after this quotation from 1 John, he wrote, "two belonging to the above-named John-or bearing the name of John-are reckoned among the Catholic epistles" (lines 68–69). How many Johannine epistles the Fragment lists is a matter of interpretation. Did the Fragmentist list one, two, or three epistles of John? Peter Katz deemed it highly unlikely that the Fragmentist meant a total of two. He asked, "How could any Canon have mentioned [only] two Johannine epistles? By their tenor and by tradition second and third are so closely connected that we should expect one only, the first, which was adduced earlier, or all three."[38] Katz contended that the Fragmentist included two epistles in *addition* to 1 John, which is *"the Catholic epistle."*[39]

Regardless, on neither side of the date-debate do scholars express much confidence in the Fragmentist's information about these epistles. Donaldson believed that *if* the Fragment's physical condition can be trusted, the Fragmentist appears to have omitted 3 John.[40] Recall that Donaldson favored an early date. However, Hahneman believed the Fragment includes 2 and 3 John, and he notes that this is consistent with the later date because these "are elsewhere found only in larger collections of the catholic epistles, which were accepted as canonical only in the fourth century."[41] Ferguson had doubts about how much can be learned from the evidence regarding these epistles. Nevertheless, he understood that this information appears to be "an anomaly for any time and place," though it lends itself more plausibly

---

[37] Victorinus of Pettau, *Commentary on the Apocalypse of the Blessed John* 11.1.

[38] Peter Katz, "The Johannine Epistles in the Muratorian Canon," *Journal of Theological Studies* 8, no. 2 (October 1957): 273.

[39] Ibid., 274.

[40] Donaldson, *A Critical History*, 212.

[41] Hahneman, *The Muratorian Fragment*, 181.

to the second century rather than to the fourth.⁴² Thus, he believed it not to be "exactly paralleled" with later lists.⁴³

The Apocalypse

The Fragmentist compared the Pauline corpus with John's epistles to the seven churches which the latter included in his Apocalypse. He recognized that "the blessed Apostle Paul, following the rule of his predecessor John, writes to no more than seven churches" (lines 47–50). Further on, he added, "it is yet shown—i.e., by this sevenfold writing—that there is one Church spread abroad through the whole world. And John too, indeed, in the Apocalypse, although he writes only to seven churches, yet addresses all" (lines 55–59). Later, he explicitly endorsed the Apocalypse by declaring "we also receive also [only] the Apocalypse of John" (lines 71–72).⁴⁴ The Fragmentist's qualification through his use of the word "*tantum*" implies that John's may have been one of several apocalypses in circulation and that his was accepted for a reason.

Scholars view this evidence from different perspectives. For example, Donaldson highlighted the Fragmentist's emphasis on the number "seven" as having a third-century parallel.⁴⁵ Like the Fragmentist, Cyprian found significance in the number when he wrote against the Jews that the seven children in 1 Sam 2:5 "are the seven Churches; whence also Paul wrote to seven Churches, and the Apocalypse sets forth seven Churches."⁴⁶ Armstrong considered this same evidence regarding seven churches to be an indication that the Fragment is a composition of Victorinus of Pettau, and therefore a third-century text.⁴⁷

Sundberg did not give attention to the content of the Fragmentist's description of the Apocalypse as much as to its placement in the order of texts. According to Sundberg, because it is located toward the end of the list, between the *Wisdom of Solomon* and the *Apocalypse of Peter*, it was considered at the time to be on "the very fringe of acceptance."⁴⁸ Like the Fragmentist, Eusebius also had reservations about the Apocalypse. He

---

⁴² Ferguson, review of *The Muratorian Fragment*, 695.

⁴³ Ibid., 696.

⁴⁴ The original Latin rendering here is "*apocalapse etiam iohanis et petri tantum recipimus.*" *Tantum* means "only," but S. D. F. Salmond omits it in his translation; see *ANF* 5:604. Those who include a translation of *tantum* as "only" are Metzger, *The Canon of the New Testament*, 305–7, and Theron, *Evidence of Tradition*, 106–13.

⁴⁵ Donaldson, *A Critical History*, 212.

⁴⁶ Cyprian, *Ad Quirinum testimonia adversus Judaeos* 1.20.

⁴⁷ Armstrong, "Victorinus of Pettau," 16–17; Victorinus of Pettau, *Commentary on the Apocalypse of the Blessed John* 1.7.

⁴⁸ Sundberg, "Canon Muratori," 21.

placed it among the "accepted writings" but conceded that "some…reject, but which others class with the accepted books."[49] Of particular interest is Eusebius's comment that it should be placed after the other accepted books; "after them is to be placed, if it really seem proper, the Apocalypse of John."[50] Sundberg contended that since the time of Dionysius, the Apocalypse faced doubts, and that these doubts manifested themselves explicitly during the fourth century in Eusebius.[51] However, Sundberg also admitted that his hypothesis faces the challenge of the Apocalypse's acceptance in Byzantium and particularly in Egypt given Athanasius's unquestioned acceptance in his *Festal Letter* 39 of 367.[52]

Ferguson countered that Sundberg placed too much stock in the order of texts found in the Fragment. He noted that "in a list something has to be last," a "fitting" location for an apocalypse.[53] In addition, Ferguson did not read much into any supposed association between the Apocalypse and the *Apocalypse of Peter*; doubts about the latter say nothing about the former. Similarly, any largescale doubt about the Apocalypse in the East is tempered by its acceptance by some there, so those doubts should not be considered any more seriously than those which Caius may have had in the West.[54] Furthermore, the statement about the catholicity of the apostles' writing does not find parallels limited to the third (with Cyprian) or fourth centuries (with Victorinus), because Tertullian made a similar statement when he declared that in Paul's individual letters "the apostle did in fact write to all."[55]

Contra Sundberg and Ferguson, William Horbury argued that the Fragmentist has deliberately placed the Apocalypse in a list of *antilegomena*, texts that were accepted by the church but not necessarily canonical.[56] Horbury made note of the fact that many Fathers treated the acceptable books of the both the Old and New Testaments together and subsequently did the same with the *antilegomena*, and then finally they dealt with the rejected texts. Given the condition of the Fragment and the missing portion which probably included the first two Gospels, Horbury inferred that this missing section probably also held a list of the received Old Testament books coming prior to the Gospels. Thus, the list of canonical New Testament books ends with the epistles of Jude and John, and the non-canonical list of acceptable texts begins with an Old Testament apocryphal

---

[49] Euseb., *Ecclesiastical History* 3.25.2, 4.
[50] Ibid., 3.25.2.
[51] Sundberg, "Canon Muratori," 26.
[52] Ibid.
[53] Ferguson, "Canon Muratori," 680.
[54] Euseb., *Ecclesiastical History* 3.28.
[55] Tert., *Against Marcion.* 5.17.
[56] Horbury, "The Wisdom of Solomon in the Muratorian Fragment," 152–56.

text, the *Wisdom of Solomon*. The Fragmentist then went on to continue listing *antilegomena* but that of the New Testament: the Apocalypse, the *Apocalypse of Peter*, and the *Shepherd of Hermas*.

Other Epistles

Hebrews

The Fragmentist made no mention of the Hebrews epistle, either among the Pauline or otherwise, and only one other catalog makes this type of omission: the Mommsen Catalog, also known as the Cheltenham Canon, of the late fourth century. Likewise, Eusebius made no explicit mention of Hebrews in his list, but may have had it in mind when he stated that Paul's epistles are among the recognized.[57] If this is the case, this practice of implicitly including Hebrews among Paul's epistles would prove consistent with Clement of Alexandria's assertion that it is indeed Pauline, but anonymous due to the Jews' unfavorable view of Paul.[58] The remainder of fourth-century lists include either Hebrews explicitly or implicitly among Paul's "fourteen" epistles.[59] Origen included Hebrews but argues it is not Pauline.[60] The Codex Claromontanus omits Hebrews, but Zahn believed this to have been accidental, and Metzger chalked it up to scribal or translator error.[61] Hahneman agreed with both Zahn and Metzger that the composer intended to include it.[62]

A few scholars have weighed in on the meaning behind the Fragmentist's omission of Hebrews. First, Muratori saw it as an indication that Caius is the composer, and thus of the second century, based on testimony by Eusebius and Jerome.[63] However, Eusebius and Jerome merely stated that Caius did not attribute Hebrews to Paul, which may or may not have suggested the latter's position on its suitability as part of a canon.[64] Second, Ferguson believed the Fragmentist's silence regarding Hebrews becomes more problematic the later the Fragment is dated.[65] Had the

---

[57] Euseb., *Ecclesiastical History* 3.25.2. Hahneman dates Eusebius's catalog prior to 325.

[58] Ibid., 6.14.2–3.

[59] See Hahneman, *The Muratorian Fragment*, 132–83 for a detailed description of fourth-century New Testament catalogs.

[60] Euseb., *Ecclesiastical History* 6.25.11–14.

[61] Theodor Zahn, *Geschichte des neutestamentlichen Kanons*, vol. 2, *Urkunden und Belege zum ersten und dritten Band* (Erlangen, DE: Deichert, 1890), 171–72; Metzger, *The Canon of the New Testament*, 230.

[62] Hahneman, *The Muratorian Fragment*, 143.

[63] Muratori, *Antiquitates italicæ mediiævi*, col. 3:851–52.

[64] Euseb., *Ecclesiastical History* 6.20.3; Jer., *On Illustrious Men* 59.

[65] Ferguson, "Canon Muratori," 681.

Fragmentist wanted to reject Hebrews, in all likelihood he would have been as explicit about it as he is with the other rejected works he mentions. Hahneman saw the Fragmentist's exposition of the Pauline corpus as "somewhat confusing" due to the way the latter stopped and started again on the topic. Hahneman implied that the Fragmentist considered Hebrews to be Pauline along with the other but that it "may have been lost in the confusion" for some reason.[66]

James

As in the case of Hebrews, the Fragment included no mention of the epistle of James. Clement of Alexandria may have included James in his reference to "Jude and the other Catholic epistles," but this cannot be known with certainty.[67] Moreover, as in the case of the Fragment, Origen made no mention and Eusebius listed it as "disputed."[68] All other lists include it with the exception of two fourth-century catalogs, the Mommsen and the Syrian. Scholars who favor an early date see James's absence from the Fragment as a point to consider. Donaldson considered its omission to be suggestive of the third century.[69] Ferguson interpreted James's absence as evidence of a second-century composition; its omission shows that the Fragment is "not exactly paralleled in the fourth century."[70] On the other side of the debate, Hahneman had no explanation for its omission, just that it is "extraordinary."[71]

The Petrine Epistles

As with Hebrews and James, the Fragmentist made no mention of any epistle of Peter. As in the case of James, Clement of Alexandria may have included at least one of them in his catholic epistles, but whether he had it in mind is unknown.[72] Origen included one "catholic" epistle of Peter as "acknowledged" but a second as "disputed."[73] In a like fashion, Eusebius stated that "the epistle of Peter must be recognized" but that "the second epistle of Peter" is disputed.[74] All other lists include at least one epistle of Peter with the exception of the fourth-century Syrian catalog, which has neither.

---

[66] Hahneman, *The Muratorian Fragment*, 181.
[67] Euseb., *Ecclesiastical History* 6.14.1.
[68] Ibid., 6.25.3–14; 3.25.1–7.
[69] Donaldson, *A Critical History*, 212.
[70] Ferguson, review of *The Muratorian Fragment,* 695.
[71] Hahneman, *The Muratorian Fragment*, 181.
[72] Euseb., *Ecclesiastical History* 6.14.1.
[73] Ibid., 6.25.5, 8.
[74] Ibid., 3.25.2, 3.

As with James, the Fragmentist's omission of the Petrine epistles give the appearance that the Fragment is earlier rather than later. For Donaldson, the omission of Peter points to a third-century context.[75] Just as with James, Ferguson highlighted that this silence is more indicative of an earlier context rather than a later one.[76] Hahneman did not explain the omission but simply noted what he considers the unusual nature of a fourth-century list not including 1 Peter.[77]

Jude

The Fragmentist accepted Jude in his declaration that "the Epistle of Jude" is "reckoned among the Catholic epistles" (lines 68–69). Clement of Alexandria included Jude among the canonical texts and "the other Catholic epistles, but Origen made no mention of it."[78] Eusebius listed it among the disputed texts.[79] As for the fourth-century catalogs, all include James except the Mommsen and the Syrian, with Cyril of Jerusalem and Amphliochus possibly implicitly including it among their seven "catholic epistles."

In contrast to James's absence, the presence of Jude appears to place the Fragment later. Hahneman viewed Jude's presence in the Fragment as evidence of a fourth-century context because it was typically "found only in larger collections of the catholic epistles, which were accepted as canonical only in the fourth century."[80] Ferguson did not make explicit mention of Jude's inclusion by the Fragmentist, but he simply stated that the information provided by the Fragment on the catholic epistles appears to be anomalous for any date. Nevertheless, he still considered it more likely to be earlier rather than later.[81]

Disputed Texts

Wisdom of Solomon

The Fragmentist expressed his acceptance of the *Wisdom of Solomon* with the words, "and the book of *Wisdom*, written by the friends of Solomon in his honor," appearing to list it as received among the catholic epistles and the Apocalypse (lines 68–71). The author of *Barnabas* (ca. 70–135) cited *Wisdom* as authoritative by linking it closely with a quotation from the

---

[75] Donaldson, *A Critical History*, 212.
[76] Ferguson, review of *The Muratorian Fragment*, 695.
[77] Hahneman, *The Muratorian Fragment*, 181.
[78] Euseb., *Ecclesiastical History* 6.14.1; 6.25.3–14.
[79] Ibid., 3.25.3.
[80] Hahneman, *The Muratorian Fragment*, 181.
[81] Ferguson, review of *The Muratorian Fragment*, 694.

Septuagint translation of Isaiah.[82] Because of this, Metzger believed that Pseudo-Barnabas viewed *Wisdom* as being among the writings of the prophets.[83] Of *Wisdom*, Epiphanius stated that the Jews considered it canonical but that this was "disputed."[84] Thus, it appears that *Wisdom* met with Jewish skepticism but Christian acceptance. That being said, Horbury believed that the place of *Wisdom* in the list serves as indication that the Fragmentist considered it an accepted Old Testament text, but a disputed one.[85]

Such acceptance also makes itself apparent in *1 Clement* and in Irenæus's *Against Heresies*. Tregelles believed that *1 Clement* 3 featured a quote from *Wisdom* 2:24.[86] Interestingly, Tregelles believed that *Wisdom* was a recent (i.e., Christian era) book; so recent that he saw its author alluding to Rom 5:12.[87] This would mean that either *Wisdom* is a first-century composition or possibly an older text with early Christian interpolations. Also, Irenæus indicated that he considered the text authoritative as he quoted from *Wisdom* 6:19.[88] Eusebius interpreted this use by Irenæus as an acknowledgement of canonical authority, that Irenæus was furnishing an account of the traditions handed down to him "concerning the canonical books."[89] After noting how Irenæus considered the *Shepherd of Hermas* to be Scripture, Eusebius made this remark: "And he [Irenæus] uses almost the precise words of the *Wisdom of Solomon*, saying...."[90] Eusebius also stated that in one of Irenæus's works he "mentions the Epistle to the Hebrews and the so-called *Wisdom of Solomon*, making quotations from them."[91] In light of all this, Tregelles believed that "there must have been some cause which led Eusebius, or other earlier authors whom he may have followed, to speak of this book amongst Christian writings, much as it is introduced in the Muratorian fragment."[92]

Sundberg considered the Fragmentist's reference here to be evidence of a fourth-century context because he viewed the Fragment's list to be a canon of the New Testament in the strictest sense of the term. Given his understanding that this is the case, it would follow that *Wisdom* does not

---

[82] *Wisdom of Solomon* 2:12; Isaiah 3:9–10; *Barnabas* 6 (*ANF* 1:140n19). The dates for *Barnabas* are from Quasten, *Patrology*, vol. 1, 90–91.
[83] Metzger, *The Canon of the New Testament*, 57.
[84] Epiph., *Refutation of All Heresies* 1.6.4.
[85] Horbury, "The Wisdom of Solomon," 152–56.
[86] Tregelles, *Canon Muratorianus*, 55.
[87] Ibid., 54.
[88] Irenæus, *Against Heresies* 4.38.3.
[89] Euseb., *Ecclesiastical History* 5.8.1.
[90] Ibid.
[91] Ibid., 5.26.
[92] S. Prideaux Tregelles, "On a Passage in the Muratorian Canon," *The Journal of Classical and Sacred Philology*, 2 (March 1855): 41.

have a place in the Old Testament canon. Sundberg saw this as consistent with Eusebius, Athanasius, and Epiphanius.[93] In other words, by the time the Fragment was written, it had become clear that *Wisdom* could only find a place in a New Testament list; the Old Testament was complete and did not include *Wisdom*, at least in the East. However, Ferguson countered Sundberg's conclusions by highlighting Melito's omission of *Wisdom* from his Old Testament as well as the fact that what Sundberg viewed as Eusebius's treatment of *Wisdom* actually belongs to Irenæus.[94] Ferguson went on to point to Clement's use of *Wisdom* (mentioned above), the possibility that the writer of Hebrews quoted from it, and Tertullian's treatment of it as authoritative where he quoted from *Wisdom* 1:1 on two occasions in his anti-Marcionite polemics.[95] Nevertheless, Ferguson conceded that it is unknown whether these considered *Wisdom* to be in the Old or New Testament.[96]

Because the Fragmentist did not attribute *Wisdom* to Solomon, Hahneman saw this as evidence of a late date.[97] Only the earliest church fathers considered Solomon to have been the author. These include Clement of Alexandria, Tertullian, Cyprian, Lactantius, and Cyril of Jerusalem, among others.[98] Not until Augustine does one see an attribution to any other than Solomon, yet Augustine, like the Fragmentist, considered it canonical Scripture.[99] Thus, not until the late fourth century does a context present itself for the Fragmentist's view of *Wisdom*.

Armstrong found a parallel similar to the Fragmentist's use of the word *catholica* in reference to *Wisdom*. Armstrong noted that this is an "extremely uncommon construction in earliest Latin Christian literature."[100] However, Victorinus of Pettau used it in his commentary on the

---

[93] Sundberg, "Canon Muratori," 15–18, 17n58; Euseb., *Ecclesiastical History* 5.8.1–8; Athanasius, *Festal Letter* 39; Epiph., *Refutation of All Heresies* 1.1.8; 76.

[94] Ferguson, "Canon Muratori," 679. Eusebius writes in *Ecclesiastical History* 4.26.13 that Melito considered as part of the Jewish Scriptures "the Proverbs of Solomon, Wisdom also," but this "Wisdom" here mentioned is commonly considered by scholars to refer to Proverbs. See *NPNF* 2:1:200n17, 2:1:206n36.

[95] Ferguson, "Canon Muratori," 679; *Wisdom of Solomon* 7.25; Hebrews 1:3; Tert., *Prescription Against Heretics* 7; idem, *Against the Valentinians* 2.

[96] Ferguson, "Canon Muratori," 679.

[97] Hahneman, *The Muratorian Fragment*, 201.

[98] Clement of Alexandria, *Miscellanies* 6.11; Tert., *Against the Valentinians* 2.2; Cyprian, *To Fortunatus: Exhortation to Martyrdom* 2; Lactantius, *Epitome of the Divine Institutes* 42; Cyril of Jerusalem, *On the Catechetical Lectures* 9.2.

[99] Hahneman, *The Muratorian Fragment*, 201.

[100] Armstrong, "Victorinus of Pettau," 25.

Apocalypse.[101] Armstrong also conceded the fact that Tertullian used the expression in similar way.[102]

Apocalypse of Peter

Along with the Apocalypse, the Fragmentist also accepted the *Apocalypse of Peter* but remarked that "some amongst us" do not allow it to be read in the church (lines 70–73). Clement of Alexandria also accepted the *Apocalypse of Peter* as Scripture and appears to have quoted from it.[103] Methodius quoted from it and called it one of the "inspired writings."[104] Nevertheless, Eusebius listed it among the rejected books. He also remarked that it was not universally accepted and that citations from it cannot be found among any "ecclesiastical writer, ancient or modern," though this latter remark may be an exaggeration.[105] Writing between 439 and 450, regarding the period between 324 and 425, Sozomen testified that "the book entitled the *Apocalypse of Peter*, which was considered altogether spurious by the ancients, is still read in some of the churches of Palestine."[106]

Sundberg and Hahneman found parallels for the Fragmentist's cautionary tone regarding the *Apocalypse of Peter* in the fourth century.[107] Up until that time, the work appears to have been widely circulated and accepted.[108] Consistent with this, Hahneman observed that no second-century writer expressed doubts like those of the Fragmentist.

Notwithstanding the early acceptance, during the fourth century some expressed doubts, namely Eusebius, Jerome, and the scribe of the Codex Claromontanus, while others still seem to have accepted it including

---

[101] Victorinus of Pettau, *Commentary on the Apocalypse of the Blessed John* 1.7, 4.5, 12.4.

[102] Armstrong, "Victorinus of Pettau," 25n76; Tert., *Prescription Against Heretics* 30.

[103] Euseb., *Ecclesiastical History* 6.14.1; Clement of Alexandria, *Extracts from the Prophets* 48.

[104] Methodius, *The Banquet of the Ten Virgins*, Theophila 6.

[105] Euseb., *Ecclesiastical History* 3.25.4; idem, *Ecclesiastical History* 3.3.2 (*NPNF* 2:1:134n11); Sundberg, "Canon Muratori," 28.

[106] Johannes Quasten, *Patrology*, vol. 3, *The Golden Age of Greek Patristic Literature* (Westminster, MD: Christian Classics, 1950), 534; Sozomen, *Ecclesiastical History* 7.19.

[107] Sundberg, "Canon Muratori," 26–34; Hahneman, *The Muratorian Fragment*, 205–8.

[108] According to Hahneman, witnesses to this circulation include "Theophilus of Antioch, Methodius of Tyre, Eusebius in Caesarea, the Stichometry of Nicephorus in Jerusalem, Macarius in Syria, Jerome in Bethlehem, and Sozomen, a native of Bethelia in Palestine (exceptions are Clement of Alexandria and the probably Alexandrian catalogue in the Codex Claromontanus)," thus it appears that most known NT manuscripts included it. Hahneman, *The Muratorian Fragment*, 208.

Methodius and Sozomen. Horbury agreed that this ambivalence coheres with the Fragmentist's including it in the *antilegomena*, but Horbury did not agree this leads to a second-century date conclusion.[109] Ferguson downplayed the perceived similarity between the Fragmentist's and Eusebius's views on the *Apocalypse of Peter*, interpreting the Fragmentist as more sanguine about the otherwise questioned work.[110]

This apparent sanguinity may support a third-century date due to a parallel perceived by Armstrong between the Fragmentist and Victorinus of Pettau. Armstrong highlighted a quote from Victorinus in which the latter identified the *Apocalypse of Peter* as Scripture. Armstrong concluded, "The phenomenal rarity of authors who accepted the *Apocalypse of Peter* speaks all the more forcefully for a Victorinan theory of authorship."[111] The early acceptance of the *Apocalypse of Peter* and the doubts regarding it that came about later appear to place the Fragment in that transition period perhaps in the third century.

Shepherd of Hermas

With regard to the *Shepherd of Hermas*, the Fragmentist wrote,
"The Pastor, moreover, did Hermas write very recently in our times in the city of Rome, while his brother bishop Pius sat in the chair of the Church of Rome. And therefore, it also ought to be read; but it cannot be made public in the Church to the people, nor placed among the prophets, as their number is complete, nor among the apostles to the end of time." (lines 73–80)

Scholars give special attention to two items in this passage: the date of *Shepherd's* composition (*nuperrime temporibus nostris*) and the reception of *Shepherd*. They give special consideration to the impacts that these items have on determining the Fragment's date due to their reference to time.

Nuperrime temporibus nostris

Second- and third-century proponents translate the expression *nuperrime temporibus nostris* as "very recently in our times." Muratori believed this shows that Caius would have had opportunity to write the Fragment as he lived during the period in question.[112] Donaldson entertained the possibility that "in our times" may be the writer's way of distinguishing between the apostolic and post-apostolic eras. If this is possible, one cannot insist on an early date.[113] Like Donaldson, Salmon did not think that the expression "in

---

[109] Horbury, "The Wisdom of Solomon," 154, 159.
[110] Ferguson, "Canon Muratori," 680.
[111] Armstrong, "Victorinus of Pettau," 28.
[112] Muratori, *Antiquitates italicæ mediiævi*, col. 3:852.
[113] Donaldson, *A Critical History*, 212.

our times" should be "too severely pressed," and he also thought that the Fragmentist could have even been writing fifty to sixty years after Pius's death and still legitimately have used such an expression.[114] In this way, Salmon allowed for his understanding that the Fragmentist is a contemporary of Zephyrinus. However, Zahn asserted that even if the term *nuperrime* could allow for an interpretation which points to separate apostolic and post-apostolic periods, one must understand that the expression *temporibus nostris* is conclusive that the author had to have been born prior to Pius's death.[115] In this way, proponents of the Early Hypothesis insist that the Fragmentist is a contemporary of Pius and could not have feasibly written his work later than the third century. In other words, the question is not whether the Fragmentist distinguishes between apostolic and post-apostolic eras; it is clear from line 80 that he does. Rather, the issue is whether or not he lived and wrote during or at least shortly after, Pius's lifetime. Proponents of the Early Hypothesis say he did.

This interpretation of *nuperrime temporibus nostris* persisted as the general consensus for over two hundred years. Still, Sundberg questioned it.[116] First, Sundberg doubted that *nuperrime* must only be translated as "very recently." He argued that another viable translation is "most recently." This opens the possibility that the Fragmentist (or at least some Latin translator) did not necessarily mean that *Shepherd* was written as recently as were the other books he lists, but instead it could mean that *Shepherd* was the most recently written in the list. Ferguson agreed with Sundberg that this is a possibility, but Ferguson contended that Sundberg's translation does not necessarily rule out a second-century date either. Ferguson did not believe Sundberg's alternative interpretation to be "the most natural meaning."[117] Hahneman agreed with Sundberg that the possibilities are open, but he did so primarily in light of the chance that the Fragment in its extant form is a translation. Therefore, Hahneman expressed caution that "there may be 'limited value' in dating the Fragment upon this simple three-word Latin phrase."[118]

Second, Sundberg did not believe that one must interpret the phrase "in our times" to mean during our lifetime.[119] According to him, another possible interpretation can be found in the understanding that early church writers set apart "the apostolic time from subsequent periods of church

---

[114] Salmon, "Muratorian Fragment," 1002.
[115] Zahn, "Muratorian Fragment," 54. Rothschild, "The Muratorian Fragment," 69–70. Rothschild calls this the "plain reading."
[116] Sundberg, "Canon Muratori," 8–9.
[117] Ferguson, "Canon Muratori," 678.
[118] Hahneman, *The Muratorian Fragment*, 34.
[119] Sundberg, "Canon Muratori," 9–11.

history."[120] In other words, when the Fragmentist wrote "our times," he could have meant the times since the death of the apostle John. For example, Sundberg grounded his position in the fact that Irenæus used a similar expression when describing the Apocalypse as having been written during the reign of Domitian, "almost in our generation" (σχεδόν επί της ημετέρας γενεάς).[121] Surely, Irenæus did not mean that the Apocalypse was written during his lifetime or that of his readers.[122] On the other hand, Ferguson believed instead that the quote Sundberg cited from Irenæus argues *against* Sundberg's interpretation.[123] Ferguson contended that Irenæus was using the expression "in our generation" in reference to his lifetime because he stated that the Apocalypse was written "*almost*" as recently as "our generation," especially given the probability that John wrote it during the early 90s and Irenæus was born as early as the 120s. Ferguson also cited Eusebius who stated that "the generation of those that had been deemed worthy to hear" the apostles "had passed away"; it appears that Eusebius equated "generation" (i.e., γενεάς) with lifetime.[124]

In short, Early Hypothesis proponents consider the Fragmentist's comment that *Shepherd* was written *nuperrime temporibus nostris* to be remarkable. Late Hypothesis proponents see the comment as inconclusive either way. Sundberg and Hahneman preferred to look elsewhere for evidence of the Fragment's date.[125] Hahneman summed up the problem as follows:

> *The real point of the argument in the Fragment's statements about the Shepherd is not that it is heretical, but that it was written too late to be considered apostolic. The temporal references of "nuperrime" and "temporibus nostris" in this case should perhaps then be read as relating only to the Shepherd of Hermas and the apostolic age, and not to the date of the Fragment itself. The argument in the Fragment for a late dating of the Shepherd need not correlate it with the lifetime of the Fragmentist, but only with that of Pius of Rome. The language of the Fragment can be read as making its case against it without reference to the dating of the Fragmentist.*[126]

---

[120] Sundberg, "Canon Muratori," 9; Armstrong, "Victorinus of Pettau," 23–25. Armstrong also highlights this distinction in his defense of Victorinan authorship of the Fragment.

[121] Euseb., *Ecclesiastical History* 5.8.6 (*NPNF* 2:1:222), (*PG* 20:449).

[122] Sundberg, "Canon Muratori," 10. Rothschild, "The Muratorian Fragment," 70–72. Rothschild calls this the "periodic reading."

[123] Ferguson, "Canon Muratori," 678.

[124] Euseb., *Ecclesiastical History* 3.32.8.

[125] Sundberg, "Canon Muratori," 11; Hahneman, *The Muratorian Fragment*, 34, 72.

[126] Hahneman, *The Muratorian Fragment*, 36.

Reception of the *Shepherd of Hermas*

The Fragmentist allowed for the reading of *Shepherd*, but he proscribed its public reading and denied it a place among the writings of the prophets or the apostles due to its having been written after their time. Arguably, both Irenæus and Clement of Alexandria accepted *Shepherd* as authoritative Scripture, quoting from it and alluding to it approvingly.[127] Tertullian quoted *Shepherd* in order to justify a point with his readers, who ostensibly accepted it, but whether at this point Tertullian himself accepted it or not remains unclear.[128] Nevertheless, most scholars see an explicit rejection of *Shepherd* by Tertullian during his Montanist years; according to him the universal church had also rejected it as "apocryphal and false."[129] On the other hand, in Alexandria, Origen apparently accepted it even though he knew that not all agreed with him. He noted that *Shepherd* is "a Scripture which is in circulation in the church, but not acknowledged by all to be divine."[130] Eusebius also acknowledged that *Shepherd* was not universally acknowledged but disputed.[131] Those who accepted it had read it publically in church, and "most of the ancient writers used it," among these being Irenæus.[132] Nevertheless, Eusebius did not recognize *Shepherd* at all; he rejected it without qualification.[133] Athanasius did not include *Shepherd* in his canon, but allowed for its limited use "by those who newly join us, and who wish for instruction in the word of godliness."[134]

Salmon believed that based on the evidence of how the Fragmentist treats *Shepherd*, the Fragment was composed during the bishopric of Zephyrinus of Rome, between the times that Tertullian wrote *Prayer* (ca. 200) and *Modesty* (ca. 217).[135] This places the date in the beginning of the third century. Zahn noted that the issue of using *Shepherd* in public worship presented itself most prominently around 200, not as late as the fourth century.[136]

---

[127] Irenæus, *Against Heresies* 4.20.2 quoted Shepherd of Hermas, *Mandate* 1; Clement of Alexandria, *Miscellanies* 1.17, 29; 2.1, 9, 12 quoted and alluded to Shepherd of Hermas, *Vision* 3.4, 8, 13; *Mandate* 4.2, 11; *Similitude* 9.16.

[128] Tert., *Prayer* 16.

[129] Tert., *Modesty* 10, 20.

[130] Origen, *First Principles* 1.3.3, 2.1.5, 3.2.4, 4.1.11; *Commentary on Matthew* 14.21. Origen quotes from Shepherd of Hermas, *Mandate* 1, 6.2.

[131] Euseb., *Ecclesiastical History* 3.3.6–7.

[132] Ibid., 3.3.6, 5.8.7.

[133] Euseb., *Ecclesiastical History* 3.25.4.

[134] Athanasius, *Festal Letter* 39.

[135] Salmon, "Muratorian Fragment," 1002–3; Quasten, *Patrology*, vol. 2, 296, 313.

[136] Zahn, "Muratorian Fragment," 54.

Against this, because *Shepherd* does not appear in any New Testament lists after Eusebius's censure of the text, Sundberg viewed Eusebius's time as the transition point with regard to sentiment about *Shepherd*; previously it had been accepted and disputed, but by the time Eusebius wrote his *Ecclesiastical History* it had come to be rejected.[137] Notwithstanding this transition apparent by the time of Eusebius and later Athanasius, Ferguson maintained that the evidence in the Fragment with regard to the reception of *Shepherd* could still allow for a second-century context. The Fragmentist may have had Irenæus and Clement in mind when he approved of *Shepherd's* private use but not of its ecclesial reading.[138] Further, Ferguson did not think that Eusebius marks a transition point, but rather that he was describing a condition in history that had existed since Tertullian.

Hahneman saw the Fragmentist's comments about *Shepherd* as consistent with a fourth-century context. Tertullian's rejection was an exception due to that Father's sectarian bent, not because of a wholesale consensus by the western church, so it does not necessarily indicate an early context.[139] In other words, *Shepherd* was generally accepted in the East until after Origen and in the West until the time of Jerome. In response to Hahneman, Ferguson highlighted the understanding that *Shepherd* itself shows evidence of being a composite work, possibly spread out over a period of time.[140] Thus, it is possible that a portion of it was written earlier, during the time of Clement of Rome (see *Shepherd of Hermas* 1.2.4), and that its final form was published while Pius was bishop of Rome.

This means that Hermas would have had a long career which Ferguson argued was not an impossibility. If Hermas gave Clement a copy around 99, toward the end of the latter's episcopacy, forty-one years later, at the beginning of Pius's bishopric, the much older Hermas may have finished it. This means it would have been written after the age of the apostles and during the time of Pius, as the Fragmentist attests, *as well as* during the time of Clement as *Shepherd* attests.[141] Contra the notion of a Fraternity "Legend," if Pius was born around 81, it is not inconceivable for him to have had a brother close to the same age.[142] Quasten put it this way: "The two dates are accounted for by the way in which the book was compiled. The

---

[137] Sundberg, "Canon Muratori," 13–15.
[138] Ferguson, "Canon Muratori," 678–79.
[139] Hahneman, *The Muratorian Fragment*, 70.
[140] Ferguson, review of *The Muratorian Fragment*, 692.
[141] Hahneman, *The Muratorian Fragment*, 53, 71. This is contra Hahneman's insistence that the Fragmentist could not have been a contemporary of Hermas or Pius. Also, the date during Clement's time coheres with Hahneman's belief that *Shepherd* was written around 100.
[142] Ibid., 52. This is contra Hahneman's supposition that the two were not brothers on the grounds of the time span.

older portion would most likely go back to Clement's day while the present redaction would be of Pius's time. Critical examination of the contents leads to the same conclusion. This shows that parts of the work belong to different periods."[143] For these reasons and more, Rothschild's claim that the Fragmentist's testimony regarding *Shepherd* is fraught with inconsistencies and errors seems doubtful.[144] In conclusion, the link between *Shepherd* and Pius place the Fragment squarely in the second or third centuries, but its rejection allows for a Fragment written as late as the fourth.

Pseudo-Pauline Epistles

After the Fragmentist listed and described the Pauline Epistles, he identified at least two supposed Pauline pseudepigrapha, and he mentioned a few other works. About these he stated, "There are [epistles] also in circulation one to the Laodiceans, and another to the Alexandrians, forged under the name of Paul, and addressed against the heresy of Marcion; and there are also several others which cannot be received into the Catholic Church, for it is not suitable for gall to be mingled with honey." (lines 63–68)

According to Tertullian, the Marcionites referred to the canonical epistle to the Ephesians as having been written to the Laodiceans by Paul.[145] Because the Fragmentist listed Ephesians earlier, he either misunderstood that these were the same epistle, or he understood them to be two separate epistles. Epiphanius related that in Marcion's supposed canon he included both the Ephesian epistle and "parts of the so-called Epistle to the Laodiceans."[146] Jerome mentioned a putatively Pauline epistle written to the Laodiceans of which he said, though it is read by some, "it is rejected by everyone;" he listed this in addition to Ephesians.[147]

Attempts to identify the Alexandrian epistle have fallen short; scholars simply do not have an extant work to which the Fragmentist is likely referring. Hahneman points out that due to apparent corruptions in the text, it is possible that the reference to forgery only applies to the Alexandrian epistle as related to Marcion, or that it refers to neither epistle,

---

[143] Quasten, *Patrology*, vol. 1, 92–93.

[144] Rothschild, "The Muratorian Fragment," 72–74. Rothschild contends that it is unlikely that poverty-stricken Hermas could have been a bishop's brother, that Pius's bishopric is too late to have taken place during *Shepherd's* writing, that Pius's brother was probably not named "Hermas," and that it is illogical for the Fragmentist to receive *Shepherd*, a book written after the apostles' time.

[145] Tert., *Against Marcion* 5.17. Several of the earliest manuscripts of Ephesians lack the phrase "in Ephesus." These manuscripts include p^{46}, ℵ, B, 424, 1739, Marcion, Tertullian, Origen, Ephraem, manuscripts according to Basil. Kurt Aland, et al., eds., *The Greek New Testament*, 3rd ed. (New York: United Bible Societies, 1975), 664.

[146] Epiph., *Refutation of All Heresies* 42.9.4. Cf., 42.11.9, 42.13.1.

[147] Jer., *On Illustrious Men* 5.

only to some other works related to Marcion.[148] Nevertheless, scholarship has weighed in on how these references enhance an understanding of the Fragment's date. First, Muratori believed that during the time of Caius the Laodicean epistle was being circulated, so Muratori simply assumed that this supposed pseudonymous work was flourishing during the second century.[149]

Second, Zahn saw the presence of the Laodicean epistle in fourth-century New Testament manuscripts as the "belated influence" of the past; an influence against which the Fragmentist protested as a "live" issue of his day.[150] In other words, Zahn saw no reason to believe the mention of this epistle indicates a fourth-century date for the Fragment. Third, Hahneman asserted of the Laodicean epistle, "there is no evidence of its existence earlier than the late fourth century," this notwithstanding evidence that the Marcionites believed in one, though they may have inadvertently been referring to Ephesians according to Tertullian.[151] Hahneman saw a parallel between the Fragment and Epiphanius, who also listed both Ephesians and Laodiceans. If the Fragment is second-century, it is unique with respect to Laodiceans. Regardless, there existed within the early third century, or earlier, the perception (albeit a Marcionite one) that an epistle purported to have been written by Paul (whether true or not), and purported to have been written to the Laodiceans (whether true or not).[152] Nevertheless, establishing a date for the Fragment based on this evidence remains difficult. Ferguson conceded as much when he admitted that he could only justify an early date if the Fragmentist was referring to Laodiceans, the Marcionite revision of Ephesians. On the other hand, Ferguson noted that the Fragmentist probably did not do this because Ephesians is mentioned among Paul's orthonymous writings (line 51).[153] If this is the case, the Fragmentist may have been referring to the Latin Laodicean epistle, in which case the Fragment must be dated much later. Finally, Rothschild believes that either the Fragmentist was wrong about Ephesians and Laodiceans, in which case it is probably an unreliable fourth-century work posing as a second-century work, or the Fragmentist was referring to the Latin Laodicean epistle of which there is no second- or third-century attestation.[154]

---

[148] Hahneman, *The Muratorian Fragment*, 196–97.

[149] Muratori, *Antiquitates italicæ mediiævi*, col. 3:853.

[150] Zahn, "Muratorian Fragment," 55.

[151] Hahneman, *The Muratorian Fragment*, 200.

[152] Tert., *Against Marcion* 5.17. *Encyclopedia of Early Christianity*, 2nd ed., s.v. "Marcionite Prologues"; the so-called "Marcionite Prologues" bear resemblance to Marcion's order of the Pauline epistles, but they do not exhibit a great deal of Marcion's teachings, and do not seem to contribute to this present debate.

[153] Ferguson, "Canon Muratori," 681.

[154] Rothschild, "The Muratorian Fragment," 76–77.

The Catalogue of Heresies

Toward the end of the Fragment, the author expressed his rejection of the work of certain individuals. He declared, "Of the writings of Arsinous, called also Valentinus, or of Miltiades, we receive nothing at all. Those are rejected too who wrote the new Book of Psalms for Marcion, together with Basilides and the founder of the Asian Cataphrygian" (lines 81–85). In one of his anti-Marcionite works, Tertullian mentioned what he considered to be a heretical psalter written by Valentinus.[155] Whether this is the same psalm book mentioned by the Fragmentist is uncertain, but that it was of the same general persuasion is likely.

As with the other evidence presented here, Fragment scholars view this "catalogue of heresies" as supporting their respective positions on its date. Muratori cautioned that the "Mitiades" in the Fragment must not be confused with Miltiades of which both Eusebius and Jerome spoke and who wrote for the church catholic.[156] Donaldson did not see the value in dating the Fragment based on this passage due to what he considers to be its corrupted condition. Even if one could correctly interpret the Fragmentist's mention of the Cataphrygians as a condemnation, this does not necessarily place the Fragment prior to Tertullian because it may have been Montanism's spread in Africa which prompted this reference.[157] Salmon saw the Cataphrygian mention as an indication of the Fragment having been written during Zephyrinus's bishopric.[158]

On the other hand, Zahn saw it quite the opposite. For him, the Fragment appears to be one written after the Roman church had condemned the doctrines of Montanus, Valentinus, Basilides, and Marcion, thus no earlier than 195.[159] In addition, Ferguson asserted that the "heresies mentioned are those of the second century" (he associates Basilides and Valentinus with Gnosticism).[160] Since other known fourth- and fifth-century writers against heresy (e.g., Epiphanius and Theodoret) listed heretics of their own day along with those of the second century, Ferguson argued that if the Fragment is a fourth-century work, one can reasonably expect to see something similar here.[161] Hahneman considered the catalogue of heresies evidence of a fourth-century date for three reasons.

---

[155] Tert., *The Flesh of Christ* 20.
[156] Muratori, *Antiquitates italicæ mediiævi*, col. 3:854. In place of the Fragment's "Mitiades" some translators have transcribed "Miltiades." Euseb., *Ecclesiastical History* 5.17.1–5, 5.28.4. Jer., *On Illustrious Men* 39.
[157] Donaldson, *A Critical History*, 212–13.
[158] Salmon, "Muratorian Fragment," 1003.
[159] Zahn, "Muratorian Canon," 54.
[160] Ferguson, "Canon Muratori," 681.
[161] Ferguson, review of *The Muratorian Fragment*, 696.

First, he believed the Fragmentist betrayed a dependence on Eusebius because he mistakenly identified Mitiades as a Montanist due to a possible copyist error in Eusebius.[162] Second, Hahneman took notice of the absence of references to Cataphrygians prior to the fourth century; up until that time, the prefix had not yet been added to the term "Phrygian."[163] Third, he also noted silence until the fourth-century regarding a Marcionite psalter.[164]

Armstrong looked to the evidence here to support his argument that Victorinus of Pettau authored the Fragment. He saw parallels between the two in Victorinus's commentary on the Apocalypse in the latter's condemnation of the Montanists.[165] Also, if Pseudo-Tertullian's *Against Heresies* belongs to Victorinus (and Armstrong believed it does), Armstrong contended that this argues even more conclusively for his claim primarily in the way that document contests the doctrines of the "Cataphrygians," Marcion, and Valentinus.[166] Rothschild believes that the list of rejected dissenters "looks less anti-Montanist or anti-Marcionite than like a medley of stereotypical second-century heretics jumbled together to exude a disapproving aura for an audience either unaware or uninterested in the facts," this in support of her contention that the Fragment constitutes a later work attempting to portray itself as an earlier one.[167]

Ecclesiastical Context

The Doctrine of the Gospel

After his treatment of the Gospels, the Fragmentist highlighted a theme which runs through them for the universal church "as regards the faith of believers" (lines 18–19). He then explicated what is ostensibly a *regula fidei* formula: "the Lord's nativity, His passion, His resurrection, His conversation with His disciples, and His twofold advent,—the first in the humiliation of rejection, which is now past, and the second in the glory of royal power, which is yet in the future" (lines 20–26).

Both Donaldson and Ferguson viewed this statement as indicative of an early context for the Fragment. Its simplicity and content show similarities with similar formulas found in Ignatius, Justin Martyr, Aristides,

---

[162] Hahneman, *The Muratorian Fragment*, 209–11.
[163] Ibid., 211–13.
[164] Ibid., 213.
[165] Armstrong, "Victorinus of Pettau," 28; Victorinus of Pettau, *Commentary on the Apocalypse of the Blessed John*, 2.4, 10.2.
[166] Armstrong, "Victorinus of Pettau," 28–29; Pseudo-Tertullian, *Against Heresies* 4, 6.
[167] Rothschild, "The Muratorian Fragment," 76.

Irenæus, and Tertullian.[168] Though this "rule of faith" is structurally dissimilar to that of Victorinus of Pettau in his commentary on the Apocalypse, Armstrong noted that they both follow immediately after the writers' exposition of the Fourth Gospel and Victorinus's versions compare closely to the Fragment's in other ways as well.[169]

The Church

In two ways, the Fragment offered a glimpse into ecclesial social context. First, throughout the Fragment, the author made reference to the all-important reception of texts by the church at large by highlighting the otherwise assumed criticality of catholicity. He noted that the personal epistles of Paul, though not written to entire churches per se, are "hallowed in the esteem of the Catholic Church" (lines 59–63). On the other hand, the pseudo-Pauline "cannot be received into the Catholic Church" (lines 64–67). Additionally, the epistles of Jude and John are "reckoned among the Catholic" (lines 68–69). Second, the Fragmentist held the personal epistles of Paul to be just as vital for the "regulation of ecclesiastical discipline" as the apostle's public epistles (lines 62–63).

Donaldson asserted that the phrases "the Catholic Church" and "ecclesiastical discipline" belong to the late second to early third centuries and not prior, though Ignatius refers to the catholic church as early as 117.[170] Because the Fragment in its current form may be a translation, Ferguson conceded that comparisons made between its idiolect and that of other documents can yield only limited fruit.[171] Nevertheless, he pointed out a parallel between the Fragment's notion of *ecclesiasticae disciplinae* and a similar idea throughout Tertullian's work.[172] In addition, at one point, the Fragment uses the term "catholic" substantively rather than attributively as in the other two times. Armstrong found this remarkable due to the paucity of instances where such a substantive construction of the adjective *catholica* was employed in early Christian literature.[173] Victorinus of Pettau used this construction in his commentary on the Apocalypse, so Armstrong saw a

---

[168] Donaldson, *A Critical History*, 212; Ferguson, "Canon Muratori," 681, 681n17, 682; Ferguson, review of *The Muratorian Fragment*, 696; Ignatius, *To the Trallians* 9; Justin Martyr, *First Apology* 31; Aristides, *Apology* 2; Irenæus, *Against Heresies* 1.10; Tert., *Prescription Against Heretics* 13; idem, *The Veiling of Virgins* 1; idem, *Against Praxeas* 2.

[169] Armstrong, "Victorinus of Pettau," 9; Victorinus of Pettau, *Commentary on the Apocalypse of the Blessed John* 1.2, 3; 3.1; 5.3.

[170] Donaldson, *A Critical History*, 212; Ignatius, *To the Smyrnaeans* 8.

[171] Ferguson, "Canon Muratori," 678.

[172] Ferguson, "Canon Muratori," 678; Tert., *Prescription Against Heretics* 36, 44; idem, *Prayer*, passim; idem, *The Veiling of Virgins* 16; idem, *Against Marcion* 5.21.

[173] Armstrong, "Victorinus of Pettau," 25.

parallel here.[174] However, Armstrong also conceded that Victorinus more frequently made use of the attributive construction of *catholica*, and he conceded that Tertullian used the term substantively as well.[175]

The Chair

In describing a bishopric, in this case Pius's, the Fragmentist stated that Pius "sat in the chair of the Church of Rome" (lines 75–76). Regarding this expression, Donaldson observed that it has no parallel in the period from about 110 to 180, nor does Tertullian use it.[176] However, he noted that Cyprian used similar expressions at times.[177] According to Salmon, the expression's implication that a mono-episcopacy prevailed in Rome betrays a time much later than that of Pius, during whose ministry the constitution of the church did not call for a single occupant of the bishop's chair.[178] Ferguson considered this expression to be parallel to Irenæus's idea of a chair of magisterium.[179]

Church Reading of the Prophets and the Apostles

In his distinction between books that "ought to be read" but "cannot be made public in the Church to the people," the Fragmentist implied a difference between the Old and New Testaments with his explicit mention of two separate categories of writings: those which are "among the prophets" and those which are "among the apostles" (lines 77–80). Ferguson highlighted the fact that Justin Martyr makes just such a distinction, as well.[180] Whereas the Fragmentist linked these two categories to public reading in the church, so, too, Justin wrote that on Sundays at the Christian meetings, "the memoirs of the apostles or the writings of the prophets are read."[181] Rothschild adds to this with her observation that other second-century works make this distinction between the prophets and the apostles in the same manner; these include Ignatius, Polycarp, and the *Didache*, but she believes the

---

[174] Victorinus of Pettau, *Commentary on the Apocalypse of the Blessed John*, 1.7.

[175] Victorinus of Pettau, *Commentary on the Apocalypse of the Blessed John*, 4.4, 12.4; Tert., *Prescription Against Heresies* 30.2.

[176] Donaldson, *A Critical History*, 209, 212.

[177] Cyprian, *To the People, Concerning Five Schismatic Presbyters of the Faction of Felicissimus* 5; idem, *To Antonianus About Cornelius and Novatian* 9.

[178] Salmon, "Muratorian Fragment," 1002.

[179] Ferguson, "Canon Muratori," 678; Irenæus, *Demonstration of the Apostolic Teaching* 2.

[180] Ferguson, "Canon Muratori," 681; Ferguson, review of *The Muratorian Fragment*, 696.

[181] Justin, *First Apology* 67.

Fragmentist is merely imitating this supposedly earlier notion rather than speaking about the context in which he found himself.[182]

Summary

This chapter has enumerated the evidence upon which Muratorian Fragment scholars typically consider regarding the date of its composition. In addition, it has offered brief expositions on their interpretations of that evidence. In some cases, evidence is used by both camps, while in others, individual items are only considered important by proponents on one side of the debate. However, in all cases, it is absolutely certain that scholars' assumptions color the evidence they examine. The combination of assumptions with evidence then leads to the various, and at times conflicting, interpretations they proffer. In other words, scholars' hypotheses derive from their interpretations of the evidence rather than on the evidence directly, and those interpretations result from the assumptions the scholars bring with them to the debate.

In applying the Harman-McCullagh Criteria to answer the research question, the study examined whether or not, and to what degree, each item of evidence listed above implies the hypotheses. Moreover, because these hypotheses are, albeit indirectly, products of scholars' assumptions, the study considered to what extent unsubstantiated assumptions play a role in coloring scholars' interpretation of the evidence. To that end, the following chapter features a description of both the Early and Late Hypotheses, and it identifies the assumptions made by scholars on each side of the debate.

---

[182] Rothschild, "The Muratorian Fragment," 77n112; Ignatius, *To the Philadelphians* 9; Polycarp, *To the Philippians* 6; *Didache* 11.

A Date: The Hypotheses

Inasmuch as the study calls for an examination of how well the two hypotheses under consideration explain the evidence, the preceding chapter offered a catalog of the evidence to which scholars point in support of their positions. The present chapter features descriptions of these hypotheses, first of the Early Hypothesis and then of the Late Hypothesis. Where applicable, it offers discussion regarding potential counters to the reasons driving each of them as well as exposure to their basic assumptions and apparent indiscretions in logic.

The Early Hypothesis

Since Muratori's publication of the Fragment in 1740, the belief that it constitutes a second- or third-century composition prevailed among scholars for over two hundred years. Scholars who subscribe to the Early Hypothesis include Muratori, Hug, Credner, Donaldson, Tregelles, Salmon, Zahn, Westcott, and Quasten. After the hypothesis faced Sundberg's challenge in the 1960s, the Early Hypothesis persisted in the work of Ferguson, Verheyden, Balla, and Armstrong. These contend that the Early Hypothesis best explains the evidence through three lines of reasoning. First, the Fragmentist implied that he was a contemporary of Pius. Second, the Fragment exhibits literary features similar to those found in second- and third-century literature. Third, the Fragment possesses elements which seem to betray an apparent second- or third-century historical/theological context. This section offers a discussion of some of the issues involving a subscription to the Early Hypothesis with its supporting reasons and the evidence upon which those reasons are supposedly based.

Reason #1:
The Fragmentist, a Contemporary of Pius

The Plain Reading

Proponents of the Early Hypothesis conclude that the Fragment is a second- or third-century composition because they maintain that the Fragmentist claimed to be a contemporary of Pius, the bishop of Rome. The Fragmentist states that the *Shepherd of Hermas* was written "very recently in our times (*nuperrime temporibus nostris*) in the city of Rome, while his brother bishop Pius sat in the chair of the Church of Rome" (lines 73–77). It is a recognized fact among church historians that Pius was bishop of Rome from about 138 to 155.[1]

The interpretation of the expression "in our times," as equating to the lifetime of Pius, appears on the surface to be a logical understanding of the text. Among the scholars who read the Fragment with this meaning are Muratori, Tregelles, Zahn, Westcott, and Ferguson.[2] Westcott maintained that this interpretation was the best inference because it did not derive from interpreting the passage "loosely."[3] Likewise, Ferguson held to the notion that this was "the most natural meaning."[4] Rothschild dubbed this type of interpretation the "Plain Reading."[5]

The Periodic Reading

However, others believe the Fragmentist had a broader meaning in mind when referring to the time of *Shepherd's* writing as "in our times," and this can be seen if one employs what has come to be called a "Periodic Reading."[6] A periodic reading, while allowing for the possibility that the plain reading may be valid, also allowed for the possibility that the Fragmentist was referring to the post-apostolic period in general. In other words, the Fragmentist was making a distinction between the times of the apostles and his own. For example, both Donaldson and Salmon, reluctant to stake their understanding of the Fragment's date on the plain reading, allowed for a periodic reading. Nevertheless, these still argued for an early date albeit for other reasons.[7]

Of these two hermeneutic methods, only the plain reading requires a period of time tied to Pius's lifespan. The periodic reading has no such restriction; the period began with the death of the last apostle and extends indefinitely into the future, with no *terminus ad quem*. This possibility means that it is no longer necessary to consider the Fragmentist and Pius to be contemporaries, and by implication, no longer necessary to date the Fragment in the second century. As such, it allows for the Fragment to have

---

[1] *Encyclopedia of Early Christianity*, 2nd ed., s.v. "Pius I (d. ca. 155)."
[2] Muratori, *Antiquitates italicæ mediiævi*, col. 3:852; Tregelles, *Canon Muratorianus*, 64; Zahn, *Geschichte des neutestamentlichen Kanons*, 340, 438; Westcott, *A General Survey*, 215n1; Ferguson, "Canon Muratori," 678.
[3] Westcott, *A General Survey*, 215n1
[4] Ferguson, "Canon Muratori," 678.
[5] Rothschild, "The Muratorian Fragment," 69.
[6] Ibid., 70.
[7] Donaldson, *A Critical History*, 212. Salmon, "Muratorian Fragment," 1002.

been written either during Pius's lifetime *or* during a subsequent time period. Sundberg, in his development of the Late Hypothesis, capitalized on this possibility. He questioned the assumption that "in our times" meant within Pius's lifetime, and this opening provided him with the opportunity to posit the Fragment's date in the fourth century.[8]

However, Sundberg did not remain content to simply allow for the likelihood of an early date. In several of the church fathers, notably Ignatius, Polycarp, Hegesippus, and Eusebius, he observed a distinction made between the time of the apostles and the remainder of church history, and he likened the Fragment's reference to "our times" as an indication of a similar distinction. Of special interest to Sundberg's case is Irenæus's statement that the Apocalypse was written "almost in our generation."[9]

It would be surprising that Irenæus could use such language to describe a lapse of time approaching a century apart from the fact that he is utilizing the tradition which differentiates between apostolic and subsequent time. It is clear that he believed that the Apocalypse of John was written about the end of the apostolic period, i.e., "almost in our own generation" (σχεδὸν ἐπί τῆς ἡμετέρας γενεᾶς). And the similarity of the language used by Irenæus to describe the time in which the Apocalypse of John was written to the language used in the Muratorian canon to describe the time in which the *Shepherd of Hermas* was written leaves poorly founded the argument that the words "temporibus nostris" can mean nothing else than within the lifetime of the author.[10]

With his reference to a century's "lapse of time," it appears that Sundberg began to go beyond any allowance for an early date but was moving completely *away* from such a possibility. Interestingly, Sundberg equated the meaning of the two expressions: the Fragmentist's "in our times," and Irenæus's "in our generation." For him, they both mean "in the post-apostolic period." Hahneman agreed with Sundberg and further argued that should one interpret Irenæus as meaning "our lifetime," doing so would put undue tension on the term "almost"; it is less problematic to have "almost" mean "almost in the post-apostolic period" than to have it mean "almost in our lifetime" considering that the latter would need to encompass a distance in time of about sixty to one hundred years.[11] Hahneman's periodic reading also makes better sense considering Irenæus's statement that the Apocalypse was written "not a long time ago," and it accords better with the Fragmentist's contrast between *Shepherd* and the writings of the apostles.[12]

---

[8] Sundberg, "Canon Muratori," 9.
[9] Irenæus, *Against Heresies* 5.30.3.
[10] Sundberg, "Canon Muratori," 10.
[11] Hahneman, *The Muratorian Fragment*, 35.
[12] Ibid., 35–36.

Ferguson argued against the conclusion of Sundberg and Hahneman by noting that while the Fragmentist and Irenæus have similar expressions, their intentions were different, and in fact contrary. He believed that whereas the Fragmentist sought to increase the distance between *Shepherd* and "our times," Irenæus sought to decrease the distance between the Apocalypse and "our generation." Ferguson contended that "if the words 'our times' and 'our generation' are indeed parallel, then the Irenæus passage argues against Sundberg by unequivocally putting Hermas in the lifetime of the author of the *Canon*."[13] Thus, while the terms may indeed be parallel, the authors' intended uses for those terms were not. In this way, Ferguson negates the validity of Irenæus's statement as an exactly parallel passage with which to compare the Fragment, and takes the steam out of Sundberg's and Hahneman's dependence upon a periodic reading.

Through their employment of a plain reading, Early Hypothesis proponents interpret "in our times" as meaning in the lifetime of the author of the Fragment because they assume that this hermeneutic approach is to be preferred. What evidence do they bring in support of their presumption? In support of the plain reading, Ferguson offers three other examples of instances where "in our times" means "in our lifetime." The author of *1 Clement* (ca. 96 CE) speaks of the apostles having been put to death "in our own generation."[14] Eusebius speaks of a generation who had heard the apostles and then passed away; to hear them, they had to have been contemporaries.[15] In addition, Eusebius quotes an anti-Montanist as having personally witnessed some martyrdoms "in our time."[16]

On the other hand, in support of a presumptively periodic reading, scholars cite evidence for a distinction between the apostolic and post-apostolic eras.[17] Hegesippus described his time as one of heresy which followed the period during which the church had as yet been uncorrupted as he saw it, before the "sacred college of apostles had suffered death."[18] Eusebius makes explicit reference to an apostolic age.[19] However, while it is true that these latter examples which scholars proffer as support of the periodic reading are evidence of a distinction between the apostolic and post-apostolic ages, they are not evidence that a periodic reading should be preferred over a plain reading in the case of the Fragment.

Moreover, though of considerable interest to the problem of understanding the Fragmentist's reference to the date of *Shepherd*, little has

---

[13] Ferguson, "Canon Muratori," 678.
[14] *1 Clement* 5.
[15] Euseb., *Ecclesiastical History* 3.32.8.
[16] Ibid., 5.16.22.
[17] Sundberg, "Canon Muratori," 9.
[18] Euseb., *Ecclesiastical History* 4.22.4, 3.32.8.
[19] Ibid., 3.31.6.

been said by scholars with regard to the mention of *Pius* in support of either of the two readings. Why did the Fragmentist mention his bishopric at all? Given the Fragmentist's intention to distinguish between *Shepherd* and the apostles' writing, he could have simply stated that *Shepherd* was written in "our" times and therefore not to be considered among the apostolic works; in this case, there is no reason to insert a word about Pius and his seat in Rome. Instead, it appears that while the Fragmentist may have indeed been speaking of a post-apostolic period with his reference to "our time," he may, in addition to this, have chosen to set a delimiter on the timeframe of *Shepherd* within that period.

By the Fragmentist's account, *Shepherd* was written in the post-apostolic era, but apparently he believed it to have been written during a specific portion of that era, namely the time of Pius's bishopric. The existence of such a statement regarding a precise timeframe fits less problematically in a plain reading than in a periodic reading. If the Fragmentist intended a periodic reading the statement is unnecessary, but if he intended a plain reading, the mention of Pius adds extra weight to the Fragmentist's overall intended contention that *Shepherd* should not be considered with the apostles because both he and his audience can recall personally when it was authored.[20]

In short, Early Hypothesis proponents believe the Fragment is a second- or third-century composition because the Fragmentist implied that he is a contemporary of Pius. In interpreting the evidence for this belief, they employ a plain reading to interpret the Fragmentist's statement that *Shepherd* was written "in our times" during Pius's bishopric. This plain reading leads to an interpretation of "in our times" as meaning "in our lifetime." Support for the assumption that the plain reading should be preferred is found in patristic literature where it is clear that the writer was referring to his own lifetime when using the same expression the Fragmentist used to date *Shepherd*.

In addition, given the Fragmentist's intention to distinguish *Shepherd* from the apostolic writings, his reference to Pius's bishopric only offers value to an understanding of the text if a plain reading is employed (as opposed to a periodic reading). Thus, adherents to the Early Hypothesis believe it explains the evidence (i.e. "in our times . . . while . . . bishop Pius

---

[20] Sundberg hinted at the possibility that the Fragmentist simply misunderstood the situation in Rome because he did not live closely enough to Pius's time to understand the situation in Rome insofar as he seems to suggest that Rome's was a mono-episcopacy at the time. Sundberg, "Canon Muratori," 10n30, 12n33. Hahneman believed that the reason the Fragmentist mentioned Pius was due to a desire to refute the supposed apostolicity of *Shepherd*. However, this mention of Pius would then be unnecessary if, as Hahneman contends, the readers clearly understood "in our times" to mean the post-apostolic era. Hahneman, *The Muratorian Fragment*, 52.

sat in the chair of the Church of Rome") because it assumes a plain reading, a reading which is preferred over a periodic reading due to its having been substantiated by similar use in other early Christian works.

Reason #2:
Literary "Parallels" in Second- and Third-Century Literature

In addition to their direct inference from the Fragmentist's statement regarding the contemporaneity of Pius's bishopric, Early Hypothesis proponents also reason that the Fragment is early because they believe it features literary parallels with known second- and third-century writings. Early Hypothesis proponents cite four items of evidence in support of their premise that the Fragment possesses literary features parallel to literary features found in the second and third century.

First, the Fragmentist and Irenæus referred to Luke's Gospel using the same expression; they both called it *euangelii librum secundum Lucam* (i.e. "book of the Gospel according to Luke") (line 2).[21] Second, the Fragmentist and third-century writers place significance on the number "seven" (lines 47–50, 55–59).[22] Armstrong sees Victorinus of Pettau do this, and Donaldson notes something similar in Cyprian. Third, the Fragmentist, Tertullian, and Victorinus of Pettau all used an uncommon construction of the word *catholica* (line 69).[23] Fourth, the Fragmentist, Irenæus, and Cyprian characterize the bishop's chair similarly (lines 75–76).[24]

At this point it is important to highlight two critical assumptions that Early Hypothesis proponents make when considering literary parallels which appear to exist in the Fragment and in second- and third-century literature. First, they assume that language changes over time.[25] According

---

[21] Stanton, "The Fourfold Gospel," 323; Irenæus, *Against Heresies* 3.11.7. Quasten, *Patrology*, vol. 1, 291. This Latin translation of the Greek original comes from the West around the late third to early fourth centuries, when Latin flourished, and thus is, in all likelihood, a reliable one.

[22] Donaldson, *A Critical History*, 212; Cyprian, *To Quirinius: Testimonies against the Jews* 1.20; Armstrong, "Victorinus of Pettau," 16–17; Victorinus of Pettau, *Commentary on the Apocalypse of the Blessed John* 1.7.

[23] Armstrong, "Victorinus of Pettau," 25, 25n76; Victorinus of Pettau, *Commentary on the Apocalypse of the Blessed John* 1.7, 4.5, 12.4; Tert., *Prescription Against Heretics* 30.

[24] Ferguson, "Canon Muratori," 678; Irenæus, *Demonstration of the Apostolic Teaching* 2; Donaldson, *A Critical History*, 209, 212; Cyprian, *To the People, Concerning Five Schismatic Presbyters of the Faction of Felicissimus* 5; idem, *To Antonianus About Cornelius and Novatian* 9.

[25] Late Hypothesis proponents also make this assumption when they cite literary parallels between the Fragment and fourth-century writings as a reason for their conclusion regarding the Fragment's date.

to Professor of Historical Linguistics Theodora Bynon, this is not an unreasonable assumption. She maintains the following:

> *That language does in fact change during the course of time soon becomes evident when documents written in the same language but at different periods in time are subjected to examination . . . it may fairly be assumed that such texts are a representative sample of the spoken language as it was when they were committed to writing . . . . This means that it is possible to abstract the grammatical structure of the language of each period from the documents and in this way a series of synchronic grammars may be set up and compared. The differences in their successive structures may then be interpreted as reflecting the historical development of the language.*[26]

Professor Emeritus of Linguistics Lyle Campbell agrees. He acknowledges that "change in language is inevitable . . . . All languages change all the time (except dead ones). Language change is just a fact of life; it cannot be prevented or avoided."[27]

However, Bynon also issues a cautionary note lest interpreters of historical literature place *too* much stock in perceived changes, and this leads to the second assumption that Early Hypothesis proponents make in their consideration of parallels. They assume that expressions used in the second and third centuries were not used in the fourth but by that time had gone "out of vogue." In other words, in order to make the assertion that, for example, the Fragment is likely a third-century composition, and not a later one, because a third-century church father (e.g. Cyprian) uses the same verbal expression, one must believe that the use of that expression went out of vogue by 300. Bynon believes that in order to systematically study the change in language over time, a time lapse of four to five centuries is "optimal."[28] Longer periods may mean that one is not necessarily dealing with the "same language"; shorter ones mean that an insufficient amount of change has taken place upon which to base a rule.[29] What does this mean for the consideration of literary parallels in dating the Fragment? How valuable is this evidence in the debate?

---

[26] Theodora Bynon, *Historical Linguistics* (Cambridge: Cambridge University Press, 1977), 2.
[27] Lyle Campbell, *Historical Linguistics: An Introduction* (Edinburgh: Edinburgh University Press, 1998), 3.
[28] Bynon, *Historical Linguistics*, 6.
[29] Ibid.

The citation of literary parallels as evidence in support of a hypothesized date for the Fragment is valuable, but this value is limited insofar as the difference in time (i.e. from the mid-second century through the fourth), a period of about 250 years, falls below Bynon's threshold. While one is still treating the "same language," not enough time has passed to form a rule regarding the use of certain expression. In the case of the Early Hypothesis, these expressions include the way the Fragmentist and second- to third-century writer use the terms: the "book of the Gospel of Luke," the use of the number "seven," the term *catholica*, and the bishop's chair. It is not unthinkable that if these expressions were used in the second or third, they would also find parlance in the fourth. Thus, while Early Hypothesis proponents may be safe to in basing their conclusion on the notion that language change is a reasonable expectation, it is not so apparent that second-century literary expressions would have passed entirely out of vogue by the fourth century. Thus, the identification of apparent literary "parallels" may not be strong reason to believe the Fragment was composed in the second or third centuries.

Reason #3:
Indications of an Early Historical/Theological Context

Along with perceived literary parallels, Early Hypothesis proponents also reason that the Fragment is early because it seems to possess elements which betray a second- to third-century historical/theological context. These elements fall into two general categories. First, the reception which the Fragmentist affords the various texts he mentions seems similar to the way that these texts were received by known second- and third-century writers. Second, within the Fragment are theological notions consistent with those common during those two centuries.

The Treatment of Texts

First, the manner in which the Fragmentist treats the various texts in question seems more befitting an earlier historical context. According to Early Hypothesis proponents, the manner in which the Fragmentist characterized two of the received texts more likely points to an early date as opposed to a later one. First, in his treatment of Luke's Gospel, the Fragmentist refrained from linking the apostolic authority of Paul with the Lucan corpus. Ferguson contends that by the time of Irenæus, Luke's writings bore the authority of Paul had become an explicit acknowledgement.[30] Anything short of this would more than likely betray an

---

[30] Ferguson, "Canon Muratori," 681.

earlier time. Inasmuch as the Fragmentist leaves out the authority of Paul and merely mentions his companionship with Luke, he seems to be writing from a time pre-dating Irenæus.

Also, the Fragmentist's treatment of the Fourth Gospel appears to be apologetic in nature. Because by the fourth century the Fourth Gospel had been widely received, Early Hypothesis proponents argue that such a defensive position by the Fragmentist would have been unnecessary.[31] Such a posture would have been more at home during the second century, when the Alogi had challenged the reception of both the Fourth Gospel and the Apocalypse, believing them to have been written by Cerinthus. Therefore, since the Fragmentist makes a case for the acceptance of the Fourth Gospel, and the Alogi did not accept it, he probably knew about their concerns and may have been addressing them here. Because some in the second century polemicized in favor of the Johannine corpus, it is reasonable to believe that this was a "live" issue in the second century, so the argument goes.[32]

Furthermore, while texts like Luke and John enjoyed widespread favor, others were not so readily accepted, and the reluctance expressed by the Fragmentist when addressing these reflects a second- to third-century context, according to the Early Hypothesis. First, the *Apocalypse of Peter* seems to have been universally received, but not acceptable for reading in the church (lines 71–73). Armstrong highlighted a similarly positive attitude in Victorinus of Pettau, and he noted that the Fragment is the only New Testament list which accepts it.[33] By the fourth century, Eusebius did not share the Fragmentist's sentiment regarding the *Apocalypse of Peter*. He listed it among those which some thought were pseudepigraphic.[34] Ferguson conceded that while the Fragmentist did not express wholesale acceptance, his does not seem as negative as the position held by Eusebius in the fourth century.[35]

Additionally, as with the *Apocalypse of Peter*, the Fragmentist accepted *Shepherd of Hermas* but did not permit it to be read in the church (lines 73–80). Salmon noted that while *Shepherd* was accepted as Scripture early, by the later years of Tertullian it had become shrouded in doubt.[36] Zahn held that the question of its public reading reached its zenith around 200, and then diminished so that by the time of Eusebius the issue had resolved itself in the classification of *Shepherd* as pseudepigrapha.[37]

---

[31] Stanton, "The Fourfold Gospel," 324.
[32] Ferguson, "Canon Muratori," 681.
[33] Armstrong, "Victorinus of Pettau," 27–28.
[34] Euseb., *Ecclesiastical History* 3.25.4.
[35] Ferguson, "Canon Muratori," 680.
[36] Salmon, "Muratorian Fragment," 1002–3.
[37] Zahn, "Muratorian Fragment," 54; Euseb., *Ecclesiastical History* 3.25.4.

However, whereas Salmon saw the change in attitude toward *Shepherd of Hermas* as having manifested between Tertullian's writing of *Prayer* and *Modesty* (ca. from 200 to 217), Sundberg argued that this change did not take place until Eusebius.[38] Ferguson counters this with the possibility that Eusebius expressed a pre-existing sentiment.[39] Nevertheless, at least on the surface, the Fragmentist's attitude toward *Shepherd* does not go quite so far to the negative as Eusebius's. It seems more likely that the former's reception of *Shepherd* matches that of writers in the second century than that of those in the fourth.

In addition to listing texts which were received and some which were disputed, the Fragmentist made explicit mention of some which were not to be accepted for any reason. The names associated with these writings are Arsinous, Valentinus, Miltiades, Marcion, Basilides, and the Cataphrygians (lines 81–84). It is widely acknowledged by scholars that these names are associated with belief systems which flourished during the second century. For this reason, Ferguson argued for a second-century date and bolstered his claim with the observation that fourth-century writers had explicitly spoken against belief systems current in their own day which they deemed to be threats to Christianity.[40] Had the Fragmentist been writing in the fourth century, it would be more reasonable that he would have mentioned these latter beliefs rather than that he merely reach back two hundred years. Armstrong saw the possibility for Victorinian authorship here due to Victorinus of Pettau having spoken against Montanism, Marcionism, and Valentinus.[41]

While the Fragmentist explicitly treated the aforementioned texts either approvingly or otherwise, he omitted several canonical New Testament texts altogether. These include Hebrews, James, and the Petrine Epistle. Early Hypothesis proponents reason that as time went on, it seems less likely that books which came to be recognized or outright rejected would be ignored.[42] To them, the absence of their mention may be an indication that the Fragmentist had not known about these books or possibly that neither he nor anyone within his circle had yet been exposed to them in order to render a judgment. Late Hypothesis proponents react to these omissions by conceding that they are unusual, and they do not offer any explanation for them other than that the Fragmentist may have not communicated clearly in this case.[43]

---

[38] Sundberg, "Canon Muratori," 13–14.
[39] Ferguson, "Canon Muratori," 678–79.
[40] Ferguson, review of *The Muratorian Fragment*, 696.
[41] Armstrong, "Victorinus of Pettau," 28–29.
[42] Ferguson, "Canon Muratori," 681; Ferguson, review of *The Muratorian Fragment*, 695.
[43] Hahneman, *The Muratorian Fragment*, 181.

Fragmentist Theology

According to the Early Hypothesis, the theology of the Fragmentist seems to be more at home in the second or third centuries rather than in the fourth. This hypothesis is supported by three areas of evidence. First, it appears that the Fragmentist placed an apparent *regula fidei* after his treatment of the Fourth Gospel (lines 18–26). A similar formula is seen in early writers such as Ignatius, Justin Martyr, Aristides, Irenæus, Tertullian, and Victorinus of Pettau.[44] Second, the Fragmentist emphasizes the importance of both the "catholic church" and the "ecclesiastical discipline" (lines 59–69), two features which have parallel emphases in the second and third centuries.[45] Third, as in the case of Justin Martyr, the Fragmentist considers the "prophets and the apostles" to be a standard of authority when evaluating texts for public use in the church (lines 77–80), and Ferguson views this as evidence for an early context.[46] Rothschild also sees a similar function for the prophets and the apostles in Ignatius, Polycarp, and the *Didache*.[47]

Though scholars who disagree with the Early Hypothesis have not mounted arguments against these three reasons, at least one cautionary note is in order about one of the items of evidence cited. In his calling attention to the Fragmentist's not making mention of Luke's Pauline authority to write, Ferguson's reasoning may have succumbed to the informal logical fallacy of arguing from silence. Perhaps even more devastating to his logic is that the consideration of this as evidence may constitute a formal fallacy known as "Denying the Antecedent," a situation which would render the Early Hypothesis an unreliable argument with regard to this particular line of evidence. Ferguson reasons that if the Fragmentist had mentioned Luke's Pauline authority, this would represent a later development due to what he sees as an expansion of their connection.[48] Thus, anything shy of linking the Lucan corpus with Paul's authority would more likely be an early postulation. To deny the antecedent is to make an inference "which involves denying that the antecedent holds [in this case denying the idea that Pauline authority in the Lucan corpus was a present understanding during the Fragment's writing] and then concluding that the negation of the consequent [in this case a negation that the Fragment is a later work] must also hold."[49]

---

[44] Donaldson, *A Critical History*, 212; Ferguson, "Canon Muratori," 681, 681n17, 682; Ferguson, review of *The Muratorian Fragment*, 696; Armstrong, "Victorinus of Pettau," 9.

[45] Donaldson, *A Critical History*, 212; Ferguson, "Canon Muratori," 678; Armstrong, "Victorinus of Pettau," 25n76.

[46] Ferguson, "Canon Muratori," 681; Ferguson, review of *The Muratorian Fragment*, 696.

[47] Rothschild, "The Muratorian Fragment," 77n112.

[48] Ferguson, "Canon Muratori," 681.

[49] Paul Tomassi, *Logic* (London: Routledge, 1999), 379.

In short, Early Hypothesis proponents believe the Fragment is a second- or third-century composition because the Fragment has features which indicate that it may have a second- to third-century historical/theological context. It treats the texts in question in much the same way that early writers did, and it highlights several theological themes which seem to have enjoyed the spotlight during the second and third centuries. That said, in one area Early Hypothesis reasoning may exhibit weakness inasmuch as a relatively small portion of it may be the result of fallacious logic based in part on the Fragmentist's silence or ignorance.

In closing, the Early Hypothesis is an attempt by some scholars to explain the evidence present in the Fragment by dating its composition in the late second to early third centuries. They conclude that it is early for three reasons: the Fragmentist claims to be a contemporary of Pius, perceived literary parallels, and indications of an early context. Of these three, the first reason offers the greatest promise in supporting the Early Hypothesis's claim to explain the evidence. The other two reasons, while somewhat sound, suffer to a degree from assumptions that lack full substantiation and from faulty logic.

The Late Hypothesis

In the late twentieth century, Sundberg and then Hahneman challenged the traditional consensus that the Fragment was a pre-fourth-century composition. The notion that the Fragment was composed in the fourth century finds credence among scholars such as Zimmerman, Hahneman, McDonald, and Rothschild. Sundberg and Hahneman argued that the Late Hypothesis best explains the evidence through three lines of reasoning. First, the Fragment's appearance to be a canon can only mean it is a fourth-century composition. Second, the Fragmentist betrays a dependence on Eusebius's *Ecclesiastical History* (ca. 303). Third, the Fragment possesses elements which seem to point to its having been composed in a fourth-century historical/theological context. This section offers a discussion of some of the issues involving a subscription to the Late Hypothesis with its supporting reasons and the evidence upon which those reasons are based.

Reason #1:
The Fragment's Designation as a Canon

Late Hypothesis proponents believe that because the Fragment is practically a "canon," it cannot pre-date the fourth century. This reason for the Late Hypothesis is rooted in three premises. First, the Fragmentist knew of a closed Old Testament canon.[50] Second, the Old Testament canon was not fixed until Athanasius.[51] Third, it is unlikely that the church would have defined a New Testament canon, such as the Fragment, one and a half centuries prior to its doing so for the Old Testament. Hahneman believes the Muratorian Fragment as traditionally dated at the end of the second century contrasts greatly with the establishing of the Old Testament in the fourth century. The Fragment clearly represents a New Testament canon. To accept its traditional date would suggest that the church was engaged in defining a New Testament canon more than 150 years before it began fixing an Old Testament canon. While this is not impossible, it is unlikely, and it must have been such a consideration that encouraged Sundberg to reconsider the date of the Fragment.[52]

The first of these premises, that the Fragmentist had a closed Old Testament canon, appears to be likely in some sense. In speaking of the *Shepherd of Hermas*, the Fragmentist declared that it cannot be read among the prophets because their number is "complete" (lines 73–79). Sundberg noted that the term "prophets" was used by the church as a designation for the writings of the Old Testament, and thus it appears that the Fragmentist wrote during a time when no texts could be added to that particular list.[53] Furthermore, this also seems evident if Horbury's theory about the Fragment is correct. Recall that in Chapter 3, this study notes how Horbury left open the possibility that the missing piece from the beginning of the Fragment may have contained a list of Old Testament texts, particularly given the remarkably strange location of the *Wisdom of Solomon* in the list.[54]

Sundberg assumed that the Fragment represented only texts which its author considered as part of his New Testament and that he did not consider the Old Testament at all.[55] For Sundberg, the inclusion of *Wisdom of Solomon* in such a "New Testament canon" as the Fragment meant that the Old Testament had to have been closed by then.

The second of the premises, that this Old Testament canon (i.e. the Prophets) was not fixed until the time of Athanasius, is not without its difficulties. For example, the possibility that a similar type of limitation to the Old Testament existed during the time of Justin goes against Sundberg's belief that this condition could have only obtained in the fourth century. Justin remarked that during Christian meetings, "the writings of the prophets are read;" it seems more reasonable to believe that this list was discreet than

---

[50] Sundberg, "Canon Muratori," 15.
[51] Sundberg, "The Old Testament," 223.
[52] Hahneman, *The Muratorian Fragment*, 83.
[53] Sundberg, "Canon Muratori," 15–16.
[54] Horbury, "The Wisdom of Solomon in the Muratorian Fragment," 152–56.
[55] Sundberg, "Canon Muratori," 17–18.

to intimate that it would be open to anyone's idea of what was acceptable.[56] Also, Melito of Sardis reported that he had "learned accurately the books of the Old Testament," implying that it was possible to "know" them inaccurately.[57]

The third premise states that the church did not define a New Testament canon until the fourth century because it seems unlikely that the church would have done such a thing prior to the closing of the Old Testament. This does not follow. For example, that the church had limited its acceptance to only four Gospels is apparent as early as Irenæus.[58] Thus it does not appear to be necessarily the case that Christians were reluctant to make such restricting decisions when it came to the question of sacred texts.

Moreover, there is reason to believe that the Fragmentist did not intend his catalogue to be considered in the way that a canonical list would have been used. Hahneman offered some insight into his view of "canon," and what he inferred was Sundberg's view as well. According to Hahneman, "canon" is then a closed collection of "scripture," to which nothing can be added and from which nothing can be subtracted. Whereas the concept of canon pre-supposes the existence of scriptures, the concept of scripture does not necessarily entail the notion of canon. It is entirely possible to possess scriptures without having a canon, and this was in fact the situation in the first few centuries of the Church.[59]

Stanton's determination that the Fragment is more of an introduction about the degree of authority held by the various supposed sacred texts of Christianity takes some of the power out of Hahneman's contention that the Fragment as canon could not be second-century. Stanton also noted the fact that the other copies of the Fragment's text found in the Benedictine manuscripts are prologues, not lists consistent with the commonly accepted nature of a canon.[60] In fact, none of the wording in the Fragment is as limiting as Hahneman's notion of canon, insofar as a canon is that "to which nothing can be added and from which nothing can be subtracted."[61] At the most the Fragmentist ensured that his readers knew about the rejected heretical writings, but he did not explicitly declare that the canon was closed, as Irenæus did with the Gospels. Even given Hahneman's definition of canon coupled with his belief that the canon was solidified in the fourth century, his conclusions contradict the evidence. Several of the fourth-century canons include texts that others do not and omit texts that

---

[56] Justin, *First Apology* 67; Ferguson, "Canon Muratori," 681.

[57] Euseb., *Ecclesiastical History* 3.26.14.

[58] "It is not possible that the Gospels can be either more or fewer in number than they are." Irenæus, *Against Heresies* 3.11.8.

[59] Hahneman, *The Muratorian Fragment*, 73.

[60] Stanton, "The Fourfold Gospel," 323.

[61] Hahneman, *The Muratorian Fragment*, 73.

others include.⁶² Thus it would appear that a true canon as Hahneman understood the term had not obtained even by the end of the fourth century as he claimed.

In short, Late Hypothesis Reason #1 is not without problems. In particular, two problems present themselves. First, while the overall argument, consisting of the three premises, constitutes sound deduction, it is invalid. Its last two premises are doubtful. The second problem with Reason #1 lies in the degree to which the third premise is dependent upon Hahneman's unsubstantiated assumption that the church would not have restricted its list of sacred Christian texts until after it had done so for its sacred Jewish texts. Also, that the Fragment constitutes a canon in the way Hahneman defines the term is not a foregone conclusion.

Reason #2:
The Fragmentist's Apparent Dependence on Eusebius

Proponents of the Late Hypothesis also conclude that the Fragment is a fourth-century composition because they maintain that the Fragment shows a dependence on Eusebius's *Ecclesiastical History* in its reference to Miltiades. At the end of the Fragment, in his Catalogue of Heresies, the Fragmentist states that he and his people do not accept the writings of one "Miltiades" (line 81). Hahneman maintained that this inclusion of Miltiades in this list of heretics is "extraordinary" if it is to be believed accurate.⁶³ Hahneman supposed it may be that the Fragmentist had read Eusebius's mistaken reference to a certain Montanist in which Eusebius accidently rendered to him the appellation of "Miltiades." Hahneman argues that more than likely this Montanist was actually one "Alcibiades," that Eusebius had gotten his name wrong, and that the Fragmentist simply copied what Eusebius had written.

An Orthodox (and a Montanist?) Miltiades

Most references to Miltiades in the literature speak of an orthodox anti-Montanist. Tertullian, though eventually a Montanist himself, spoke in high regard for Miltiades in his polemic *Against the Valentinians*, calling him the "sophist of the churches" and counting him among the likes of Justin and Irenæus.⁶⁴ Tertullian's mention of him here means that Miltiades was probably an anti-Gnostic who flourished during the reign of Marcus Aurelius and was apparently known in North Africa.⁶⁵ Known in the East as

---

⁶² Ibid., 132–56.
⁶³ Hahneman, *The Muratorian Fragment*, 211.
⁶⁴ Tert., *Against the Valentinians* 5.
⁶⁵ *NPNF* 2:1:233n1.

well, Eusebius states that Miltiades authored three books: one against Montanism, one against the Greeks, and a third against the Jews.[66] Eusebius considered him to be of like mind as Justin, Tatian, and Clement of Alexandria.[67] Jerome named his books, *Against the Nations and the Jews* and an *Apology* to the emperors of his lifetime, probably Marcus Antoninus, Marcus Aurelius, or Commodus.[68] That Jerome mentions him means he was known in Rome as well as in the East and in North Africa.

Hahneman believed that Eusebius inadvertently called this anti-Montanist "Alcibiades" at one point. In discussing Miltiades's authorship of an anti-Montanist book, Eusebius made reference to the book by attributing it to Alcibiades, and Hahneman thought this attribution to be an error on both Eusebius's part and that of his amanuensis.[69] Down further in the text, Eusebius once again refers to this person as "Miltiades" as he rightly should, according to Hahneman.[70] If Eusebius confused the two men, as Hahneman claims, there was only one Miltiades, and he was not a Montanist. For Hahneman, there simply is no evidence of a Montanist named Miltiades.[71]

However, Professor of Church History Arthur C. McGiffert suggested that Eusebius possibly also refers to another Miltiades who was indeed a Montanist. In one place (*EH* 5.3.4), Eusebius refers to this Montanist as "Alcibiades," but both Salmon and McGiffert believed this could represent an error.[72] Because Eusebius had just written of an orthodox confessor named Alcibiades, these two scholars offer that Eusebius still had him in mind when turning to describe the Montanist Miltiades and that he (or his amanuensis) had inadvertently written "Alcibiades."[73] For this reason, McGiffert also believes against the belief of several other scholars that where the manuscripts and versions have "Miltiades" later where they refer to this Montanist (5.16.3), no change to "Alcibiades" is warranted.[74] These scholars believe that there is no Montanist named Miltiades, and that Eusebius wrote "Miltiades" in error in 5.16.3; for them it should read "Alcibiades."[75] Nevertheless, while McGiffert does not insist on the existence of a Montanist Miltiades, he does suggest the possibility. He

---

[66] Euseb., *Ecclesiastical History* 5.17.1, 5.
[67] Ibid., 5.28.4.
[68] Jer., *On Illustrious Men* 39. See also Jer., *Epistle 70, to Magnus an Orator of Rome* 4.
[69] Euseb., *Ecclesiastical History* 5.17.1; thus all the manuscripts and versions. Hahneman, *The Muratorian Fragment*, 209–10.
[70] Euseb., *Ecclesiastical History* 5.17.5; Hahneman, *The Muratorian Fragment*, 210.
[71] Hahneman, *The Muratorian Fragment*, 210.
[72] *NPNF* 2:1:218n3; 230n7.
[73] Euseb., *Ecclesiastical History* 5.3.2, cf. 5.3.4.
[74] *NPNF* 2:1:230n7.
[75] Ibid.

concludes that, "Until we get more light from some quarter we must be content to let the matter rest, leaving the reason for the use of Miltiades's name in this connection unexplained. There is, of course, nothing strange in the existence of a Montanist named Miltiades."[76]

A Montanist (and an Orthodox?) Alcibiades

In addition to orthodox Miltiades (and possibly a Montanist Miltiades as seen above), Eusebius also mentioned a Montanist named Alcibiades.[77] He listed this individual in the company of Theodotus as well as with Montanus, himself.[78] Hahneman believed that in 5.16.3, Eusebius accidently called this Alcibiades "Miltiades" where he wrote of the "heresy of those who are called after Miltiades"; he actually meant Alcibiades here.[79]

However, McGiffert preferred to hold to the manuscript evidence, and insisted that there existed an anti-Montanist Alcibiades. He believed that the "Miltiades" of *EH* 5.17.1a is an overlooked scribal error, and that had Eusebius been paying attention, he would have ensured 5.17.1a read as 5.17.1b reads, with "Alcibiades" instead.[80] Nevertheless, McGiffert concedes that, "Of the Alcibiades who wrote the anti-Montanistic treatise referred to, we know nothing."[81]

In summary, Hahneman argued that Eusebius mistakenly recorded "Miltiades" as a Montanist.[82] The Fragmentist read this not knowing that it was an error and as a result listed Miltiades among the heretics rather than among the orthodox. This means that Eusebius must pre-date the Fragmentist, and therefore the Fragment must be a fourth-century composition.

On the other hand, against Hahneman, it is possible that the Fragmentist is not referring to a "Miltiades" at all.[83] The text of the Fragment actually reads "mitiad(ei)*is*" not "Miltiades"; Hahneman assumed that it referred to Miltiades, and he admitted as much.[84] Like Hahneman, Tregelles, who personally examined the Fragment, saw no reason to doubt that Miltiades was the intended referent.[85] In addition, the manuscripts with the Fragment's text discovered at the Benedictine monastery at Monte

---

[76] *NPNF* 2:1:230n7.
[77] Euseb., *Ecclesiastical History* 5.3.4.
[78] Ibid.
[79] Hahneman, *The Muratorian Fragment*, 210.
[80] *NPNF* 2:1:233–34n1.
[81] Ibid.
[82] Euseb., *Ecclesiastical History* 5.16.3; Hahneman, *The Muratorian Fragment*, 210–11.
[83] *NPNF* 2:1:230n7.
[84] Hahneman, *The Muratorian Fragment*, 209.
[85] Tregelles, *Canon Muratorianus*, 65.

Cassino have Mitiadis, Mi(ti)adis, and Mitididis.[86] No existing Latin transcript of the Fragment's contents reads "Miltiades," and McGiffert suggested that it is "doubtful whether a Miltiades is mentioned at all in that document [i.e. the Fragment]."[87]

Three possible explanations present themselves. First, the Fragmentist read and copied Eusebius's erroneous use of "Miltiades" believing that this was the name of a Montanist. This is possible, but there is no evidence which makes it more likely than the following two scenarios. Second, there was a heretic with the same name as the orthodox polemicist Miltiades, and this was the individual to whom the Fragmentist referred. Like option one, this, too, is possible, but the textual evidence suggests otherwise, and points more to the third option. The third option is that the Fragmentist was referring to one "Mitiades," a heretic, possibly a Montanist, possibly a Gnostic. Not only is the third option possible, it appears to be more likely given the fact that the Benedictine documents also have Mitiadis, Mi(ti)adis, and Mitididis, all of which also lack the letter "L". In addition, as Hahneman concedes, "The Latin of the excerpts in the later Benedictine manuscripts is significantly better than that in Muratori's Fragment and this suggests a source for the Benedictine manuscripts not directly dependent upon the Muratorian Fragment."[88] In other words, there is no reason to believe the Fragmentist had Miltiades in mind, whether this supposed individual was the renowned orthodox polemicist (based on Eusebius's error) or an unknown heretic.

The Late Hypothesis reasons that the Fragment is a fourth-century composition because of a perceived dependence upon Eusebius. However, this perception is rooted in at least two unsubstantiated assumptions. First, it is rooted in the presupposition that Eusebius allowed a scribal error in *EH* 5.16.3 when he wrote "Miltiades" instead of "Alcibiades"; a supposition for which there is no conclusive evidence. Second, it is dependent upon the notion that "Miltiades" is misspelled in the Ambrosian Fragment and the Benedictine manuscripts as well as in the likely source upon which these copies are alleged to be dependent.

Reason #3:
Indications of a Late Historical/Theological Context

In the same way proponents of the Early Hypothesis perceive elements in the Fragment which betray an early historical/theological context, so those

---

[86] Hahneman, *The Muratorian Fragment*, 29, 209; Rothschild, "The Muratorian Fragment," 75.

[87] *NPNF* 2:1:230n7.

[88] Hahneman, *The Muratorian Fragment*, 10.

of the Late Hypothesis see indications of a later context. These indications of a late context fall into two general categories. First, the way the Fragmentist treats certain texts seems consistent with how others in the fourth century treated those same texts. Second, the Fragment appears to possess certain idiosyncrasies, or "peculiarities" which have parallels in other literature known to have obtained during the fourth century.[89]

Of special significance to this portion of the study, which deals with the reasoning behind the Late Hypothesis, is a comment made by Sundberg in "Canon Muratori." In response to Tregelles's comparison of the Fragment with authorities of the second century, Sundberg established the standard by which to judge the evidences pointing to the Fragment as a fourth-century composition. These evidences consist of "features in the canon which *cannot* be paralleled within the second-century church fathers and which find parallels *only* in substantially later materials [emphases added]."[90] Ferguson held Hahneman to Sundberg's standard when evaluating *The Muratorian Fragment*. Ferguson, like Sundberg, believed that in order to conclusively show the Fragment to be a fourth-century work, "There must be in the contents of the Fragment something only possible in the fourth century or something impossible in the second century."[91]

The Treatment of Texts

The Late Hypothesis argues that the Fragmentist treated the texts in question in the same manner that only fourth-century writers treated them. For example, the discussion regarding the *Wisdom of Solomon* may be of the greatest import regarding the question of how well the Late Hypothesis explains the evidence. While one could argue about how the Fragmentist received the Apocalypse, the *Apocalypse of Peter*, and the *Shepherd of Hermas*, the problem of *Wisdom* is the foundation for Sundberg's overall contention regarding the Fragment's date and its status as a canon. However, as well as being an integral part of the Late Hypothesis, the Fragmentist's mention of *Wisdom* may also be its Achilles Heel.

Both Sundberg and Hahneman make much of the Fragmentist's inclusion of the *Wisdom of Solomon* in what they presuppose is a New Testament list.[92] Hahneman reiterates Sundberg's argument that the Fragment's inclusion of *Wisdom* in its New Testament means its exclusion

---

[89] Hahneman, *The Muratorian Fragment*, 183–214.
[90] Sundberg, "Canon Muratori," 12.
[91] Ferguson, review of *The Muratorian Fragment*, 691.
[92] Sundberg, "Canon Muratori," 16–18; Hahneman, *The Muratorian Fragment*, 201.

from the Old.[93] This has parallels in Athanasius and Epiphanius, who also exclude *Wisdom* from the Old Testament. It is for this reason, along with others, that Sundberg believes the Fragment reflects a fourth-century situation, one in which the Old Testament would have finally been closed. The Fragmentist had to include *Wisdom* here, in this supposed New Testament list, because he could not consider it among the Old Testament texts.

However, this view of Sundberg's is not without its difficulties. First, unlike the Fragmentist, Athanasius does not place *Wisdom* in his New Testament list.[94] Therefore, it cannot be said that in this regard the Fragment is parallel with all fourth century New Testament lists. Even more problematic for Sundberg's case is the fact that Irenæus, like the Fragmentist, includes *Wisdom* in his New Testament, thus with regard to its reception of a text, the Fragment has a parallel in the second century.[95] This fact invalidates the reason to believe that the Fragment could *only* have existed within a fourth-century milieu.

Furthermore, the Fragment's location of *Wisdom* in its list has parallels which led Horbury to believe that the Fragmentist may not have considered it as part of his New Testament but rather as a part of his Old Testament.[96] Contrary to Sundberg and Hahneman, Horbury suggested that the Fragmentist had intended to list *Wisdom* as Old Testament antilegomena. This suggestion is based on what appears to be the common "practice of listing the disputed books of both Testaments together."[97] Horbury believed the first, and missing, part of the Fragmentist's list included the accepted Old Testament books (and ostensibly the Gospels of Matthew and Mark). Within the extant portion of the document, the author continued with the accepted books of the New Testament, beginning with Luke and continuing through John's epistles. Next, having finished with the accepted texts, the Fragmentist began his list of antilegomena, starting with the Old Testament, of which there is only one book in that category, i.e. *Wisdom*, and continuing with the New Testament antilegomena the Apocalypse through the *Shepherd of Herma*s. After this, he concludes with the rejected texts, the Catalogue of Heresies. In other words, Horbury believes the Fragment was meant to be organized as follows:

---

[93] Sundberg, "Canon Muratori," 16.
[94] Athanasius, *Festal Letter* 39.
[95] Euseb., *Ecclesiastical History* 5.8.1–8; Sundberg, "Canon Muratori," 17.
[96] Horbury, "The Wisdom of Solomon in the Muratorian Fragment," 152–56.
[97] Ibid., 152.

1. Received Texts (Old and New Testaments)
2. Disputed Texts (Old [*Wisdom*] and New [Apocalypse, *Apocalypse of Peter*, *Shepherd of Hermas*] Testaments)
3. Rejected Texts (Old and New Testaments)

Horbury cites several examples of writers who list the antilegomena of both the Old and New Testaments together.[98] When listing the texts of Clement of Alexandria, Eusebius began the disputed portion with *Wisdom*.[99] Athanasius, Epiphanius, Rufinus, and Jerome did the same.[100] Therefore, it appears more likely that *Wisdom* was never considered a New Testament book and that it has always been counted among the Old; there is no direct evidence that it should be counted in the New, merely the speculation of Late Hypothesis proponents.

With regard to the Fragmentist's treatment of other texts, Hahneman remarked that the mentions of Jude and the *Apocalypse of Peter* are an indication of a fourth-century context, but according to Eusebius, Clement of Alexandria considered these to be canonical Scripture as well; so, their acceptance was not merely a fourth-century phenomenon.[101] To be precise, Eusebius, in the fourth century, was not as accepting of Jude or of the *Apocalypse of Peter* as the Fragmentist or Clement were.[102]

In short, the Late Hypothesis reasons that the reception that the Fragment affords to the texts in question mirrors that of the fourth century and that in no case does it find parallels prior to that period. However, as has been demonstrated above, this is simply not borne out by the evidence. In several instances, earlier writers come close to expressing an attitude similar to that of the Fragmentist regarding these texts. Moreover, the place of the *Wisdom of Solomon*, which is critical for Sundberg's case, seems to parallel other works which place that text among the Old Testament antilegomena rather than among the books of the New Testament. Given Sundberg's stated criterion that features within the Fragment must not have parallels in the centuries preceding the fourth, it remains unclear how the Late Hypothesis proponents can place dependence upon the way the Fragment treats certain texts to support their overall claim.

---

[98] Horbury, "The Wisdom of Solomon in the Muratorian Fragment," 153–54.

[99] Euseb., *Ecclesiastical History* 6.13.6–6.14.1.

[100] Athanasius, *Festal Letter* 39.7; Epiph., *Refutation of All Heresies* 76.5; Rufinus, *Commentary on the Apostles' Creed* 37–38; Jer., *Preface to the Books of Samuel and Kings*.

[101] Hahneman, *The Muratorian Fragment*, 181; Euseb., *Ecclesiastical History* 6.14.1.

[102] Euseb., *Ecclesiastical History* 3.15.3, 6.14.1.

"Peculiarities"

The Fragment has features which Late Hypothesis proponents claim are peculiar to the fourth century. First, the Fragmentist, in his enumeration of the Gospels, listed Luke's as the third (*tertium*), and John's as the fourth (*quarti*) (lines 2, 9). Scholars assume that the missing beginning of the Fragment included Matthew and Mark, and likely in that order. Hahneman states that such an order would fit well in the fourth century but would be unusual. As noted in Chapter 3, this order is not unique to the fourth century, as Irenæus listed them similarly on one occasion.[103] While statistically the likelihood of such an order is more prevalent in fourth-century works, it does not require a fourth-century context.

Second, Hahneman considered certain statements made by the Fragmentist about the Fourth Gospel to be evidence of a fourth-century context, such as his reference to "bishops" having encouraged John to write as well as the statement that John participated in a fast prior to his receiving the inspiration for the book (lines 10–11). According to Hahneman, these are notions that show theological development; a development which does not pre-date 300.[104] Third, the Fragmentist called the book of Acts the "Acts of all the Apostles" (line 34), an elaboration which Hahneman views as more necessary in the fourth century than earlier due to the proliferation of apocryphal "*Acts*."[105] Again, the supposed need for this cannot be considered peculiar to the fourth century as there were other apocryphal "*Acts*" in the second century from which disambiguation may have also required.

Finally, with regard to the Catalogue of Heresies found toward the end of the Fragment, Late Hypothesis proponents believe it shows a fourth-century context for two reasons. First, the Fragmentist's designation of the Montanists as "Cataphrygians" seems more at home in the fourth century than earlier, when writers had called them "Phrygians" (line 84).[106] Second, there is no mention of a Marcionite Psalter until the fourth century (line 83). In both of these suppositions, Hahneman is committing the informal logical fallacy of arguing from silence. The apparent absence of such phenomena in extant writings prior to the fourth century does not necessarily (or even probably) lead to the conclusion that they did not occur before that time, and one need not conclude that because of their absence, the Fragment could only have been obtained in the fourth century.

In closing, the Late Hypothesis is an attempt by some scholars to explain the evidence present in the Fragment by dating its composition in the

---

[103] Irenæus, *Against Heresies* 3.1.1.
[104] Hahneman, The Muratorian Fragment, 188–90.
[105] Ibid., 193–94.
[106] Ibid., 211–13.

fourth century. They conclude that it is late for three reasons: the Fragment as a canon can only be fourth century, it shows a dependence on Eusebius, and it possesses features which were only known in a fourth-century context. However, each of these reasons has remarkable problems. First, there is reason to doubt that the Fragment was intended to function as a New Testament canon in the sense in which Late Hypothesis proponents understand the term; it may not have been a canon, per se, and it may not have been merely a *New Testament* list. Second, there is reason to doubt that the Fragmentist intended to include Eusebius's "Miltiades" among his heretics; he may have been referring to an otherwise unknown person named "Mitiades." Third, there is evidence of second- and third-century writers treating texts in a manner similar to that of the Fragmentist; such phenomena are thus not unique to the fourth century as Sundberg claimed. The reasons which Late Hypothesis proponents offer for their claim find their bases in a few unsubstantiated assumptions, contradictory evidence, and arguments from silence.

Summary

This chapter has described the Early and the Late Hypotheses. The proponents of the Early Hypothesis conclude that it is the best explanation of the evidence for three reasons. First, they maintain that, based on a plain reading of the text, the Fragmentist implied that he was a contemporary of Pius. Second, according to the Early Hypothesis the Fragment possesses literary parallels found in works known to be of the second and third centuries. Third, the Fragment contains historical and theological features which point to its having been composed during the second or third centuries. The reasons furnished by Early Hypothesis proponents are based on several assumptions. First, they assume that a plain reading of "in our times" is to be preferred over a period reading; an assumption that is not without historical precedence. In addition, they assume that language changes over time. Again, in light of the work of historical linguists, this assumption is reasonable. Third, they assume that language typical of the second and third centuries would have gone out of vogue by the fourth. However, historical linguists maintain that a longer time lapse would be necessary for this to be the case. The Early Hypothesis also suffers from faulty logic to a relatively small degree. In some cases it makes its argument from the silence of the Fragment on certain texts, and, to some extent, it also commits the formal logical fallacy known as "Denying the Antecedent."

Late Hypothesis proponents hold to their position for three reasons as well. First, they believe that because the Fragment is canon, based on their understanding of the term, it could not have obtained prior to the fourth century. However, there is doubt about the validity of these reasons due to the possibility that the Fragment may not constitute a canon as they have defined it, and due to the questionable assertion that the church did not beginning restricting the books it held as authoritative until the fourth century. Second, Hahneman argues that the Fragmentist depended on Eusebius, and that the former based his writing on a scribal error committed by the latter. However, there is credible reason to believe that this is simply not the case. Third, the Late Hypothesists believe that the features within the Fragment which indicate its time period are only found in the fourth century; an assertion which has been shown to be contrary to the evidence that several of these features are also found in earlier writings.

In these ways, both hypotheses attempt to explain the evidence. Each hypothesis comes as the result of reasons based on the available evidence, and are the products of this evidence combined with scholars' interpretations of that evidence. The evidence (Chapter 3) implies that, to a lesser or greater degree, as the case may be, and the hypotheses (Chapter 4) based on various reasons explains the evidence, to a lesser or greater degree. In the next chapter, the study weighs each of the hypotheses based on the five Harman-McCullagh criteria, *plausibility*, *explanatory scope*, *explanatory power*, *credibility*, and *simplicity*.

4

Weighing the Hypotheses

The previous chapters have offered a general overview of the Fragment and some of its problems, a list of the evidence which scholars cite when attempting to determine the date of its composition, and a description of each of the two hypotheses which derive from scholars' interpretation of that evidence. In this chapter, the study weighs each of the hypotheses using the five Harman-McCullagh criteria. It considers the plausibility, explanatory scope, explanatory power, credibility, and simplicity of each hypothesis.

The Early Hypothesis

By way of review, the reader will recall that scholars who conclude the Fragment is a second- or third-century composition reach that conclusion for three reasons. First, they understand the Fragmentist to have been a contemporary of Pius. Second, they perceive literary parallels in both the Fragment and Christian literature from the second and third centuries. Third, they observe contextual features in the Fragment which have commonalities with literature known to have been composed during the second and third centuries.

Plausibility

In order to determine the plausibility of the Early Hypothesis, one must ask the question: does the evidence imply that the Fragment was written during the second or third centuries and no later? In other words, unless the evidence reasonably suggests the greater likelihood that the Fragment was written prior to 301, it *does not* imply the Early Hypothesis. Conversely, if the evidence does reasonably suggest the greater likelihood that the Fragment was not written after 300, it *does* imply the Early Hypothesis.

First, Early Hypothesis proponents see significance in the way the Fragmentist refers to the Gospels of Luke and John as the "book of the Gospel according to Luke" (*euangelii librum secundum Lucam*) (line 2), and as the "fourth of the Gospels" (*quarti euangeliorum Iohannis*) (line 9), respectively. According to Stanton, these forms of identification do not appear in any fourth-century writing, but the second century furnishes evidence of their use by Irenæus.[1] Nevertheless, the absence of this type of identification for the Gospels in the fourth century, an argument from silence, does not necessarily mean the Fragment could not have been written during that period. Thus, the manner in which the Fragmentist identifies the Gospels does not imply the claim of the Early Hypothesis.

Second, in his articulation of the Early Hypothesis, Ferguson expressed his belief that because the Fragmentist referred to Paul and Luke as associates (line 4) and did not highlight the Pauline authority in the Lucan corpus. This serves as an indication that the Fragment was written early and that it may pre-date Irenæus.[2] However, the Fragmentist's unique way of referring to Paul and Luke may not have been an early development. There is no way of knowing if this type of language was used by the greater community when mentioning the two men together, or simply the Fragmentist's unique manner. In addition, given second-century references to the Pauline authority in Luke, it seems unlikely that this phenomenon was linked to any one particular period over another. Thus, the Fragmentist's omission of Pauline-Lucan authority does not imply the claim of the Early Hypothesis.

Third, the way the Fragmentist singles out the Fourth Gospel (lines 9–16) for what appears to be special treatment may serve as an indication that some may have had problems accepting its authority. Early Hypothesis proponents view this as having a greater likelihood of being necessary in the second century than in the fourth, because by the fourth century such questions had resolved themselves.[3] The Fragmentist felt the need to describe the occasion of its writing coupled with his inclusion of a sort of *regula fidei* point more readily to a date prior to the fourth century. Thus, the Fragmentist's apparent special treatment of the Fourth Gospel implies the claim of the Early Hypothesis to be more likely the case than the notion that the Fragment was written later.

Fourth, the Fragmentist apparently accepted the Apocalypse but may have included it among the antilegomena, if Horbury's theory is correct.[4] In either case, whether the Fragmentist indeed intended to list the Apocalypse among the antilegomena cannot now be known; to insist that he did or did not is merely conjecture. Also, the Fragmentist's notice of and emphasis on the number seven, highlighted by Early Hypothesis proponents, does not necessarily point to an early date. Cyprian's similar emphasis in the

---

[1] Stanton, "The Fourfold Gospel," 325; Irenæus, *Against Heresies* 3.11.7.
[2] Ferguson, "Canon Muratori," 681.
[3] Zahn, "Muratorian Canon," 54; Ferguson, "Canon Muratori," 681, 681n19; Stanton, "The Fourfold Gospel," 324.
[4] Horbury, "The Wisdom of Solomon in the Muratorian Fragment," 152–56.

third century may have been an influence on the Fragmentist and led to its inclusion in the latter's work. The evidence regarding the Apocalypse does not imply that the Fragment must pre-date the fourth century, so it does not imply the Early Hypothesis.

Fifth, the Fragmentist does not mention Hebrews at all, and Ferguson viewed this as less problematic for an earlier date than for a later one.[5] That Caius rejected Hebrews is unclear; and even if he had, were he the Fragmentist, as Muratori believed, he likely would have still listed it among the rejected texts.[6] While Ferguson's logic regarding the slim chance of a fourth-century list omitting Hebrews is valid, it is nonetheless possible that such could be the case. Several of the lists from the fourth century either include Hebrews by implication among Paul's epistles or omit it outright.[7] While limited in number, the Fragment does have parallels among the fourth century lists with respect to Hebrews. Thus, the absence of Hebrews in the Fragment does not imply the Early Hypothesis.

Sixth, the Fragmentist also leaves out any mention of James. The case of James's omission is similar to that of Hebrews. Because fourth-century lists omit it altogether, there remains a chance that the Fragment is of the fourth century. Therefore, the omission of James does not imply that the Fragment is early.

Seventh, no epistle of Peter is listed in the Fragment. While this omission flummoxes Late Hypothesis proponents, other scholars see this as suggestive of an early date. This appears to be the case especially given the fact that only one fourth-century catalogue (the Syrian) leaves the Petrine epistles out. Thus the likelihood that the Fragment is reflective of an early context seems greater. While admittedly an argument from silence, with no comment on these epistles either positive or negative, it may seem more reasonable to conclude that this absence implies the Early Hypothesis over the Late Hypothesis, due primarily to the fact that every later list includes Peter's epistles except one. Nevertheless, because the Fragment is silent, it cannot be said that this silence implies an early date.

Eighth, with regard to the *Apocalypse of Peter*, Armstrong saw a parallel in the Fragment and in the work of Victorinus of Pettau inasmuch as it appears Victorinus accepted it as Scripture.[8] This suggests an early date. However, the Fragmentist notes that some had reservations about its being read in church (lines 71–73). This does not indicate a clear parallel with Victorinus. In addition, given similar reservations noted by fourth-century

---

[5] Ferguson, "Canon Muratori," 681.
[6] Muratori, *Antiquitates italicæ mediiævi*, col. 3:851–52.
[7] Hahneman, *The Muratorian Fragment*, 134–35.
[8] Armstrong, "Victorinus of Pettau," 28.

writers, it cannot be reasonably believed that the evidence points to an early date.[9]

Ninth, the Fragmentist's comments regarding the date of *Shepherd of Hermas* suggest that he wrote prior to the fourth century. Assuming a plain reading of the text (and as seen above, there is evidence to suggest this is the most reasonable reading), the Fragmentist lived and possibly wrote during the lifetime of Pius. Arguably, this evidence is the most suggestive of an early date and implies the Early Hypothesis more strongly than any of the other evidence. With regard to the question over the public reading of *Shepherd*, though apparently resolved by the fourth century, the Fragmentist's remarks do not necessarily imply an earlier date.[10] The view that *Shepherd* should be read, just not publically in church, is not unique to the second or third centuries.

Tenth, though the heresies are mentioned toward the end of the Fragment obtained during the second century, their censure herein does not necessarily point to an early date. While it may appear to be reasonable to conclude that the Fragment is early based on this evidence, the evidence regarding these heresies may be incomplete due to their location at the point where the Fragment ends as a result of some damage which prevents scholars from knowing how the text concludes. Ferguson noted that these were early heretical teachings, and he made the observation that were the Fragment of the fourth century, the author likely would have included a condemnation of contemporary heresies.[11] However, one cannot not know this given the placement of the list toward the end of the document. Perhaps the author did include a list of fourth-century heresies. Thus, the evidence in the Fragment regarding the catalogue of heresies does not imply the Early Hypothesis.

Eleventh, the presence of a type of *regula fidei* in the Fragment suggests an early date (lines 18–26). Similar forms, which seem rather free in their makeup, are not found after Irenæus and Tertullian. More "fixed" formulas do not appear until around the beginning of the third century with Hippolytus's baptismal formula.[12] Had the Fragmentist written in the fourth century, he would more likely have deferred to the Nicene Creed or used another fixed form rather than make a free-form confession of faith. Thus it appears more likely that this free-from *regula fidei* betrays an early date; it would seem out of place after the third century. The Fragmentist's inclusion of this confession implies the Early Hypothesis.

---

[9] Sundberg, "Canon Muratori," 26–34; Hahneman, *The Muratorian Fragment*, 205–8.

[10] Zahn, "Muratorian Fragment," 54.

[11] Ferguson, review of *The Muratorian Fragment*, 696.

[12] J. N. D. Kelly, *Early Christian Creeds*, 2nd ed. (London: Longmans, Green and Co., 1960), 88–89.

Twelfth, while Early Hypothesis proponents cite evidence from the Fragment regarding its mention of the "catholic church" and "ecclesiastical discipline," the author's use of these terms does not rule out its having been written after the third century. Parallels can be found in Tertullian and Victorinus of Pettau, and it is likely that these terms do not pre-date the second century, but their presence in the Fragment does not limit it to having been written early.[13] Thus, the use of these terms does not imply the Early Hypothesis as some have tried to claim.[14]

Thirteenth, as with the case of the Fragmentist's references to the "catholic church," his expression regarding the bishop's chair also does not rule out a post-third-century date. Though similar expressions are found in the third century, it would be a leap of logic to conclude that such terminology is limited to the early time period.[15] Therefore, it cannot be said that the evidence found in the Fragment regarding the episcopal chair implies the Early Hypothesis.

Finally, Ferguson highlights the parallel in Justin Martyr regarding the reading of the prophets and the apostles, which seems to mirror the Fragmentist's remark (line 79–80).[16] Others who use the term "prophets and apostles" in a technical sense include Ignatius, Polycarp, and the *Didache*.[17] However, once Tertullian refers to these authoritative writings as the "Old Testament" and the "New Testament" in *Against Praxeas*, the use of "prophets and apostles" used in a technical sense is not seen again.[18] Thus, it appears unlikely that the Fragmentist would have used such an expression in the fourth century. It seems more likely that he would have employed the current terminology; that is, the Old and New Testaments. This does not constitute an argument from silence, because writers after Tertullian were not silent; they simply replaced the terms used to express the same idea. In light of this, the Fragmentist's use of the expression "prophets and apostles" points to a second-century context and therefore implies the Early Hypothesis.

In summary, some of the evidence implies the hypothesis that the Fragment is a late second- to early third-century composition. The evidence cited which does not imply the Early Hypothesis consists of the way the Fragmentist identifies the Gospels, the association of Luke and Paul, the

---

[13] Tert., *Prescription Against Heretics* 36, 44; idem, *Prayer*, passim; idem, *The Veiling of Virgins* 16; idem, *Against Marcion* 5.21; Victorinus of Pettau, *Commentary on the Apocalypse of the Blessed John*, 1.7; Donaldson, *A Critical History*, 212.

[14] Armstrong, "Victorinus of Pettau," 25.

[15] Cyprian, *To the People, Concerning Five Schismatic Presbyters of the Faction of Felicissimus* 5; idem, *To Antonianus About Cornelius and Novatian* 9.

[16] Justin, *First Apology* 67.

[17] Ignatius, *To the Philadelphians* 9; Polycarp, *To the Philippians* 6; *Didache* 11.

[18] Tert., *Against Praxeas* 15.

Fragmentist's treatment of the Apocalypse, the *Apocalypse of Peter*, his characterization of the reception of the *Shepherd of Hermas*, his omission of Hebrews, James, and the Petrine epistles, his list of heresies, his characterization of the church, and his understanding of the bishop's "chair." On the other hand, the evidence cited which implies the Early Hypothesis is as follows: the Fragmentist's defense of the Fourth Gospel, his dating of *Shepherd*, his inclusion of what appears to be a nascent *regula fidei*, and his use of the expression "prophets and apostles" instead of "Old and New Testaments." In short, of the fifteen items of evidence cited by Early Hypothesis proponents in support of their position, four items imply their conclusion.

Next, the study examined the Early Hypothesis's *explanatory scope*.

Explanatory Scope

Assessing the explanatory scope of the Early Hypothesis requires asking the following question: what (i.e. how much) evidence does the hypothesis explain, or at least attempt to explain? The hypothesis which has an explanation for the greatest amount of evidence is preferred. The Early Hypothesis has an explanation for all of the evidence cited by scholars regarding the Fragment's date with the exception of four items. The first item of evidence for which the Early Hypothesis has no explanation consists of the Fragmentist's identification of the book of Acts as the "Acts of all the apostles" (line 34). While Late Hypothesis proponents see this as evidence for their claim, the Early Hypothesis does not address the issue at all. Nevertheless, while it may appear that the Fragment was disambiguating the book of Acts from supposed apocryphal "Acts" of the fourth century, there were also apocryphal "Acts" in the second and third centuries. It remains possible that the Fragmentist was disambiguating Luke's work from these.

Second, the Early Hypothesis cannot explain the Fragmentist's treatment of the Johannine epistles (lines 68–69). The Fragment appears to mention only two of the epistles, and scholars debate about how this is to be understood.[19] Both Donaldson and Ferguson see issues with the condition of the text, and while these are the only two Early Hypothesis proponents who address the question, neither of them express the slightest degree of certainty in their understanding of the passage.[20]

Third, the Early Hypothesis does not attempt to explain the Fragmentist's omission of James. Ferguson does not specifically refer to the

---

[19] Katz, "The Johannine Epistles," 273–74.

[20] Donaldson, *A Critical History*, 212; Ferguson, review of *The Muratorian Fragment*, 695–96.

problem of James. Instead, in general terms, he laments the difficulty in understanding the Fragmentist's treatment of the general epistles.[21]

Finally, proponents of the Early Hypothesis do not proffer an explanation for the presence of the pseudo-Pauline works mentioned in the Fragment (lines 63–65). Rather, they simply declare that there is no reason to believe that these are fourth-century works. Ferguson conceded that looking to this evidence for clues regarding the date of the Fragment is difficult unless one knows whether the author was confusing Paul's Ephesian epistle with that of the one supposedly addressed to the Laodiceans.[22]

In summary, the Early Hypothesis explains the preponderance of evidence cited in support of the Fragment's date. In short, it explains eighteen of the total twenty-two items of evidence relevant to the debate.

Next, the study examined the Early Hypothesis's *explanatory power*.

Explanatory Power

For any hypothesis to be preferred, it must powerfully explain the evidence it cites in support of its reasons to be believed. In the case of the Early Hypothesis, it must demonstrate that the phenomena which it cites as evidence for its claim find themselves more "at home" in the second or third centuries than in the fourth. In other words, it cannot merely be possible that the evidence comes from an early context; it must be plausible to likely that this is the case. The Early Hypothesis demonstrates a remarkable amount of explanatory power in the way it explains the existence of five phenomena found within the Fragment. First, and arguably the most compelling, the Early Hypothesis explains the Fragmentist's statement that he is a contemporary of Pius. Of note is the link between this "temporal" declaration and the very question of date. The proposition that Pius was bishop in Rome "in our times" offers a direct response to the question of when the Fragment was written. A Late Hypothesis arguments to the contrary notwithstanding, the plain reading of the text is epistemically superior to the periodic reading proposed by Sundberg and his subscribers.

In addition, whereas the Late Hypothesis does not in any way explain why the Fragmentist mentioned Pius, Early Hypothesis proponents understand that by referencing his bishopric, the Fragmentist was offering a precise time period in support of his own argument that the *Shepherd of Hermas* was too recent to be considered among the apostles. Thus, with regard to the Fragment's evidence in reference to Pius, the Early

---

[21] Ferguson, review of *The Muratorian Fragment*, 695–96.
[22] Ferguson, "Canon Muratori," 681.

Hypothesis's explanation seems likely to be true and contributes to its consideration as the preferred hypothesis.

On the other hand, the Early Hypothesis does not powerfully explain the second reason to conclude an early date for the Fragment; the perceived literary parallels with second- and third-century works could just as possibly exist in fourth-century writings. In other words, there is no compelling reason to believe that the Fragmentist's nomenclature for the Gospels, his emphasis on the number seven, his use of an uncommon construction of the term *catholica*, or his understanding regarding the bishop's authority in "the chair" must be limited to the early period. Each of these could just as possibly have been used in the fourth century; their use is not limited to a particular time period.

However, some of the features which indicate an early historical/theological context are best explained by the Early Hypothesis. In other words, they are best understood as having been obtained prior to the fourth century. First, the Fragmentist's apologetic tone in his description of the Fourth Gospel's background serves to justify its authority. This was more likely to have been needed earlier rather than later as observed above.

Second, the manner in which the Fragmentist measures the *Shepherd of Hermas's* suitability seems more at home prior to the fourth century, though it is more likely that this question was resolved to a greater degree in the years following the third century. He compares *Shepherd* with the "prophets and the apostles," a technical term for the biblical canon, terminology which was replaced in the fourth century with the designation of the "Old and New Testaments." Third, as noted above, the inclusion of an informal *regula fidei* had later been replaced by more fixed formulas of faith statements. Thus, it seems more likely that the Fragmentist would have offered up his free-form confession prior to the creeds and baptismal formulas which became the norm in the fourth century. Fourth, the Early Hypothesis serves as the best explanation for the omission of the Petrine epistles. Though admittedly an argument for silence, the overwhelming majority of fourth-century catalogues include at least one of Peter's epistles. That the Fragment has neither seems more likely to fit within an early context than in a later one.

In summary, the Early Hypothesis potently explains the evidence which it cites in support of its reasons to be believed. While it is merely possible that the Fragment has literary parallels in the second and third centuries, it is likely that the Fragmentist was a contemporary of Pius and that the Fragmentist was composed in an early historical/theological context. In short, the Early Hypothesis appears to cogently explain the evidence behind two of the three reasons for its conclusion that the Fragment is a second- or third-century composition.

Next, the study examined the Early Hypothesis's *credibility*.

Credibility

Hypotheses that are credible are those for which there is little to no evidence suggesting they are unlikely to be true, and, conversely, credible hypotheses do not make it unlikely for any of the evidence to be true. In other words, preferred hypotheses correspond to reality. While the Early Hypothesis does not cast any of the relevant evidence in a negative light, at first glance there may be reason to believe the Early Hypothesis is unlikely. This comes about due to problems related to the evidence in the Fragment regarding the *Shepherd of Hermas*; arguably, and ironically, the strongest element within the Early Hypothesis's claim. Hahneman casts doubt on the believability of the Fragmentist's testimony regarding the date of *Shepherd's* composition on the tradition that Hermas and Pius were brothers, and on the conclusion that the Fragmentist's portrayal of the *Shepherd's* reception should lead to the early dating. Nevertheless, though Hahneman casts doubt upon the Early Hypothesis's credibility, did the evidence he furnished disconfirm it?

First, Hahneman argued that the *Shepherd of Hermas* was written not during Pius's bishopric (140–155), but over thirty years earlier (i.e. pre-110). Throughout the third chapter of his book on the Fragment, Hahneman cites a variety of evidence which suggests an early date for *Shepherd*, as early as toward the end of the first century, possibly while John the apostle was still living.[23] According to Hahneman, having *Shepherd* written during the first century or early second century, rather than the late second century, better explains the author's reference to Clement of Rome, the apparent plurality of Roman bishops at the time of writing, and the ongoing persecution which seems to be that of either Domitian or Trajan. Therefore, Hahneman concludes that it is impossible for *Shepherd* to have been written by Hermas during the period between 140 and 155.

However, Ferguson contends that this need not be the case. Hermas could have begun writing the *Shepherd of Hermas* in the late first century and completed it at, or around, the mid-second century point. Clement of Rome's bishopric ended in 99 and Pius's began in 140, a space of forty-one years. It is not inconceivable for the author of *Shepherd* to have completed the composition of his work over a forty-year period. Admittedly, as Ferguson notes, this would have meant "a long career" for Hermas.[24] Ferguson adds that, "*Shepherd* gives many indications of being a composite work, if not of composite authorship; the date of the materials is not necessarily the date of final writing, editing, or redacting."[25]

So too Quasten, who held that there is no reason to doubt *Shepherd's* reference to Clement and the Fragmentist's assertion that he and

---

[23] Hahneman, *The Muratorian Fragment*, 37–43.
[24] Ferguson, review of *The Muratorian Fragment*, 692.
[25] Ibid.

its author were contemporaries. "The two dates [i.e. Clement's and Pius's] are accounted for by the way in which the book was compiled. The older portions most likely go back to Clement's day while the present work would be of Pius's time. Critical examination of the contents leads to the same conclusion. This shows that parts of the work belong to different periods."[26]

Furthermore, as Hill highlights, having the Fragmentist make such statements about *Shepherd* in the fourth century seems to create more problems than having him do so in the second.[27]

Second, Hahneman believed it "unlikely that the Hermas of the *Shepherd* was the brother of Pius."[28] In support of this, Hahneman leans upon his supposition that *Shepherd* was written much earlier than the Fragmentist would lead one to believe, but as also seen above, this need not be the case. Additionally, however, Hahneman doubts a fraternal relationship between Hermas and Pius the bishop for three other reasons. First, Hermas was a slave and would not have known who his parents were.[29] Second, "Hermas" is a Greek name and Pius a Latin one. Third, Hermas never mentioned a brother.

However, the link (or "non-link" as the case may be) between Hermas and Pius is irrelevant. Early Hypothesis proponents who cite this passage in the Fragment as evidence usually focus on the connection between Pius and the Fragment, not the connection between Hermas and Pius.[30] The Fragmentist claims that Pius was bishop "in our times."

Regardless of who Hermas was, or who the Fragmentist perceived wrote the *Shepherd of Hermas*, or when the Fragmentist believed it was written, the fact remains that the Fragmentist appears to be aware that Pius was bishop of Rome in his lifetime and counts on this fact as an essential part of his argument; an argument which would have failed if his readers did not believe this to be the case.

Finally, Hahneman believes that the reception of the *Shepherd of Hermas* as portrayed by the Fragmentist points to a fourth-century context. Many second- and third-century writers accepted *Shepherd,* and at times appeared to equate it with canonical, authoritative Scripture. According to Hahneman, this acceptance began to evaporate with Eusebius, and doubts about the full suitability of *Shepherd* continued through the fourth century.[31] In a way similar to these fourth-century Fathers, the Fragmentist also

---

[26] Quasten, *Patrology*, vol. 1, 92–93.

[27] Hill, "The Debate Over the Muratorian Fragment and the Development of the Canon," 439.

[28] Hahneman, *The Muratorian Fragment*, 52.

[29] Shepherd of Hermas, *Vision* 1.

[30] Holmes, review of *The Muratorian Fragment*, 595; Schnabel, "The Muratorian Fragment," 246.

[31] Hahneman, *The Muratorian Fragment*, 66–69.

expressed that some had reservations about *Shepherd* (lines 73–80). Thus, Hahneman infers that the Fragment is from the fourth century.

In reaction to Hahneman's view of the reception of the *Shepherd of Hermas*, Schnabel speculates that Irenæus may have cited *Shepherd* as Scripture due to his assumption that Hermas was Paul's associate (Rom 16:14).[32] Also, in Ferguson's view, this type of acceptance by Irenæus and others in the second century may have been that against which the Fragmentist was polemicizing.[33] In addition, Tertullian, in his invective against *Shepherd,* cites its wholesale rejection "by every council of Churches . . . among apocryphal and false (writings)."[34] Hahneman doubted the factuality of Tertullian's statement, but as Hill pointed out, "Tertullian may have been given to flamboyance, but it was hardly his custom to appeal to historical precedents of his own imagination, especially when his appeal entailed an implicit challenge to his opponents to check his sources."[35]

As far as Eusebius's apparent skepticism is concerned, Ferguson believed Eusebius was pointing to a regard for *Shepherd* which likely predated himself.[36] Moreover, there remains the possibility that the Fragmentist himself accepted *Shepherd* as worthy of serious consideration for personal use, but not for public edification.

It appears then in the final analysis that, while Hahneman makes a case which casts some doubt on the credibility of the Early Hypothesis, his case does not render the hypothesis unlikely. Hahneman also makes much of the poor condition of the Fragment where this passage is located. He declares that the traditional dating of the Fragment in the second century is "rash in view of the known poor transcription and the suspected careless translation of the manuscript." However, as Ferguson and Schnabel point out, the condition of the Fragment works against Hahneman's argument just as much as it does against any interpretation of the manuscript.[37] Therefore, Hahneman's case notwithstanding, one can conclude that there is no evidence which renders the Early Hypothesis to be unlikely and that the hypothesis thus exhibits credibility.

Next, the study considered the Early Hypothesis's *simplicity*.

---

[32] Schnabel, "The Muratorian Fragment," 247.

[33] Ferguson, "Canon Muratori," 678–79.

[34] Tert., *Modesty* 10.

[35] Hahneman, *The Muratorian Fragment*, 63; Hill, "The Debate Over the Muratorian Fragment and the Development of the Canon," 440; so too Ferguson, "Canon Muratori," 679.

[36] Ferguson, "Canon Muratori," 679.

[37] Hahneman, *The Muratorian Fragment*, 72; Ferguson, review of *The Muratorian Fragment*, 691; Schnabel, "The Muratorian Fragment," 246.

Simplicity

In the evaluation of a hypothesis's simplicity, one must ask if its proponents make unsubstantiated assumptions either in linking the evidence to its premises or in defending it against counterarguments. Hypotheses which have fewer ad hoc components (i.e. statements not backed by evidence) are to be preferred. In the development and defense of their conclusion, Early Hypothesis proponents make four assumptions, three of which are evidenced and one that is not.[38]

First, and already discussed in detail above, the Early Hypothesis depends on the assumption that the expression *temporibus nostris* should be read plainly. This assumption is based on evidence found in other ancient church writings in which the authors use such terminology in a literal sense. In other words, when this expression is used elsewhere it refers to the author's lifetime.

Second, in their reasoning that the Fragment possesses literary features with parallels in the second century, thus attempting to render the fourth century a less likely context, Early Hypothesis proponents make the assumption that language changes over time. The evidence appears to support this assumption. This is borne out by research in the field of historical linguistics.[39]

The third assumption appears in the defense of the hypothesis. In reaction to Hahneman's assertion that Irenæus and Clement of Alexandria appear to have accepted the *Shepherd of Hermas* without reservation, indicating a fourth-century context given the Fragmentist's caveat, Ferguson makes an assumption. He speculates that the Fragmentist was arguing against the type of acceptance of *Shepherd* which Irenæus and Clement espoused. Contra Hahneman, there is evidence to support Ferguson's supposition inasmuch as Tertullian mentioned the rejection of *Shepherd* by church councils. Not all accepted *Shepherd* in the second century. This fact means that the Fragment would not be out of place in that period with regard to *Shepherd's* reception.

Finally, Early Hypothesis proponents make one unsubstantiated assumption. They assume that language makes noticeable change over two and one-half centuries; change drastic enough to allow for the assignment of dates to literature for which there is no other external evidence. However, research in the field of historical linguistics suggests that this is not enough

---

[38] In the case of Early Hypothesis, Reason #3, which deals with the historical/theological context question, the hypothesis commits a logical fallacy in its understanding of the Lucan-Pauline association, but such fallaciousness does not constitute an unsubstantiated assumption and is therefore not included in this section. Reason #3 remains strong due to its dependence on other evidence.

[39] Bynon, *Historical Linguistics*, 2; Campbell, *Historical Linguistics* 3.

time. The dating of literature based on language change is not reliable within fewer than four hundred years.[40] Anything shorter may not be sufficient to notice a difference.

In summary, most of the assumptions that Early Hypothesis proponents make are substantiated by evidence. The simplicity of the hypothesis is marred by one unsubstantiated assumption which effects one of the three reasons to believe the hypothesis true, that of the supposed literary parallels between the Fragment and literature of the second and third centuries. The other reasons are left intact.

To recapitulate, in the foregoing section, the study weighed the Early Hypothesis by judging it against the Harman-McCullagh criteria of plausibility, explanatory scope, explanatory power, credibility, and simplicity. It found that the hypothesis is implied by four of the fifteen evidences cited (27%), that it explains eighteen of the total twenty-two evidences cited by both sides (82%), that it powerfully explains two of the three reasons to be believed (66%), that no evidence contradicts it (100%), and that one of its three assumptions are unsubstantiated (66%), for an overall average score of 68%.

Next, the study weighed the Late Hypothesis using the same criteria. Those findings follow.

The Late Hypothesis

Scholars who subscribe to the Late Hypothesis do so for three reasons. First, they claim that because the Fragment constitutes a canon of the New Testament, it was not likely to have been composed prior to the fourth century, insofar as they assume that there were no formal canons prior to that time. Second, they contend that the Fragmentist demonstrates an apparent dependence upon the work of Eusebius. Third, in their view, the Fragment exhibits features which betray a fourth-century historical/theological context.

Plausibility

The plausibility of the Late Hypothesis depends on the answer to the following question: does the evidence imply that the Fragment was written during the fourth century and no earlier? In other words, unless the evidence reasonably suggests the greater likelihood that the Fragment was written after 300, it *does not* imply the Late Hypothesis. Conversely, if the evidence does reasonably suggest the greater likelihood that the Fragment was not written before 301, it *does* imply the Late Hypothesis.

---

[40] Bynon, *Historical Linguistics*, 6.

First, Late Hypothesis proponents argue that because the Fragment exhibits an adherence to the notion that there are only four authoritative Gospels, it was likely to have been written during the fourth century and not before.[41] For them, up until that time, the number of Gospels was not restricted. However, there is evidence from the second and third centuries that several of the church fathers were adamant that there were only four recognized Gospels.[42] Therefore, it does not appear that the evidence in the Fragment regarding the number of accepted Gospels implies that it was written in the fourth century and no earlier.

Second, Hahneman observed the order of the Gospels in the Fragment as evidence for a fourth-century date stating that it would be unusual to see this order early.[43] However, Irenæus listed them in this order.[44] As a result, though this order is rare prior to the fourth century, one cannot be insistent on a fourth-century date for the Fragment based on this. The Gospel order in the Fragment is not exclusively implicative of a fourth century date. Granted, while it may lean in that direction, the evidence on its face does not imply that it was composed in the fourth century.

Third, where the Fragmentist designates the book of Acts as the "Acts of all the Apostles," Late Hypothesis proponents view this as indicative of a fourth-century date.[45] They contend that due to the proliferation of apocryphal "Acts" such specificity was necessary to disambiguate this text from others which were not about the acts of "all" the apostles, a specification required in the fourth century. However, there is reason to believe that such disambiguation was called for as early as the second century, as well. During that earlier period, a number of apocryphal Acts were making their way around.[46] Therefore, the arguments of those who see a fourth-century Fragment notwithstanding, this evidence does not imply the Late Hypothesis.

Fourth, Hahneman argued that the way the Fragmentist described the origin of the Fourth Gospel betrays a fourth-century context because according to the former, John was urged to write it by the "bishops." Early sources claim that John was encouraged by his γνώριμοι.[47] According to

---

[41] Hahneman, *The Muratorian Fragment*, 109–10.

[42] Clement of Alexandria, *Miscellanies* 3.13, "Primum quidera, in nobis traditis quatuor Evangeliis non habemus hoc dictum, sed in eo, quod est secundum Ægyptios"; Origen, *Homilies in Luke*, Homily 1; Irenæus, *Against Heresies* 3.11.8; Tert., *Against Marcion* 4.2.

[43] Hahneman, *The Muratorian Fragment*, 183, 187.

[44] Irenæus, *Against Heresies* 3.1.1.

[45] Hahneman, *The Muratorian Fragment*, 192–96.

[46] Quasten, *Patrology*, vol. 1, 133–42.

[47] Translated as "friends" by McGiffert (*NPNF* 2:1:261) in Euseb., *Ecclesiastical History* 6.14.7, and as *discipuli* by Rufinus in his translation of Eusebius (per Hahneman, *The Muratorian Fragment*, 189).

Hahneman, not until the fourth century does it become known that John wrote at the behest of "bishops." Hahneman assumes that, "With the passage of time the identity of those who urged John to write his gospel became more important, as did the gospel itself. In Jerome's retelling and in Victorinus' story those who urged John are *episcopi*; this introduction of bishops into the tradition is probably a later element."[48]

However, as noted above, the acceptance of the Fourth Gospel was less likely a contentious issue by the fourth century than it had been earlier; the need to identify it with the authority of bishops would have been of greater significance in the second century than in subsequent centuries. Perhaps this is why Victorinus of Pettau, writing in the third century of a tradition that more than likely predated him, stated that John was compelled by the bishops around him.[49] Thus, it does not seem necessary to limit such references to the fourth century; the evidence here does not point exclusively to a fourth-century context and therefore does not imply the Late Hypothesis.

Fifth, Hahneman sees the Fragmentist's inclusion of the Johannine epistles as evidence of the fourth century theory because they are "found only in larger collections of the catholic epistles, which were accepted as canonical only in the fourth century."[50] However, against this Origen included the Johannine epistles, acknowledging that some questioned their authenticity.[51] Also, Origen seems to have possessed some idea of a canonical list.[52] In addition, contra Hahneman's suggestion that the epistles of John were in fourth-century lists and "accepted as canonical" is Eusebius's inclusion of these epistles among his disputed texts.[53] Therefore, it is unlikely that the Fragmentist's mention of the Johannine epistles is evidence of the Late Hypothesis, at least not for the reasons that Hahneman suggests. However, the evidence here does appear to imply a late date for another reason. In the Fragment, the authority of the Johannine epistles is accepted without qualification, something which cannot be said of Origen's or Eusebius's accounting. In every fourth-century catalogue after Eusebius's (ca. 303, quite early in the fourth century), the epistles of John are accepted as canonical just as it is in the Fragment. When all the evidence is considered, it may be that the Johannine epistles moved from a situation in which they were disputed (Origen and Eusebius in the third and early fourth

---

[48] Hahneman, *The Muratorian Fragment*, 190.
[49] Victorinus of Pettau, *Commentary on the Apocalypse of the Blessed John* 11.1.
[50] Hahneman, *The Muratorian Fragment*, 181.
[51] Euseb., *Ecclesiastical History* 6.25.10.
[52] Ibid., 6.25.1, 3.
[53] Euseb., *Ecclesiastical History* 3.25.3; Hahneman, *The Muratorian Fragment*, 181.

centuries) to one in which they were accepted (post-Eusebius, most of fourth century, and the Fragment).[54] Thus, this evidence regarding the Johannine epistles points more toward a late date than to an early one, and therefore implies the Late Hypothesis.

Sixth, Sundberg believed the evidence in the Fragment regarding the Apocalypse pointed toward its having been written in the fourth century. The Apocalypse's placement in the list among the disputed texts (i.e. the *Apocalypse of Peter*), according to Sundberg, betrays a later date when doubts about the Apocalypse began to arise.[55] However, several factors mitigate against the likelihood of this. First, as a matter of fact, the Fragmentist accepts the Apocalypse without question. He merely lists it here in proximity to another apocalypse, probably more for organization's sake than as an indication of the text's acceptability. Toward the beginning of the Fragment, the author compares the Apocalypse with the epistles of Paul, stating that it was written for the whole church (lines 39–59). Second, in Origen, the Apocalypse is accepted and it is attributed to John, as it is in the Fragment.[56] Therefore, it cannot be said that the Fragmentist's remarks about the Apocalypse could make sense in only a fourth-century context, and they no not imply the Late Hypothesis.

Eighth, as in the case of the Johannine epistles, Hahneman sees the mention of Jude as indicative of the fourth century.[57] However, whereas the inclusion of the Johannine epistles implies the Late Hypothesis, the inclusion of Jude cannot be understood as having a place only in the fourth century. Clement of Alexandria included Jude in his canon, known through Eusebius's explicit reference.[58] Therefore, in contrast to the other general epistles, this evidence in the Fragment does not imply the Late Hypothesis.

Ninth, in consequence of his presupposition that formal canons of the Old and New Testaments were unknown until the fourth century, Sundberg concluded that the Fragment is a fourth-century canon due its inclusion of the *Wisdom of Solomon*.[59] Had the Old Testament canon not been closed by this time, the Fragmentist would not have been compelled to place this respected text among his books of the New Testament. Moreover, Epiphanius included *Wisdom* in his New Testament, a point that Ferguson concedes.[60] Additionally, Hahneman considered the Fragmentist's denial of

---

[54] Euseb., *Ecclesiastical History* 6.14.1. Clement of Alexandria accepted the general epistles but of these only Jude is certain. It is unclear if Clement had James, the Petrine epistles, or the Johannine epistles in mind.

[55] Sundberg, "Canon Muratori," 21.

[56] Euseb., *Ecclesiastical History* 6.25.9.

[57] Hahneman, *The Muratorian Fragment*, 181.

[58] Euseb., *Ecclesiastical History* 6.14.1.

[59] Sundberg, "Canon Muratori," 16.

[60] Epiph., *Refutation of All Heresies* 1.1.8; 76; Ferguson, "Canon Muratori," 679.

Solomonic authorship evidence of a late date.⁶¹ Many of the early Fathers attribute *Wisdom* to Solomon, unlike the Fragmentist who attributed it to Solomon's friends; the later church fathers did not hold that Solomon authored it.⁶² Nevertheless, a couple of factors cast doubt on these suppositions. First, Irenæus considered *Wisdom* to be among his New Testament Scriptures.⁶³ Second, there is Horbury's suggestion that *Wisdom* in the Fragment is among the antilegomena, not a part of a New Testament canonical category.⁶⁴ Third, the Late Hypothesis's consideration of *Wisdom* depends on its assumption that exclusive canonical lists of the New Testament did not obtain until the fourth century, an assumption that has not been substantiated. These possibilities cast doubt on the conclusion that the evidence in the Fragment with respect to *Wisdom* implies the Late Hypothesis.

Tenth, the manner in which the Fragmentist described the reception of the *Apocalypse of Peter* implies the Late Hypothesis. It was accepted, but not allowed by all to be read in church (lines 71–73). Such a qualification would appear out of place prior to the fourth century. Clement of Alexandria accepted it as Scripture, and Methodius (d. 311) quotes from the *Apocalypse of Peter*, assuming it to be of "the inspired writings."⁶⁵ Not until the fourth century did this text come to be received with some doubt. In light of the evidence regarding the *Apocalypse of Peter*, the Fragment appears to have been written during the fourth century.

Eleventh, in the Fragment, the *Shepherd of Hermas* is acceptable private reading material, but not to be read publically in church due to its non-apostolicity (lines 73–80). Late Hypothesis proponents consider this to be evidence of a fourth-century context. While it is true that Irenæus and Clement of Alexandria appear to have accepted *Shepherd*, quoting authoritatively from it, whether they believed it should be read publically as part of the church's liturgy or if they considered it apostolic cannot be known.⁶⁶ By the time of Tertullian, it had come to be rejected by several synods.⁶⁷ It may be that these synods explain why Origen, Eusebius, and Athanasius came to acknowledge its circulation in the church with the understanding that it was questioned by some, yet was still seen as

---

⁶¹ Hahneman, *The Muratorian Fragment*, 201.
⁶² For a list of these see Hahneman, *The Muratorian Fragment*, 201.
⁶³ Euseb., *Ecclesiastical History* 5.8.8. Cf. Irenæus, *Against Heresies* 4.38.3.
⁶⁴ Horbury, "The Wisdom of Solomon," 152–56.
⁶⁵ Methodius, *The Banquet of the Ten Virgins*, Theophila 6.
⁶⁶ Irenæus, *Against Heresies* 4.20.2 quoted Shepherd of Hermas, *Mandate* 1; Clement of Alexandria, *Miscellanies* 1.17, 29; 2.1, 9, 12 quoted and alluded to Shepherd of Hermas, *Vision* 3.4, 8, 13; *Mandate* 4.2, 11; *Similitude* 9.16.
⁶⁷ Tert., *Modesty* 10, 20.

somewhat useful.[68] Therefore, whereas Sundberg held that Eusebius marked the turning point for Shepherd, the evidence points more toward the time of Tertullian.[69] Therefore, the Fragmentist may be reflecting a sentiment in place around the early third century, or possibly earlier, depending on the time of the synods mentioned by Tertullian.[70] As a result of this, it does not appear that the evidence about the reception of *Shepherd* implies the Late Hypothesis.

Twelfth, with regard to his reference to a pseudo-Pauline epistle to the Laodiceans, Hahneman assumes that the Fragmentist is writing of a distinct epistle, which should not be confused with the known canonical epistle to the Ephesians (a question for some scholars), because this is mentioned in another part of the Fragment. For Hahneman this must be the Latin Laodicean epistle, of which the earliest evidence is from around the fifth century. In addition, Hahneman noted that there was no evidence of the existence of such a Laodicean epistle prior to the late fourth century.[71] As a matter of fact, by Hahneman's own admission, there is no evidence of such an epistle prior to the fifth century. Thus, the evidence within the Fragment with reference to a pseudo-Pauline epistle to the Laodiceans does not imply the Late Hypothesis.

Finally, Hahneman believed that evidence from the Fragmentist's catalogue heresies points to a fourth-century date.[72] First, he argued that the inclusion of Mitiades in the list betrays a dependence upon Eusebius; a notion which has been shown to be unlikely in this book. Second, that the Montanists were known as "Cataphrygians" prior to the fourth century is unlikely, according to Hahneman. Third, he posited that there was no reference to a Marcionite psalter prior to the fourth century. These last two reasons proffered by Hahneman are arguments from silence. The absence of earlier mention neither necessitates nor makes a later date more likely. Thus, the evidence from the Fragment's catalogue of heresies does not imply that it constitutes a fourth-century composition.

In summary, very little of the presented evidence validates the hypothesis that the Fragment is a fourth-century composition. The evidence cited which does not imply the Late Hypothesis consists of the Fragment's Fourfold Gospel, the Gospel order, the Fragmentist's defense of the Fourth Gospel, his title for Acts, his regard for the *Wisdom of Solomon*, his

---

[68] Origen, *First Principles* 1.3.3, 2.1.5, 3.2.4, 4.1.11; *Commentary on Matthew* 14.21. Origen quotes from Shepherd of Hermas, *Mandate* 1, 6.2; Euseb., *Ecclesiastical History* 3.3.6–7, 3.25.4; Athanasius, *Festal Letter* 39.

[69] Sundberg, "Canon Muratori," 13–14.

[70] This dating depends on Quasten's assessment of when Tertullian wrote Modesty. Quasten, *Patrology*, vol. 2, 313.

[71] Hahneman, *The Muratorian Fragment*, 197–200.

[72] Ibid., 209–13.

inclusion of Jude, his treatment of the Apocalypse, his reception of the *Shepherd of Hermas*, his mention of the pseudo-Pauline epistles, and his list of heresies. However, the evidence cited which implies the Late Hypothesis consists of his characterization of the reception of the *Apocalypse of Peter* and his inclusion of the Johannine epistles. In short, of the twelve items of evidence cited by Late Hypothesis proponents in support of their position, only two items imply their conclusion.

Next, the study considered the Late Hypothesis's *explanatory scope*.

Explanatory Scope

In order to weigh the Late Hypothesis's explanatory scope, the study asked what (i.e. how much) evidence the hypothesis explains, or at least attempt to explain? The hypothesis which has an explanation for the greatest amount of evidence is preferred. The Late Hypothesis explains most of the evidence cited by scholars regarding the Fragment's date with the exception of eight items. Five of these unexplained evidence items are cited by Early Hypothesis proponents in support of their position. These items are not even mentioned by those who subscribe to the Late Hypothesis. They include the way the Fragmentist identifies the Gospels, the apparent *regula fidei*, the Fragmentist's expression regarding the church and the bishop's chair, and his use of the prophets and the apostles as a litmus test of authority. The other three items of evidence, the Fragmentist's omission of Hebrews, James, and the Petrine epistles, are simply shrugged off as confused or anomalous.

Nevertheless, the Late Hypothesis has an explanation for most of the evidence cited in support of the Fragment's date. In short, it explains fourteen of the total twenty-two items of evidence relevant to the debate.

Next, the study assessed the Late Hypothesis's *explanatory power*.

Explanatory Power

Believable hypotheses powerfully explain the relevant evidence. For this to be the case with the Late Hypothesis, it must demonstrate that the phenomena which it cites as evidence for its claim were more likely to occur in the fourth century and not before. In other words, it cannot merely be possible that the evidence comes from a later context, it must be likely. The Late Hypothesis exhibits little explanatory power in the way it explains the evidence. First, because Late Hypothesis proponents assume the Old Testament canon must have been closed when the Fragment was written, they explain the Fragmentist's declaration that the *Shepherd of Hermas* cannot be included among the prophets and the apostles because their time is past. It is for this reason, coupled with an assumption that this "closing" did not take place *until* the fourth century, that they conclude the Fragment is a fourth-century work. However, as noted above, there is reason to believe that as early as Justin Martyr and Melito of Sardis an exclusive Old Testament canon was recognized. In addition, Sundberg's assumption that formal and exclusive canons did not come to be recognized until the fourth century is not without problems. The evidence, particularly from Irenæus in his Fourfold Gospel, in support of limited acceptance of authoritative texts works against both Sundberg's and Hahneman's arguments. In the final analysis, Reason #1 of the Late Hypothesis does not explain the evidence regarding the criterion by which *Shepherd* was judged in a powerful way. In other words, the Late Hypothesis does not convincingly demonstrate that the Old Testament was still open until the fourth century, nor does it show the likelihood that the notion of a restrictive canon did not come to fruition before then. It is possible that the evidence of the Fragmentist's characterization of *Shepherd* could still be "at home" in the second century.

Second, the Late Hypothesis does not powerfully explain the Fragmentist's reference to an individual named "Miltiades." The hypothesis is dependent, in part, upon the likelihood that the Fragmentist depended on Eusebius when compiling his catalog of heresies. However, there is a greater likelihood that the Fragmentist did not have the name "Miltiades" in mind here, but rather that he intended to write "Mitiades," as indeed the text itself bears witness. The other copies of the Muratorian canon from Monte Cassino also agree with this spelling. There is no evidence to suggest that Eusebius naively copied "Miltiades" from the Fragment; though while it is possible, it does not appear likely that he did so. In addition, there is no evidence of a heretic with the same name as the allegedly orthodox Miltiades. Reason #2 to believe the Late Hypothesis does not powerfully explain the spelling of "Mitiades" in the Fragment's catalog of heresies.

Finally, the critical evidence which initially drove Sundberg to develop the Late Hypothesis is explained by the hypothesis, but not in a powerful manner. While the explanation Late Hypothesis proponents proffer with respect to the evidence in the Fragment regarding the *Wisdom of Solomon* is possible, there is reasonable doubt that the explanation is likely to be the case. According to Sundberg, "The matter that first attracted my attention to the question of place and date of the Muratorian fragment deals with the question of *Wisdom's* inclusion in the Fragmentist's list."[73]

Whereas, the Fragment's evidence regarding the date *Shepherd of Hermas* is the critical piece in the Early Hypothesis, so the evidence about *Wisdom* is for the Late. For Sundberg, it appears that the Fragmentist was writing in the fourth century after the closing of the Old Testament

---

[73] Sundberg, "Canon Muratori," 15.

compelled him to place *Wisdom* (an apparently liturgically acceptable writing) in his New Testament list between the Johannine epistles and the Apocalypse.[74]

However, Irenæus included *Wisdom* in his New Testament, as well.[75] Did he include it there for the same reason the Fragmentist did, because the Old Testament was closed? If so, the Late Hypothesis does not sufficiently explain why this evidence does not support a second-century Fragment. One cannot know. Sundberg's inference that this is the reason for the Fragment's inclusion is speculative. Irenæus's parallel inclusion means that there did exist during the second century a theological/historical context which allowed or called for it. It is possible that this was the same context and reason for the Fragmentist's inclusion.

However, on the other hand, if the Fragment was written in the fourth century, this would allow for the unconditional acceptance of the Johannine epistles as authoritative, which is apparently how the Fragmentist perceived them. Given the express reluctance to receive these universally in Origen and Eusebius's acknowledgement that not all had accepted them, it is remarkable that every other fourth-century canon does so.[76] Additionally, a fourth-century Fragment better explains the partial acceptance of the *Apocalypse of Peter*. Up until that time, the *Apocalypse of Peter* was accepted as Scripture by all, but in the Fragment and in the fourth century there was a refusal to ascribe it full authority.

In summary, the Late Hypothesis does not powerfully explain the evidence. While the Late Hypothesis is a reasonable and powerful explanation for the Fragmentist's acceptance of the Johannine epistles and the *Apocalypse of Peter*, it does not explain the Fragmentist's criterion by which he judges the *Shepherd of Hermas*, for his listing "Mitiades" in his catalogue of heresies, or for his placement of the *Wisdom of Solomon* in between the Johannine epistles and the Apocalypse. In short, the Late Hypothesis does not appear to powerfully explain the evidence behind any of the three reasons for its conclusion that the Fragment is a fourth-century composition.

Next, the study examined the Late Hypothesis's *credibility*.

Credibility

Is there evidence which renders the Late Hypothesis unlikely to be correct, or conversely does the Late Hypothesis give rise to critical doubts about the likelihood of the viability of any relevant evidence? If so, it is not a credible hypothesis and should not be preferred. As explained above, most of the

---

[74] Sundberg, "Canon Muratori," 16–18.
[75] Euseb., *Ecclesiastical History* 5.8.1–8.
[76] Ibid., 3.25.3; 6.14.1; 6.25.1, 3, 10.

evidence does not imply the Late Hypothesis, but all the evidence could exist within a fourth-century composition with the exception of one item: the evidence regarding the Fragmentist having been a contemporary of Pius. A plain reading of *temporibus nostris* points to the likelihood that that Fragment is not a fourth-century composition. As demonstrated above, the plain reading is to be preferred over the periodic reading suggested by Sundberg.

Several issues here warrant emphasis. First, the plain reading of *temporibus nostris* leads to the conclusion that the Fragmentist and Pius were contemporaries due to the expression's interpretation as meaning "in our *life*time." There is precedence for reading it this way within other ancient patristic literature, and the mention of Pius rules out the likelihood that the Fragmentist was broadly referring to a long period of time following the end of the apostolic era. Second, Sundberg concedes that his is not the only possible interpretation. Rather, he understands that his is a possible translation and that it is a viable alternative to the traditional dogmatic interpretation of the passage. This means that the argument that the author of the fragment must have been born before the death of Pius is inconclusive, and that the phrase "nuperrime temporibus nostris," understood as contrasted with the times of the prophets and of the apostles, is another viable meaning of the passage.[77]

In other words, for Sundberg neither interpretation, the plain reading nor the periodic reading, yield anything with respect to making a *positive* determination of the Fragment's date. However, in some sense, the plain reading does yield a determination *against* the Fragment's having been written in the fourth century. While Sundberg may be correct that both readings are acceptable alternatives to one another, a plain reading means that his Late Hypothesis is not credible. In short, because it is more likely that the plain reading is to be preferred over the periodic reading (based on ancient precedent), and because a plain reading casts reasonable doubt on the likelihood of the Late Hypothesis, one can conclude that the hypothesis lacks credibility.

Next, the study considered the Late Hypothesis's *simplicity*.

Simplicity

The reasons to believe the Late Hypothesis are dependent upon five assumptions, one of which is evidenced and four that are not. First, in his belief that the Fragment constitutes a formal canon, Sundberg assumed that the Fragmentist's Old Testament canon was one that was closed. There is evidence that the notion of a closed canon had obtained by the time of the

---

[77] Sundberg, "Canon Muratori," 11.

Fragment inasmuch as the Fragmentist states that the *Shepherd of Hermas* should not be read among the prophets because their time is "complete" (lines 73–79). The Fragment may serve as an example of one such closed canon.

The second premise, which underscores Sundberg's belief that the Fragment is a formal canon, holds that the Old Testament canon was not a closed canon until Athanasius. However, not only is this an unsubstantiated assumption, there is evidence to suggest that this was not the case. This evidence consists of Melito's insistence that he learn the accurate list of acceptable Old Testament books, which also must mean that there was an inaccurate list; this points to the idea of a closed Old Testament.[78]

Third, Sundberg maintains that the early church would not have settled on a restrictive list of New Testament books until it had reached a consensus on the closure of the Old Testament. This is possible and may even be likely. However, there is no way of knowing this. This is a supposition for which there is no evidence. Even if it is found likely to be true, it remains a meaningless notion for the Late Hypothesis insofar as the closure of the Old Testament seems to have been earlier (per Justin and Melito) than Sundberg and company believe it to have been. To summarize the case against Sundberg's seeing the Fragment as a formal canon: it is likely that the Old Testament was closed by the time of the Fragment; it cannot be shown to be likely that this did not take place until Athanasius; and it cannot be shown that the church would have closed the New Testament canon (in the Fragment, for example) until the Old Testament was closed. Sundberg's deductive logic is valid, but his reasons leave his argument unsound due to the lack of evidence to support them.

The final two unsubstantiated assumptions in the Late Hypothesis are Hahneman's. For him, the Late Hypothesis relies on Eusebius's dependence on the Fragment. To show this, Hahneman argued that Eusebius transcribed a scribal error when he (or his amanuensis) indiscriminately copied "Miltiades" from the Fragment. However, there is no evidence that this happened, and there are two other possible scenarios. The Fragmentist may have been referring to a known heretic named "Miltiades," but it seems more likely that the Fragmentist was referring to a heretic named "Mitiades," especially since all the extant copies agree with this spelling. Hahneman assumes that they are all misspelled. It would be more likely that Eusebius depended on the Fragment, if the text of the Fragment read "Miltiades" instead of "Mitiades," and more likely if the most well-known Miltiades was a heretic instead of an orthodox father in the church.

In summary, most of the assumptions upon which the Late Hypothesis depends are not substantiated by evidence. Two of the three

---

[78] Euseb., *Ecclesiastical History* 3.26.14.

reasons which lead to the Late Hypothesis cannot stand without the five assumptions described above, four of which are based on no evidence. Only the third reason to believe the hypothesis, that the Fragment contains elements which betray a fourth-century theological/historical context, is free of unsubstantiated assumptions. Thus, one can conclude that the Late Hypothesis does not exhibit simplicity and seems for the most part based upon ad hoc components for which there is no evidence leading to the likelihood that the hypothesis should be believed beyond a reasonable doubt.

To summarize the second half of this chapter, the study weighed the Late Hypothesis by judging it against the Harman-McCullagh criteria of plausibility, explanatory scope, explanatory power, credibility, and simplicity. It found that the hypothesis is implied by two of the twelve evidences cited (17%), that it explains fourteen of the total twenty-two evidences cited by both sides (64%), that it did not powerfully explain any of the three reasons to be believed (0%) that there is evidence which contradicts it (0%) and that four of its five assumptions are unsubstantiated (20%) for an overall average score of 20%.

The next and final section compares the two hypotheses based on the results of weighing them against the five criteria.

The Findings: A "Winner"

Judging the two hypotheses against the Harman-McCullagh criteria of plausibility, explanatory scope, explanatory power, credibility, and simplicity, this study found that the Early Hypothesis is to be preferred over the Late Hypothesis.

In the two categories plausibility and credibility, the Early Hypothesis implies more items of evidence (27%) than does the Late Hypothesis (17%). In other words, for the Early Hypothesis, three items serve as circumstantial evidence and one item (the dating of the *Shepherd of Hermas* during Pius's bishopric) serves as direct evidence. For the Late Hypothesis, two items serve as circumstantial evidence and no items serve as direct evidence. Also, the Early Hypothesis is not disconfirmed by any evidence, as is the case with the Late Hypothesis.

For the two categories of explanatory scope and power, the Early Hypothesis explains more of the total evidence (82%) than the Late (64%).

Also, the Early Hypothesis demonstrates greater explanatory power (66%). Its explanation of the evidence in support of two of its three reasons is more powerful (i.e. more reasonable) than the explanation of the Late Hypothesis for the phenomena in the Fragment (0%).

In the area of simplicity, while the Early Hypothesis is beset by one unsubstantiated assumption of its three (66%), the Late is by four out of five (20%). With an overall average percentage score of 68%, the Early

Hypothesis appears to be the best explanation in contrast to the Late Hypothesis, with an overall average percentage score of 20%.

Of remarkable import to the arguments presented by each of the two sides are two items of evidence esteemed to be particularly crucial. The Early Hypothesis depends heavily on the Fragmentist's statement about the *Shepherd of Hermas*, that it was written "in our times" during the bishopric of Pius. This evidence strongly implies a second-century date, and the hypothesis that the Fragmentist was apparently written early powerfully explains the *raison d'être* of this statement. In addition, this evidence remains viable despite the attacks upon the Early Hypothesis which come in the form of doubts about the date of *Shepherd's* composition and the denial of a fraternal relationship between Hermas and Pius. Finally, the Early Hypothesis shows its simplicity inasmuch as the plain reading of *temporibus nostris* is an evidenced assumption and preferred interpretation.

On the other hand, the Late Hypothesis depends to a crucial degree upon two things. First, it depends on unsubstantiated (and arguably irrelevant) assumptions about how and when the New Testament canon (and even the Old) developed. Second, it looks to the evidence in the Fragment with regard to the *Wisdom of Solomon*. The evidence in the Fragment about *Wisdom* does not imply that the Fragment could not have been written in the second or third centuries, nor does the Late Hypothesis well explain how Irenæus, like the Fragmentist, also included *Wisdom* among his accepted texts. By basing their conclusion on such questionable factors, proponents of the Late Hypothesis have not set themselves up to ably deal with the evidence in the Fragment about Pius, something which the Early Hypothesis proponents have competently leveraged. In the final analysis, it seems more likely that the Muratorian Fragment is a second- or third-century composition.

The Chronological Fiction Argument

The Argument

Because the Early and Late Hypotheses are both so compelling, there has arisen the suggestion that the Fragmentist, though *writing in the fourth century*, deliberately *made his manuscript appear to have been written early*. The chronological fiction argument furnishes a "conciliating position" and proffers the notion that, "The Fragment represents a fictitious attempt to provide a venerable second-century precedent for a later position on canon."[1] This suggestion acknowledges that the text does indeed "date itself to the second century but can only be a product of the . . . fourth."[2] The primary proponent of this argument, Clare K. Rothschild, understands this to be the case due to the perceived presence of "anachronisms, clichés, and mistakes," despite the Fragmentist's supposed intentions to beguile his contemporary readers into believing this to be an earlier manuscript.[3]

In order for one to take the chronological fiction argument seriously, two things must be demonstrated. First, it must be shown that the Fragment appears to be a second-century composition. This present study has already demonstrated this. Second, it must also be demonstrated that the Fragment possesses anachronisms which point more reasonably to a fourth-century context than to one of the second-century. It is this second point which Rothschild has set out to affirm.

Rothschild contends that the chronological fiction argument best explains the evidence through two lines of reasoning. First, the Fragment appears to have been composed in the second century, a matter which, again, has already been thoroughly addressed in this paper. Second, the Fragment manifests anachronisms which place its composition *de facto* in the fourth century, not in the second. These anachronisms are pieces of information which would have raised red flags in the mind of a second-century reader, but which would have gone virtually unnoticed by a reader in the fourth-

---

[1] Rothschild, "The Muratorian Fragment," 55–56n1, 59.
[2] Ibid., 79.
[3] Ibid., 59.

century.⁴ The following section offers a description of the issues involving a subscription to the chronological fiction argument regarding Reason #2 (i.e. the presence of anachronisms in the Fragment) and the evidence upon which it is supposedly based.

The Perceived Presence of Anachronisms

According to the chronological fiction argument, anachronisms show up in four major areas of the Fragment. These areas are the so-called Fraternity "Legend," the reception of the *Shepherd of Hermas*, the Catalog of Heresies, and what Rothschild designates as "Other Evidence."

First, with regard to the Fragmentist's assertion that Hermas and Pius were brothers (lines 75–77), the chronological fiction argument posits three objections, hence the designation of "legend."⁵ According to Rothschild (and Hahneman), *Shepherd* was more likely to have been written before 140, prior to Pius's bishopric.⁶ As evidence for this belief, Hahneman cites the fact that the author of *Shepherd* references Clement of Rome, that there is no evidence that the church in Rome had yet come to be led by a mono-episcopacy, and that the mention of a persecution is probably a reference to one that took place in the first century.⁷ In addition, it casts some doubt that the Fragmentist was a contemporary of Hermas or Pius, as the Fragment implies.⁸ This is due to the lack of information about a relationship between the author of *Shepherd* and Pius until the fourth century. This information does not come until the Liberian Catalog, *Carmen adversus Marcionitas* and the *Letter of Pius to Justus of Vienne*.⁹ Furthermore, no mention is made of this relationship by Irenæus, Clement of Alexandria, Origen, or Eusebius.

Second, regarding the reception of the *Shepherd of Hermas* (lines 73–80), the chronological fiction argument suggests that the Fragmentist viewed *Shepherd* as antilegomena per the Horbury theory already mentioned above. This classification is given, by Eusebius for example, to texts which were reluctantly or provisionally accepted. If the Fragmentist is indeed doing this, he is in effect accepting *Shepherd*. Thus, the Fragment is perceived by adherents to the chronological fiction argument to feature a critical

---

⁴ Rothschild, "The Muratorian Fragment," 59n11.
⁵ This present study prefers the designation "Fraternity Statement" rather than the prejudicial "Fraternity Legend."
⁶ Rothschild, "The Muratorian Fragment," 71, 72–73; Hahneman, *The Muratorian Fragment*, 71.
⁷ Shepherd of Hermas, *Vision* 2.4; Shepherd of Hermas, *Vision* 3.2 speaks of some having endured "crosses," and this may be a reference to Nero's persecution in the mid-60s; see Osiek, *The Shepherd of Hermas*, 19–20.
⁸ Rothschild, "The Muratorian Fragment," 72, 73.
⁹ Ibid., 72.

contradiction. Rothschild asks, "Why characterize composition after the close of the apostolic period if the intention is to receive the text, especially when the actual date of the text is half a century earlier? In short, Horbury's argument adds a layer of internal contradiction."[10]

On the other hand, if the Fragmentist is *not* accepting *Shepherd*, he stands in opposition to Irenæus, Tertullian, and Clement of Alexandria who accepted it early; something which would not give the appearance of a second-century context.[11]

Third, the Catalog of Heresies contains four elements that chronological fiction argument proponents view as anachronisms and believe point to a fourth-century composition, casting doubt on the likelihood that the Fragment was composed in the second century. These errors make the Fragment look "like a medley of stereotypical second-century heretics jumbled together to exude a disapproving aura for an audience either unaware or uninterested in the facts."[12]

First, the name "Arsinoi" (line 81) is unknown, unless it is to be understood as a corruption of the name Bardesanes of Edessa (154–222) who came under criticism of the eastern Father beginning in the fourth century.[13] Also, the name "Miltiades" does not make sense in a list of heretics, as Miltiades was known to oppose Gnosticism; apparently an error. Third, the Fragmentist mistakenly calls Basilides the founder of Montanism and asserts that he was from Asia Minor rather than from Alexandria, as attested in other literature.[14] Fourth, the Fragmentist calls the Montanists "Cataphrygians," a name unfamiliar until the fourth century.[15] These types of errors point to an author who was attempting to convince his readers of something but who did not have all the facts necessary to pull it off well.

According to Rothschild, this is also evident by the way the Fragmentist references an epistle written to the Laodiceans. Apparently, either the Fragmentist does not know that "Laodiceans" is another name for the supposed Pauline epistle to the Ephesians (already mentioned in the first half of the manuscript), or he is referring to the Latin version of a Laodicean epistle, which is not attested until the fourth century.[16]

Finally, Rothschild lists "Other Evidence" which indicates that the Fragment is likely a fictitious work.[17] These "anachronistic traditions" include:

---

[10] Rothschild, "The Muratorian Fragment," 74.
[11] Hahneman, *The Muratorian Fragment*, 71.
[12] Rothschild, "The Muratorian Fragment," 76.
[13] Ibid., 74–75, 75n92.
[14] Ibid., 75.
[15] Ibid., 75–76.
[16] Ibid., 76.
[17] Ibid., 77–78.

1. Order of the four gospels (lines 1–9) [Rothschild provides no further information of how this constitutes an anachronism]

2. Tradition of Luke as doctor and companion of Paul (lines 3–5) [Rothschild implies that this tradition is unknown until the fourth century]

3. Tradition that neither Paul nor Luke saw Jesus in the flesh (lines 6–8) [Rothschild implies that this tradition is unknown until the fourth century]

4. Legend about the authorship of the Fourth Gospel (lines 10–16) [Rothschild implies that this is a late tradition]

5. *Regula fidei* (lines 19–26) [no further information of how this constitutes an anachronism]

6. "Reminiscence of Jerome's Latin Vulgate" (lines 33–34) [Rothschild probably sees a dependence here on Jerome; on the other hand, she acknowledges Ferguson's suggestion about its having more to do with the Latin translation than with the Greek original]

7. Reference to Acts as treating "all" the apostles (lines 34–39)

8. Echo of *Shepherd of Hermas*, Mandate 5.1 (lines 67–68) [no further information of how this constitutes an anachronism]

9. Suggestion that *Wisdom of Solomon* was written by Philo (lines 68–70) [no further information of how this constitutes an anachronism]

10. Inclusion of the *Apocalypse of Peter* (lines 71–72) [no further information of how this constitutes an anachronism]

11. Reference to Miltiades as a Montanist (line 81)

12. Designation "prophets and apostles" (lines 79–80) [no further information of how this constitutes an anachronism]

The chronological fiction argument proposed by Rothschild is an attempt to reconcile the two long-standing theories about the Muratorian Fragment's date while considering all the evidence. On one hand, Rothschild agrees with

Early Hypothesis proponents that indeed the Fragment appears to have been written in the second century, and that giving this appearance was probably the Fragmentist's intent. On the other hand, she contends that the Fragmentist's plan has been uncovered due to the anachronisms in the manuscript which betray what she considers could only have been generated in a fourth-century context. In this way, she leans in favor of the Late Hypothesis. In the following sections, this paper will weigh the chronological fiction argument against the criteria of IBE. Does the evidence imply Rothschild's argument beyond a reasonable doubt (plausibility)? How much of the evidence does her argument explain, and does it do this in a way which makes the argument more likely to be the case than not (explanatory scope and power)? Is there any evidence which would render the argument unlikely or that the argument cannot explain (credibility)? How many unsubstantiated assumptions are necessary to make the argument (simplicity)?

Plausibility

The plausibility of the chronological fiction argument depends on the answer to the following question: does the evidence imply that the Fragment is an attempt to furnish a second-century precedent for a fourth-century position regarding the canon? More specifically, unless the evidence reasonably suggests the greater likelihood that the Fragment contains fourth-century anachronisms, it *does not* imply that it is a chronological fiction. Conversely, if the evidence reasonably suggests the greater likelihood that the Fragment contains fourth-century anachronisms, it *does* imply that it is a chronological fiction.

Rothschild cites fifteen items of evidence to support her argument. Nine of these will be weighed in this section on plausibility. The remaining six will not be considered because though Rothschild identifies them, she offers no explanation of how they are anachronistic or lead to her argument that the Fragment is a fictional work.[18]

First, Rothschild argues that the Fraternity Statement (lines 73–80) regarding the date of the *Shepherd of Hermas's* composition constitutes an anachronism. She believes that several features found in *Shepherd* foil the Fragmentist's attempt to beguile his readers into thinking his work is two hundred years old. However, as will be demonstrated here, none of these features imply that the Fragment is a work of chronological fiction. Rather, they allow for possibility that *Shepherd* was indeed written during Pius's

---

[18] The six items not considered here include the order of the Gospels, the *regula fidei*, echoes of Hermas, Wisdom's authorship by Philo, the *Apocrypha of Peter*, and the expression "prophets and apostles." Rothschild, "The Muratorian Fragment," 77–78. It is unclear how Rothschild sees these as evidence of a fourth-century context.

bishopric, just as the Fragmentist maintains. These features in *Shepherd* consist of the reference to Clement, the lack of a mono-episcopacy, a reference to persecution, a supposed fourth-century indication of Hermas's and Pius's fraternity, and the silence about this relationship in Irenæus, Clement of Alexandria, Origen, and Eusebius.

Contra both Rothschild and Hahneman, there is reason to doubt that the *Shepherd of Hermas* was more than likely complete by the time of Pius's episcopal career. First, its reference to Clement does not require a pre-Pius composition.[19] Though Hahneman argues for a date of 100 for *Shepherd* based in part on the author's reference to Clement, most scholars are not convinced that it need be the case that the book was completed by then.[20] Moreover, logically speaking, the mention of Clement does not require an early composition for *Shepherd*. As Carolyn Osiek observes,

> *If the person known as Clement of Rome was a young secretary in the Roman church at the end of the first century, and Hermas was a young man at the time of the first visions, it is quite possible that he and a brother named Pius could still be alive but elderly toward the middle of the second century. The text could have been composed over a long period of years as interaction with audiences and expanded parts were added.[21]*

Thus it remains possible that *Shepherd* was being written, revised, and expanded upon from the time of Clement (ca. 96–100) until the middle of the second century, a period of about fifty years. The possibility of an extended time period for the writing of *Shepherd* becomes particularly apparent from an observation made by Hahneman:

> *In Vision III (13.1) there is a hint that some of the apostles were still alive. In one sentence the "apostles" are listed with "the bishops, teachers, and deacons." This sentence is followed by one which reads: 'some [of them] have fallen asleep while others are still living' (13.1). This may suggest that some of the apostles were still living. Later in Similitude IX, however, the apostles appear to have all died (92.4; 93.5).[22]*

---

[19] Shepherd of Hermas, *Vision* 2.4.

[20] Hahneman, *The Muratorian Fragment*, 71; Osiek, *The Shepherd of Hermas*, 20.

[21] Osiek, *The Shepherd of Hermas*, 19; so also Quasten, *Patrology*, 1:92–93.

[22] Hahneman, *The Muratorian Fragment*, 37–38; Shepherd of Hermas, *Vision* 3.5; *Similitude* 9.15, 16.

Also, the author of *Shepherd* alludes to a plurality of elders in Rome, which means that when the book of *Visions* was written it is likely that the Roman church was not yet led by only one bishop; a point which Hahneman highlights to support his belief that *Shepherd* pre-dates Pius.[23] However, this simply means that this particular portion of *Shepherd* pre-dates Pius; it is still feasible that the latter portions were written during his bishopric. As far as the persecution is concerned, Hahneman believes it "might best be assigned then to Domitian (95), or the early years of Trajan (c. 100)."[24] And then Hahneman asserts that, "Similitude IX seems to have been written to unify the work and threaten those who had been disloyal to the church and left it," which means that they would have done this after 95.[25] Thus, there is no reason requiring that this portion be written prior to the career of Pius; it could have been written later and still make sense.

Furthermore, the fact that the fraternal relationship of Hermas and Pius is not seen in the literature until the fourth century is at most a dubious indication of an anachronism on the Fragmentist's part and at the least an argument from silence. While it is true that neither Irenæus, Clement of Alexandria, Origen, nor Eusebius mention this relationship, there is a possibility that it was known prior to the fourth century, possibly as early as the early third century. In the Liberian Catalog, an ancient list of Roman bishops, there appears to be a break in the list between bishops, and there is reason to believe that the first section of the list was written by Hippolytus (ca. 170–235).[26] Lightfoot also believes that Hippolytus wrote the note about the *Shepherd of Hermas* being written during Pius's episcopal career in order to discredit it as authoritative, probably due to its lateness.[27] The establishment in Rome, against which Hippolytus stood, is supposed to have depended upon *Shepherd* as authoritative, so its denigration in the Liberian Catalog would come as no surprise, so to add such a negative note about *Shepherd* by the time of the fourth century would be less necessary.

As Lightfoot observes, "The notice respecting the *Shepherd of Hermas* seems intended to discredit the pretensions of that work to a place in the Canon and therefore would probably be written at a time when such pretensions were still more or less seriously entertained."[28] Nevertheless, even if Lightfoot is wrong and this historical note in the Liberian Catalog did not come until the fourth century, the argument that casts the Fragmentist's reference to a fraternal relationship between Hermas and Pius as an anachronism is still an argument from silence. In short, it can be reasonably

---

[23] Shepherd of Hermas, *Vision* 2.4; Hahneman, *The Muratorian Fragment*, 38.
[24] Hahneman, *The Muratorian Fragment*, 41.
[25] Ibid.
[26] Lightfoot, *The Apostolic Fathers*, 261.
[27] Ibid., 262.
[28] Ibid.

said that none of the evidence cited to deny the contemporaneity of *Shepherd's* author and Pius makes the Fragmentist's assertion that it was being written during Pius's ecclesiastical career an anachronism. In other words, this evidence does not imply the chronological fiction argument.

The second piece of evidence of import in this discussion is in regard to the way the Fragmentist characterizes the reception of the *Shepherd of Hermas*. He declares that it ought to be read, but not publically (i.e. liturgically) in the church due to its lateness (lines 73–80). Rothschild contends that such a statement makes no sense.[29] By classifying *Shepherd* as antilegomena, the Fragmentist is accepting it to a degree. If this is the case, he is operating in contradiction with his own understanding of the text's post-apostolic date.[30] However, is the Fragmentist accepting *Shepherd*, and does his statement imply that the Fragment is a work of fiction?

First, it is not clear that the Fragmentist employs the idea of "antilegomena" (i.e. opposed) the way that Eusebius or that modern scholars have done. For the Fragmentist, the all-important issue is the function of a text with relation to the church (i.e. public use). Several of Paul's letters, though personal, are still considered sacred in the church. The Marcionite epistles cannot be received in the church. The Johannine epistles and that of Jude are used in the church, and some are only willing that the Johannine Apocalypse, and not Peter's, be read in the church. So, when the Fragment treats the *Shepherd of Hermas*, it is in relation to its acceptability in the church; it must not be read in the church apparently because books which post-date the apostles do not qualify for that particular usage. Because the Fragmentist is primarily interested in public church reading, for the Fragmentist, *Shepherd* is *not* accepted. In contrast, the way Eusebius used the term "antilegomena" seems to involve the notion of a provisional and local acceptance; the antilegomena were accepted in some places at some times, but opposed in other places at some times. For the Fragmentist, either a text is suitable for the church or it is not. The evidence does not indicate that the Fragmentist is answering question other than this, and when he does, *Shepherd* is not suitable (for this and only this question). Therefore, it cannot reasonably be concluded that the Fragmentist's statement constitutes a contradiction, error, or anachronism based on the notion of "antilegomena" as such; there simply is not enough evidence to suggest he is considering anything other than texts' suitability for public reading in church.

In addition, as noted above, the evidence regarding the *Shepherd of Hermas's* reception is inconclusive for a date; it implies neither a second- to third- nor fourth-century date of composition. However, based on the literary

---

[29] Rothschild, "The Muratorian Fragment," 74.
[30] Ibid., 73. "Horbury argues that the Fragment most likely receives *Wisdom*," and because *Shepherd* is grouped with *Wisdom* in the Fragment, the Fragment also receives *Shepherd* albeit to a limited function.

evidence, it is plausible if the issue is pressed that the Fragmentist seems at home in a very late second- to early third-context. From around 150 to 200, it appears that readers in some way accept the authority of *Shepherd*. For Clement of Alexandria it is divine revelation, Irenæus calls it scripture, and Tertullian's readers respect it.[31] However, by the beginning of the third century, there is a change in attitude toward the text. Tertullian rejects it, and Origen seems ambivalent about it, noting that some despise it.[32] By the time of Eusebius, *Shepherd*, though read by some in church, has fallen into disrepute with others. Therefore, Eusebius bins it with the "opposed," but not for the same reason as the Fragmentist. The Fragmentist's opposition to *Shepherd* was due to its post-apostolic date; Eusebius's opposition was due to the opposition of his forebears and likely his contemporaries. Because "the *Shepherd* . . . has been disputed by some," Eusebius does not place it "among the acknowledged books."[33] Thus it becomes apparent that opposition to *Shepherd* precedes Eusebius's writing here (ca. 312).

Plausibly, the opposition in the past to which Eusebius refers is similar to that voiced by the Fragmentist. So what role is left by the beginning of the third century for *Shepherd*? For the Fragmentist and his audience, it "ought indeed to be read" (line 77). Perhaps Eusebius was referring to individuals like the Fragmentist when he notes those for whom *Shepherd* was "considered quite indispensable, especially to those who need instruction in the elements of the faith."[34]

Indeed, this view may have persisted from the time of Tertullian's opposition (ca. 222) to 367, when Athanasius writes, "There are other books besides these not indeed included in the Canon, but appointed by the Fathers to be read by those who newly join us, and who wish for instruction in the word of godliness . . . the *Shepherd*."[35]

In short, the Fragmentist's reference to the *Shepherd of Hermas's* reception does not appear to be anachronistic, primarily because it does not point decisively to one time frame or another. The most than can be said is that the Fragmentist does not find *Shepherd* suitable for liturgical reading, but that he does consider it valuable for private reading. The evidence bears out that such a perspective could feasibly have obtained at any time around Tertullian's conversion to Montanism (ca. 207) through the late fourth century with Athanasius, and is not limited to the fourth.

---

[31] Clement of Alexandria, *Miscellanies* 1.29; Irenæus, *Against Heresies* 4.20.2; Tertullian, *Prayer* 16.
[32] Tertullian, *Modesty* 10, 20; Origen, *First Principles* 1.3.3, 2.1.5, 3.2.4, 4.1.11.
[33] Eusebius, *Ecclesiastical History* 3.3.6.
[34] Ibid.
[35] Athanasius, *Festal Letter* 39 (*NPNF* 2:4:552).

The third item of evidence cited on behalf of the chronological fiction argument is the Catalog of Heresies (lines 81–85). Rothschild sees four anachronisms in this section of the Fragment. First, she notes that both Hahneman and Credner suggest that the Fragmentist's mention of "Arsinoi" is a reference to Bardesanes of Edessa. Bardesanes lived from ca. 154 to 222, but he is condemned in the fourth-century literature in a way supposedly similar to that found in the Fragment.[36] Thus, Rothschild holds that the Fragmentist is doing the same, and therefore also writing in the fourth century. However, while this is possible, the Fragmentist's antagonism toward an individual pilloried in the fourth century, the identity of whom is in doubt due to a supposedly corrupted text, does not necessarily, or even plausibly, constitute an anachronism. It is just as plausible that the Fragment's Arsinoi is a second-century heretic.

Second, according to the fiction argument, if the Fragmentist's reference to "Miltiades" is the correct reading, it constitutes an error because only a second-century anti-Gnostic by that name is known, and his mention here would not make sense.[37] Rothschild is correct in this. However, it is not the case that the Fragmentist is referring to a "Mi*l*tiades" but rather one "Mitiades." Neither the Fragment nor the Benedictine manuscripts found at Monte Cassino have the former spelling; both read "Mitiades." Therefore, it is less than reasonable to conclude that the Fragmentist is confusing the two. It is not apparent that his reference here points to a likely fourth-century date.

Third, according to Rothschild, the Fragmentist mistakenly states that Basilides is from Asia Minor and is the founder of the Montanists.[38] However, this may not necessarily be the case. The statement comes at the very end of the Fragment, so it cannot be determined what follows the tear line. It is possible that the Fragmentist was ending a thought with his reference to Basilides and beginning an entirely new thought and sentence with his reference to Asia and the Cataphrygians. For example, it is possible to read it as follows: "We accept nothing whatever of Arsinous or Valentinus or Miltiades, who also composed a new book of psalms for Marcion, together with Basilides. The Asian founder of the Cataphrygians . . ."[39] Also, based on Salmond's translation, it could just as easily read, "Those are rejected too who wrote the new Book of Psalms for Marcion, together with Basilides. And the founder of the Asian Cataphrygians . . ."[40]

In other words, because it is not clear that the Fragmentist meant to say Basilides was from Asia Minor and founded the Montanists, this

---

[36] Rothschild, "The Muratorian Fragment," 75n92.
[37] Ibid., 75.
[38] Ibid.; so too Hahneman, *The Muratorian Fragment*, 28, 211.
[39] Metzger's translation, *The Canon of the New Testament*, 307.
[40] *ANF* 5:604

evidence in the Fragment does not make it clear that his statement is an error or anachronism. This evidence does not imply the Fragment is a chronological fiction.

Fourth, within the Catalog of Heresies, the Fragmentist identifies a group he calls the Cataphrygians (line 84). Rothschild believes the term "Cataphrygian" does not likely predate the fourth century. According to her, the term appears "in neither Greek nor Latin until the fourth century."[41] However, other scholars believe that Epiphanius cites a late second- to early third-century Greek source who uses the term.[42] This possibility casts doubt on the notion that the term could not have been used prior to the fourth century. Hill explains the problems with Rothschild's supposition best when he writes that a late-fourth-century Latin translator could easily have substituted *catafrygum*, the term of his day, for an original "Phrygians." Even so, we probably do have two examples of the Greek κατά Φρύγας used for the Montanists from near the beginning of the third century.

Tertullian's *Contra haereses*, a document originally written in Greek in the early to middle third century, but surviving only in a Latin translation, refers to *qui dicuntur secundum Phrygas* (7.21). Hahneman concludes it is unlikely that such represents an original Greek κατά Φρόγας, "because similar Greek phrases in the same paragraph were simply transliterated into Latin, namely 'kata Proclum' and 'kata Aeschinen'" (p. 212). What he does not tell us is that in the same paragraph we also have both the transliterated *kata Aeschinen* and the translated *secundum Aeschinen*, both presumably from a Greek κατά. Thus, *secundum* instead of a transliterated *kata* with *Phrygas* is no evidence against an assumed original κατά. Paired as it is here with *secundum Aeschinen*, what else would *secundum* have translated? Further, Hahneman has not considered an important piece of evidence from Epiphanius's *Panarion*. Since the researches of Lipsius (1865) and Voigt (1891) scholars have recognized that in Pan. 48 Epiphanius is citing a late-second or early-third-century (probably Asian) source. We find this writer too already using the phrase κατά Φρύγας for the Montanists (48.12.4).[43]

In short, evidence from the Fragment's Catalog of Heresies does not point beyond a reasonable doubt that it consists of anachronisms, and thus it does not imply the notion that the Fragment represents a work written in the fourth century purporting to have been written in the second.

The fourth item of evidence from the Fragment, which appears to Rothschild to be either an error or an anachronism, is the author's mention

---

[41] Rothschild, "The Muratorian Fragment," 76.

[42] Epiph., *Refutation of All Heresies*, 48.12.4; Hill, "The Debate Over the Muratorian Fragment and the Development of the Canon," 442.

[43] Hill, "The Debate Over the Muratorian Fragment and the Development of the Canon," 442.

of an epistle to the Laodiceans which has been "forged in Paul's name to [further] the heresy of Marcion" (lines 63–65). Rothschild believes that either the Fragmentist did not know Laodiceans was another name for the canonical epistle to the Ephesians (because he mentions Ephesians earlier) or he is referring to a Latin epistle to the Laodiceans for which there is no attestation until the fourth century.[44] However, there are other possibilities.

It remains possible that the Fragmentist knew of the name Laodiceans given for a version of Paul's epistle to the Ephesians, likely mutilated by Marcion. Writing in around 212, Tertullian elaborates on this by noting that regarding Paul's epistle, "We have it on the true tradition of the Church that this epistle was sent to the Ephesians, not to the Laodiceans. Marcion, however, was very desirous of giving it the new title (of Laodicean)."[45] Thus, though the Fragmentist may, on the other hand, be referring to a later Latin Laodiceans, it seems just as likely that, based on Tertullian's testimony, he is writing in the second century and that he is not confusing Paul's authentic Ephesians with Marcion's revision of that epistle to one called "Laodiceans." In other words, it is just as reasonable to believe that the Fragmentist is referring to a Marcionite version of Ephesians called Laodiceans as it is that he is referring to a Latin Laodiceans which may or may not have anything to do with Marcion. Therefore, this reference does not imply a late date for the Fragment.

Outside of the Fraternity Statement and the Catalog of Heresies, Rothschild also elaborates on five other items of evidence. These include the tradition of Luke as Paul's doctor/companion, the tradition that neither Luke nor Paul saw Jesus, the statement of the Fourth Gospel's authorship, apparent parallels with Jerome's Latin Vulgate, and the title "the Acts of *all* the apostles."

First, Rothschild contends that the Fragmentist could only have known about the tradition that Luke was a doctor and a companion of Paul if he had lived during the fourth century. She cites both the anti-Marcionite Prologues and the Monarchian Prologues as fourth-century evidence for the tradition and notes its absence from Papias's writing.[46] However, this does not imply that the Fragment was written in the fourth century because the tradition that Luke was a physician and companion of Paul first appears in the canonical epistle to the Colossians (4:14), which is dated around 59.[47] Therefore, the presence of this tradition in the Fragment does not point to a

---

[44] Rothschild, "The Muratorian Fragment," 76.
[45] Tert., *Against Marcion* 5.17 (ANF 3:464–65).
[46] Rothschild, "The Muratorian Fragment," 77n113.
[47] Reicke, *Re-examining Paul's Letters*, 76. According to Tacitus (*Annals* 14.27), Laodicea was destroyed by an earthquake around 61, and Reicke infers that Colosse was likely destroyed at the same time, thus rendering it unlikely that the author of Colossians wrote after this date.

fourth-century context and is not an anachronism; it does not imply the chronological fiction argument.

Next, Rothschild contends that the notion that Luke and Paul had not witnessed the life of Jesus did not obtain until the fourth century due to a similar tradition found in the Monarchian Prologue.[48] This is possible, but from the passage cited in the Prologue that this is referring to the same tradition is unclear; it is not conclusive that this tradition only first appeared in the fourth century.

In addition, the story in the Fragment regarding the authorship of the Fourth Gospel points to a fourth-century context according to the fiction argument. In the Fragment, John was encouraged to write the Gospel by his "fellow disciples" (line 10), which Armstrong believes is different from the tradition provided by Eusebius (303 CE) that Clement of Alexandria believed John to have been encouraged by his "pupils."[49] Armstrong translates Clement's term γνωρίμων as "pupils," however, it could just as readily mean "acquaintances."[50] In other words, John was familiar with these people, which makes sense if they were his fellow disciples. Clement's testimony is not contradictory to the Fragment's, it is simply less precise. The Fragmentist's use of the term *condiscipulis* here does not imply a fourth-century context.

Moreover, Rothschild cites apparent similarities between the Fragmentist's quote of 1 John 1:1–4 (lines 33–34) and Jerome's Latin Vulgate.[51] However, she also highlights Metzger's belief that these could simply be the result of a later Latin translation of an original Greek Fragment. In short, these similarities do not constitute an anachronism or point to a fictional fourth-century original composition.

Finally, with her mention of the Fragmentist's designation of Acts as that of "all" the apostles, Rothschild is probably referring to Hahneman's assertion that this expression points to a late date.[52] Hahneman maintained that such disambiguation was required in the fourth century.[53] However, as noted above, many other "Acts" were gaining popularity in the second century, and such a requirement to distinguish between them was not unique to the fourth century. In short, this designation for the book of Acts does not

---

[48] Rothschild, "The Muratorian Fragment," 78n114.

[49] Armstrong, "Victorinus of Pettau," 6.

[50] Γνωρίμων is a form of γνωρίζω which means "to make known." In other words, these were people with whom John was simply familiar, as in the case of fellow disciples. *Strong's Exhaustive Concordance of the Bible*, comp. James Strong (Peabody, MA: Hendrickson, 2004), s.v. "γνωρίζω."

[51] Rothschild, "The Muratorian Fragment," 78n117; Metzger, *The Canon of the New Testament*, 193.

[52] Rothschild, "The Muratorian Fragment," 78.

[53] Hahneman, *The Muratorian Fragment*, 192–96.

indicate a fourth-century composition, is not an anachronism, and does not imply the chronological fiction argument.

To summarize the findings regarding the chronological fiction argument's plausibility, none of the evidence (nine items) suggests the greater likelihood that the Fragment contains fourth-century anachronisms, and therefore none of it implies that it is a chronological fiction. Based on the evidence, it remains just as plausible that the Fragment is a genuine second-century work.

Next, the study examined the argument's *explanatory scope*.

Explanatory Scope

In order to weigh the chronological fiction argument's explanatory scope, the study asked what (i.e. how much) evidence does the argument explain, or at least attempt to explain? The study found that the argument does not explain most of the evidence cited by scholars regarding the Fragment's date. Of twenty-four items of evidence, the chronological fiction argument furnishes an explanation for nine.[54] The argument that the Fragment is a chronological fiction does not offer an explanation of the Fourfold Gospel; the order of the Gospels; the way the Fragmentist identifies the Gospels; the treatment of the Apocalypse; the omissions of Hebrews; James and the Petrine Epistles; the inclusion of Jude; the inclusion of the *Wisdom of Solomon*; the treatment of the *Apocalypse of Peter*; the *regula fidei*; the references to the Church; the references to the "chair"; the significance of the prophets and the apostles; and the perceived echoes of Hermas. Though Rothschild mentions some of these, she does not show how the chronological fiction argument explains them. In short, it explains nine of the twenty-four items of evidence.

Next, the study assessed the argument's *explanatory power*.

Explanatory Power

In order for the chronological fiction argument to exhibit explanatory power, it must demonstrate that the phenomena in the Fragment are more likely to constitute anachronisms than to be genuine reflections of a second-century context. It cannot merely be possible that the evidence comes from a later context, it must be more likely. The fiction argument exhibits little explanatory power in the way it explains the evidence.

---

[54] Rothschild's argument identifies two addition items of evidence that Early and Late Hypotheses proponents did not consider: the tradition that neither Luke nor Paul saw Jesus and the Fragmentist's contrast between honey and gall. However, Rothschild does not explain how the contrast between honey and gall as an "echo" of Hermas constitutes an anachronism.

The two most powerful pieces of evidence cited by Rothschild consist of the so-called "Fraternity Legend" and the Catalog of Heresies. In each of these, she perceives snippets of information which she contends could "only" have obtained during to the fourth century.[55] First, the notions that Hermas wrote the *Shepherd of Hermas* during Pius's bishopric, that Hermas and Pius were probably not brothers, and the implication that the Fragmentist was a contemporary of both are called into question by the fiction argument. However, Rothschild's argument must powerfully show that these notions are anachronistic. Primarily, Rothschild maintains that these traditions did not become known until the fourth century in the Liberian Catalogue, the *Carmen adversus Marcionitas,* and the *Letter of Pius to Justus of Vienne*; an argument from second-century silence.[56] In addition, Rothschild perceives a contradiction between the manner in which the Fragment classifies *Shepherd* as antilegomena and his stated intention to regard it unworthy for liturgical use in the church; an error which, in her view, a second-century writer would not have made. However, Rothschild must demonstrate that it is more likely that the Fragmentist was writing this around the same time that Eusebius explicitly classified *Shepherd* as antilegomena. This notwithstanding, there remains the possibility that when Eusebius refers to *Shepherd* as antilegomena, he is harkening back to the second century when writers like the Fragmentist spoke against *Shepherd* as unacceptable to church reading.

In addition to the "Fraternity Legend," Rothschild believes her theory best explains the Catalogue of Heresies. She considers it a "medley of stereotypical second-century heretics jumbled together to exude a disapproving aura for an audience either unaware or uninterested in the facts."[57] Unfortunately for the chronological fiction argument, this assertion does not powerfully demonstrate this to be the case. While Rothschild's interpretation of the various pieces of evidence point to the possibility of errors, the hypothesis that the Fragment is early holds to the reliability of the statements in the Catalog and shows that it is capable of doing so without encountering more problems or creating new ones. In other words, and as demonstrated in previous chapters, the Early Hypothesis is able to explain each of the items of evidence in the Catalogue as fitting within the second-century, and it does this without needing to resort to the idea that the Fragment did not have a firm understanding of the content; an unsubstantiated assumption on its own.

In summary, the chronological fiction argument does not powerfully explain the evidence any more than does the Early Hypothesis, which does so without having to resort to arguments from silence. Thus, it does not appear

---

[55] Rothschild, "The Muratorian Fragment," 79.
[56] Ibid., 72.
[57] Ibid., 76.

more likely that the fiction argument is a better explanation of what one finds in the Fragment. It is just as likely (or perhaps more so) that the Fragment is a second-century composition with statements genuine to that period than that it is a fourth-century composition attempting to pose as an earlier document.

Next, the fiction argument's *credibility* is considered.

Credibility

Is there any evidence which renders the chronological fiction argument unlikely? On one hand, there is no evidence which implies the likelihood that the Fragment is a fiction, thus Rothschild's argument lack plausibility, as concluded above. On the other hand, there is also no evidence which implies that the argument is unlikely. While the argument is implausible, it remains nonetheless credible. This is because assertions that ancient writings are pseudepigraphic are difficult to discount. Built into the argument that a work is false is the assumption that the author is trying to deceive his audience. Without the existence of direct evidence to contradict such an assumption, such allegations remain credible. So while Rothschild is able to doubt the veracity of the Fragment using an approach of methodological skepticism, she is at the same time able to believe that the Fragment is a ruse by coming with an equally strong amount of methodological credulity. In other words, despite a lack of direct evidence that the Fragmentist intended to deceive, she believes that he did. Yet, there is also a lack of evidence implying that he did not intend to deceive. Thus there is still the *possibility* that the chronological fiction argument is true.

Simplicity

Finally, the reasons undergirding the chronological fiction argument are predicated upon four assumptions; two substantiated by other evidence and two that are not. First, Rothschild would agree with Early Hypothesis proponents that the Fragment presents itself as a second-century composition. The two substantiated assumptions that support this reason are the presupposition that the Fragment's *temporibus nostris* should be interpreted with the Plain Reading.[58] It is only by doing this that the text could look second-century. Secondly, Rothschild also would agree that there are literary parallels in the Fragment that match similar expressions from the second century, albeit "freely excerpted from older writings."[59] As observed above, both of these assumptions are substantiated.

---

[58] Rothschild, "The Muratorian Fragment," 71.
[59] Ibid., 59.

However, two of Rothschild's assumptions are unsubstantiated by evidence. First, as with the Late Hypothesis, the chronological fiction argument assumes that there was closed canonical content which, in this case, needed to find support in the fourth-century community by means of a more ancient precedent.[60] However, there is no other example of list of New Testament texts that mirrors the Fragment found in the fourth century, so who in the fourth century would have espoused such a list? In what location would this have presented itself most acceptably? Fourth, the chronological fiction argument assumes that the Fragmentist is intent on deceiving his audience. He may have been, but there is no evidence to suggest that this is the case. At best, Rothschild could make a case that the Fragmentist is an inept historian, but even this requires evidence. In order to substantiate these two assumptions, Rothschild would need to show evidence that the Fragmentist's catalog was welcomed by others like him and that he indeed intended to deceive.

To summarize the findings of this chapter, the study weighed the chronological fiction argument against the Harman-McCullagh criteria of plausibility, explanatory scope, explanatory power, credibility, and simplicity. It found that the argument is implied by none of the nine evidences proffered by Rothschild (0%), that it explains nine of the total twenty-four evidences cited in her argument (38%), that it did not powerfully explain any of the reasons to be believed (0%), that there is no evidence which contradicts it (100%), and that two of its four assumptions are unsubstantiated (50%) for an overall average score of 38%. Thus, though the chronological fiction argument is a better explanation for the Fragment than the Late Hypothesis (with a score of 20%), it does not explain the evidence as well as the Early Hypothesis (68%). Where the fiction argument falls short is in its lack of plausibility and power, but its strength is in its credibility, because there is no evidence against it at this time.

---

[60] Rothschild, "The Muratorian Fragment," 59.

Conclusion

Recapitulation

In answer to the question of which of the two hypotheses regarding the date of the Muratorian Fragment is more likely, this study found that, by making an inference to the best explanation, the Early Hypothesis is preferred. It also found the Early Hypothesis to be preferred over Rothschild's chronological fiction argument.

This methodology consisted of weighing the two hypotheses against five criteria: *plausibility, explanatory scope, explanatory power, credibility,* and *simplicity*. First, the study considered the plausibility of each hypothesis. A hypothesis is plausible if the relevant evidence implies that hypothesis. The study found that, while some of the evidence implied the Early Hypothesis, very little evidence implied the Late Hypothesis. The Early Hypothesis is implied by the Fragmentist's apologetic tone with regard to the Fourth Gospel, his failure to mention the Petrine epistles, his understanding of the date and reception of the *Shepherd of Hermas*, his allusion to what patristic scholars call the *regula fidei*, and his use of the term "prophets and apostles" in lieu of "Old and New Testaments." In contrast, the Late Hypothesis is only implied by the Fragmentist's regard for the *Apocalypse of Peter* and his inclusion of the Johannine epistles. None of the evidence implies the chronological fiction argument. The Early Hypothesis appears to be more plausible than the Late Hypothesis or the fiction argument.

Second, the amount of evidence explained by a hypothesis constitutes its explanatory scope. When the study compared the hypotheses explanatory scope, it discovered that the Early Hypothesis possesses a broader sweep. It proves itself able to explain all but four of the items of evidence considered. The Late Hypothesis leaves eight items without explanation, and the fiction argument leaves fifteen without explanation.

With regard to the third criterion, explanatory power (the degree to which a hypothesis is able to better explain the evidence), two of the premises which scholars cite as reasons to believe the Early Hypothesis prove to be likely explanations of the evidence. It is probable that the Fragmentist and Pius were contemporaries (in the second century), and it also appears likely that the Fragment betrays the same theological/historical context seen in second- and third-century Christian literature.

On the other hand, the Late Hypothesis falls short and does not as powerfully explain the evidence. For example, it is not necessarily true, nor even more likely, that the Fragment as a formal canon should be restricted to having only obtained in the fourth century. Also, the Late Hypothesis's premise that Eusebius depended on the Fragment to write his *Ecclesiastical History* is wanting because there is another suitable (and more likely true) explanation for the Fragment's mention of one "Mitiades." Finally, the Late Hypothesis does not convincingly explain the Fragmentist's location of the *Wisdom of Solomon* within the list. The chronological fiction argument does not more powerfully explain any of the evidence. Thus, the Early Hypothesis has the greater explanatory power.

Geoffrey M. Hahneman attempted to cast doubt on the credibility (the fourth criterion) of the Early Hypothesis by bringing forth evidence to disconfirm it. Hahneman questioned the Fragmentist's attestation to the date of the composition of the *Shepherd of Hermas*, the view that Hermas and Pius were brothers, and the Early Hypothesis proponents' belief that the Fragmentist's characterization of the *Shepherd's* reception points to the second century. However, none of his objections gain traction in his effort to cite them as reasons to disconfirm the Early Hypothesis. In other words, there is no evidence which renders the Early Hypothesis to be unlikely. By way of contrast, if one accepts a plain reading of *temporibus nostris*, such an interpretation disconfirms the likelihood of the Late Hypothesis. If Pius was bishop of Rome "in our [life] times," it is impossible that the Fragmentist was writing in the fourth century. This evidence proves devastating to the Late Hypothesis's credibility, so that the Early Hypothesis appears to be more believable. Also, the chronological fiction argument, though implausible, remains credible.

Finally, the study considered the degree to which each hypothesis demonstrated simplicity of argument. To what extent did they resort to unsubstantiated ad hoc components to bolster their respective claims? The Early Hypothesis is weakened by one unsubstantiated assumption in that it is not warranted in its preconception that language changes enough over a two hundred year period to locate the time of the Fragment based on parlance. On the other hand, the Late Hypothesis suffers from comparatively less simplicity. The majority of its assumptions are not substantiated by evidence such that two of its three major premises cannot stand without four un-evidenced assumptions. The chronological fiction argument depends on four assumptions, two of which are unsubstantiated. Therefore, the Early Hypothesis demonstrates a greater simplicity.

To synopsize, in the two essential categories of plausibility and credibility, the Early Hypothesis implies more items of evidence than does the Late Hypothesis and the chronological fiction argument, and it is not disconfirmed by any evidence as is the case with the Late Hypothesis; neither is the fiction argument.

For the two categories of explanatory scope and power, the Early Hypothesis explains four more items of evidence than does the Late Hypothesis, and the Early Hypothesis demonstrates greater explanatory power in that its explanations of five items of evidence seems more likely to be the case than the Late Hypothesis is able to show for any of its explanations of the phenomena in the Fragment. The fiction argument explains less than half of the evidence and does so in a non-powerful way. In the less critical areas of credibility and simplicity, the Early Hypothesis faces no evidence disconfirming its believability while the Late Hypothesis does, and the Late Hypothesis is beset by four unsubstantiated assumptions; the Early, only one. The chronological fiction argument has two.

It is apparent that through implementing the methodology of inference to the best explanation, historians should conclude that it is more likely that the Muratorian Fragment was written during the second or third centuries than that it was written during the fourth century or that it is a fictional work from the fourth century purporting to be from the second. The foregoing study is unlike others in that it offers the discipline of Bibliology a solution to the problem of the Fragment's date. It contributes possibilities for apologetics, as well, in that it may pave the way for its methodology's use in order to resolve issues in that field as well.

Early Hypothesis	Chronological Fiction Argument	Late Hypothesis
Plausible	Implausible	Plausible
Credible	Credible	Incredible

A Plausible Interpretive Scenario

Based on the evidence and the likelihood that the Fragmentist wrote his work during the second century (or the very early third century at the latest), what types of inferences can scholars reasonably draw about the background and occasion of the Fragment's composition? Based on the likelihood that the Fragmentist lived at some point between 138 and 161, during Pius's bishopric, it seems plausible that the original manuscript was written in Greek rather than Latin, which became prominent some time later. If one were to build a profile of sorts, the Fragmentist would have been a Greek writer living in the West. He was concerned about Gnosticism, Marcionism, and Montanism. He was familiar with the ecclesiastical history of the church in Rome, and his presence near or in that city may explain the limited geographical distribution of the Muratorian text. He valued the Christian tradition passed down by the apostles as historically significant, and he emphasized the importance of the universality of the church. Proper public reading of authoritative Christian texts was important to him, and this seems to be his primary reason for writing the Fragment. He appears to be more a "man of the church," like Irenæus, than a philosopher like Justin or an historian like Eusebius. Indeed, the Fragmentist's ecclesiology mirrors that of Irenæus. Whereas the Fragmentist held that "there is one Church spread throughout the whole extent of the earth" (lines 56–57), Irenæus acknowledged "the Church . . . dispersed through the whole world, even to the ends of the earth."[1] However, as noted below, the Fragmentist's accepted list of New Testament texts does not exactly match that of Irenæus. On the other hand, one should also not be quick to rule out Justin or one of his disciples. Nevertheless, the general milieu and the man behind the work can still be characterized to a remarkable degree of accuracy and precision. At any rate, he was plausibly a second-century Greek speaker who had moved to the West and had been asked to defend the texts read liturgically in his church.

Implications for Historical Study of the New Testament Canon

This finding, that the Muratorian Fragment is probably a second- or third-century work, has several potential implications for the study of early Christianity. First, it shortens the list of possible authors, because it appears much less likely that the Fragment was written by anyone who flourished during the fourth century. Instead, especially in light of the Fragmentist's reference to his being a contemporary of Pius, it could have been written by anyone who lived during that time (ca. 138–161). Restriction to this timeframe more than likely eliminates Caius, Hippolytus, Victorinus of Pettau, Cyprian, and Polycarp.[2]

This leaves Papias (60–163), Justin Martyr (100–165), Apollinaris of Hierapolis (flourished ca. 177), Hegesippus (110–180), Melito of Sardis (c. 180), Rhodon (flourished 180–192), Polycrates of Ephesus (130–196), Victor I (d. 199), Irenæus (130–202), Clement of Alexandria (150–215), and Zephyrinus (d. 217) as possibilities.

In addition, the theology of the Fragmentist betrayed in his work means that some of these can be eliminated due to what is known about their

---

[1] Irenæus, *Against Heresies* 1.10.1.

[2] While most of these are too late, Polycarp is probably too early if the Fragmentist is indeed referring to the bishopric of Pius as a past event.

particular New Testament canons (e.g. Irenæus and Clement of Alexandria), and it means that others do not stand out simply because so little is known about their views on the same. However, of all these, Justin's life and theology pose no problems for perceiving congruence between him and the Fragmentist. This is not to say that Justin is the likely the author (or that it comes from a "Justinian School"), simply that it seems highly possible among the options. Both Justin and the Fragmentist had several things in common: they wrote apologetically, they wrote in the mid-second century, they were both familiar with the ecclesiastical politics of Rome, they both assigned significance to the liturgical reading of the prophets and the apostles, they both accepted the Apocalypse as authoritative and normative, and they both spoke out against Marcion.[3]

In addition, the Fragmentist's attitude toward the texts he lists is not inconsistent with attitudes in the early West. The rejection of the Fourth Gospel by the Alogi very possibly during Justin's lifetime is consistent with the Fragmentist's apparent need to justify its authority. Moreover, it is also in keeping with Justin's *logos* doctrine and his belief in the need to be "born again."[4] Also, the Fragmentist's omission of Hebrews is not inconsistent with the absence of Western writers' declaration of its authority, though it is alluded to; it was not accepted as early in the West as in the East.[5] Similarly, the non-mention of James is not inconsistent with the Mommsen catalog, a fourth-century Western canon. Indeed, as with these canonical New Testament texts, there is nothing inconsistent between the Fragmentist's and early western writers' attitudes toward the *Wisdom of Solomon*, the *Apocalypse of Peter*, and the *Shepherd of Hermas*.

Second, finding that the Early Hypothesis is preferred means the greater likelihood that the Fragment was originally a Greek text. Inasmuch as the western church had not begun to transition from Greek to Latin until the middle of the second century, it stands to reason that the Fragment was probably written in Greek originally.[6] Though admittedly, there is still is the slightest possibility that the original was in Latin. A Greek Fragment remains consistent with the possibility that Justin Martyr, or a Justinian School, could have composed it in the West. For example, Guignard, who has studied the language and date relationship greater than anyone, argues that the Fragment is early and Greek.[7] None of this is inconsistent with a context surrounding Justin.

---

[3] Justin, *Dialogue with Trypho* 81; idem, *First Apology* 67, 26.

[4] Zahn, "Muratorian Canon," 54; Epiph., *Refutation of All Heresies,* Proem 1.4.5, 1.5.6; Justin, *Dialogue with Trypho* 105.1; idem, *First Apology* 61.

[5] Justin, *Dialogue with Trypho* 116; Ferguson, "Canon Muratori," 681.

[6] Mohrmann, "Les Origines," 67–106.

[7] Guignard, "The Original Language of the Muratorian Fragment," 596.

Third, if the Fragment was written in the second century by Justin or his followers, it would more than likely have a western provenance. As noted above, this provenance also enjoys the consensus of Muratori, Donaldson, Salmon, Zahn, Ferguson, and Rothschild. In addition, a western provenance is consistent with the locations of the extant manuscripts' discovery in Milan and in the Benedictine monastery at Monte Cassino. There is no evidence of a "Fragment-like" catalog in the East. Also, the Fragmentist shows a familiarity with Rome. This does not necessitate a Roman origin, but does make a western one seem much more likely than an eastern.

In addition, several other factors correspond to a western context. First, the *Shepherd of Hermas* was the subject of scrutiny in the West to a greater degree than in the East, a reluctance whose echoes resound in the Fragment.[8] Second, the *Wisdom of Solomon* was considered important in the West from an early date and considered worthy of listing by the Fragmentist.[9] Third, with the exception of Caius, western acceptance of the Apocalypse in the church was firm, and the Fragmentist's emphasis on the number "seven" matches that of the Apocalyptist and Tertullian.[10] Fourth, the Fragmentist's emphasis on the bishop's chair is also found in Cyprian.[11] Fifth, the Fragmentist's *regula fidei* is not unlike similar formulas found in Justin, Irenæus, and Tertullian.[12] Finally, the Fragmentist's catalog of heresies seems like a list which would have special significance only to western readers. He wrote of Arsinous, Valentinus, Miltiades, Marcion, and Basilides. While the locations of Arsinous and this Miltiades are unknown, Valentinus "came to Rome [and] . . . flourished under Pius," thus making him a contemporary of the Fragmentist in the imperial capital.[13] It is also known that Marcion lived in Rome during the mid-second century. As for Basilides, he lived in Alexandria, which may explain why the Fragmentist, ostensibly writing from the West, referred to him as "the Asian" (line 84).[14] Lastly, the Fragmentist mentioned the Montanists who eventually had a formative influence in the West particularly on Tertullian.

---

[8] Ferguson, "Canon Muratori," 679.//
[9] Hebrews 1:3; 1 Clement 3:4, 7.5, 27.5.//
[10] Tert., *Against Marcion* 5.17.//
[11] Cyprian, *To the People, Concerning Five Schismatic Presbyters of the Faction of Felicissimus* 5; idem, *To Antonianus About Cornelius and Novatian* 9.//
[12] Justin Martyr, *First Apology* 31; Irenæus, *Against Heresies* 1.10; Tert., *Prescription Against Heretics* 13; idem, *The Veiling of Virgins* 1; idem, *Against Praxeas* 2.//
[13] Irenæus, *Against Heresies* 3.4.3.//
[14] Ibid., 1.24.1.

Further Research

The finding that the second century is the most likely timeframe for the composition of the Muratorian Fragment means more work for scholars. Further research is needed on the methodology of *inference to the best explanation*. Arguably, the methodology appears promising in answering many of the questions regarding early Christian history which have continued to flummox its students over the previous two millennia. However, in order to be considered reliable, testing needs to be conducted against questions for which the answer is already known by some. Only in blind testing can its value be confidently ascertained.

Also, with regard to the content of this present study, more research must be conducted in understanding the Fragment's probable author, language, and provenance. Answering these questions (preferably using *inference to the best explanation*) is the only way that the true significance of this present study can be realized. Coming to a consensus on the answer of who most likely wrote the Fragment will yield an understanding of this "first" of Christian canons, and may shed invaluable light on the connections between the current accepted New Testament and that of the earliest Christians.

Appendix A:
The Original Latin Fragment

The original reading of the Muratorian Fragment follows. Words in bold are rubricated in the manuscript. The letters depicted in parentheses had been erased by correctors, and the letters in italics were added by correctors, either by means of substitution or superscription.[1]

[folio 10r] quibus tamen Interfuit et ita posuit ·
tertio euangelii librum sec(a)u **ndo Lucan**
Lucas Iste medicus post ascensum $^{\overline{xpi}}$.
Cum eo Paulus quasi ut iuris studiosum.
5 Secundum adsumsisset numeni suo
ex opinione concri*b*set dñm tamen nee Ipse
(d)uidit in carne et idó pro*ut* asequi potuit ·
Ita et ad natiuitate Iohannis incipet dicere.
quarti euangeliorum Iohannis ex decipolis
10 cohortantibus condescipulis et $^{\overline{eps}}$ suis
dixit conieiunate mihi · odie triduo et quid
cuique fuerit reuelatum alterutrum
nobis ennarremus eadem nocte reue
latum andreae ex apostolis ut recognis
15 centibus cuntis Iohannis suo nomine
cun*c*ta discrib*e*ret et ideo licit uaria sin
culis euangeliorum libris principia
doceantur Nihil tamen differt creden
tium f(e)*i*dei cum uno ac principali $^{\overline{spu}}$ de
20 clarata sint in omnibus omnia de natiui
tate de passione de resurrectione
de conue*r*satione cum decipulis suis
ac de gemino eius aduentu
Primo In humilitate dispectus quod (fo

---

[1] This particular transcription of the Fragment was copied from Hahneman, *The Muratorian Fragment*, 6–7.

25 tu) secundum potentate regali pre
clarum quod foturum est. quid ergo
mirum si Iohannes tarn constanter
sincula etiã In epistulis suis proferat
dicens In semeipsu Quae uidimus oculis
30 nostris et auribus audiuimus et manus
nostrae palpauerunt haec scripsimus (uobis)
[folio10v] Sic enim non solum uisurem sed (&)
auditorem
sed et scriptoró omnium mirabiliũ dñi per ordi
nem profetetur Acta autó omniu apostolorum
35 sub uno libro scribta sunt Lucas obtime theofi
le conprindit quia sub praesentia eius singula
gerebantur sicut(e) et semote passionó Petri
euidenter declarat Sed (&) profectionó pauli
a(d)b ur
be(s) ad spaniã proficescentis Epistulae autem
40 Pauli quae a quo loco uel qua ex causa directe
sint uolen(ta)tibus intellegere Ipse declarant
Primũ omnium corintheis scysmae heresis In
terdicens deIncepsb callae*c*tis circumcisione
Romanis autẽ or(ni)dine scripturarum sed
(et)
45 principium earum (osd) esse ^{xpm} Intimans
prolexius scripsit de quibus sincolis Neces
se est ad nobis desputari Cum ipse beatus
apostolus paulus sequens prodecessoris sui
Iohannis ordinó nonnisi (c)*n*omenatĩ semptaó
50 eccles(e)*ii*s scribat ordine tali a corenthios
prima.ad efesios seconda ad philippinses ter
tia ad colosensis quarta ad calatas quin
ta ad tensaolenecinsis sexta. ad romanos
septima Uerum cor(e)intheis et *t*hesaolecen
55 sibus licet pro correbtione Itereretur una
tamen per omnem orbem terrae ecclesia
deffusa esse denoscitur Et Iohannis eñi In a
pocalebsy licet septó eccleseis scribat
tamen omnibus dicit uerũ ad filemonem una ·
60 et at titũ una et ad tymotheũ duas pro affec
to et dilectione In honore tamen eclesiae ca
tholice In ordinatione eclesiastice
[folio 11r] d(e)*i*scepline ^{scificate} sunt Fertur etiam ad
Laudecenses alia ad alexandrinos Pauli no

65 mine fincte ad he*r*esem marcionis et alia plu
ra quae In c(h)atholicam eclesiam recepi non
potest Fel enim cum melle misceri non con
cruit epistola sane Iude et superscrictio
Iohannis duas In catholica habentur Et sapi
70 entia ab amicis salomonis in honor*ḿ* ipsius
scripta apocalapse etiam Iohanis et Pe
tri tantum recip(e)*i*mus quam quidam ex nos
tris legi In eclesia nolunt Pastorem uero
nuperrim e(t) temporibus nostris In urbe
75 roma herma conscripsit sedente cathe
tra urbis romae aeclesiae Pio ᵉᵖ̄ˢ frat*r*e(r)
eius et ideo legi eum quid*ḿ* Oportet se pu
plicare uero In eclesia populo Neque inter
profe(*)tas conpletum numero Neque Inter
80 apostolos In fin*ḿ* temporum potest.
Arsinoi autem seu ualentini. uel mitiad(ei)*i*s
nihil In totum recipemus. Qui etiam nouũ
psalmorum librum marcioni conscripse
runt una cum basilide assianum catafry
85 cum con*s*itutorem . . .

Appendix B:
The Restored Latin Fragment

This appendix features David J. Theron's "restored" reading with more precise Latin spellings.[1] Words in bold are rubricated in the manuscript.

[folio10r] quibus tamen interfuit et ita posuit
tertium euangelii librum secundum Lucam
Lucas iste medicus post ascensum Christi
cum eum Paulus quasi itineris sui socium
5 secum adsumsisset nomine suo
ex opinione conscripsit — Dominum tamen nec ipse
uidit in carne — et idem prout assequi potuit
ita et a natiuitate Iohannis incepit dicere
quarti euangeliorum Iohannis ex discipulis
10 cohortantibus condiscipulis et episcopis suis
dixit conieiunate mihi hodie triduum et quid
cuique fuerit reuelatum alteratrum
nobis enarremus eadem nocte reuelatum Andreae ex apostolis ut recognis-
15 centibus cunctis Iohannes suo nomine
cuncta discriberet et ideo licet varia sin-

gulis euangeliorum libris principia
doceantur nihil tamen differt creden-
tium fidei cum uno ac principali spiritu de-
20 clarata sint in omnibus omnia de natiuitate de passione de resurrectione
de conuersatione cum discipulis suis
et de gemino eius aduentu
primum in humilitate despectus quod fu-

---

[1] Daniel J. Theron, *Evidence of Tradition: Selected Source Material for the Study of the History of the Early Church, Introduction and Canon of the New Testament* (Grand Rapids: Baker Book House, 1957), 106–13.

25 it secundum potestate regali prae-
clarum quod futurum est quid ergo

mirum si Iohannes tam constanter
singula etiam in epistolis suis proferat
dicens in semetipso quae uidimus oculis
30 nostris et auribus audiuimus et manus
nostrae palpauerunt haec scripsimus uobis
 [folio10v] Sic enim non solum uisorem sed et auditorem
sed et scriptorem omnium mirabilium Domini per ordinem profitetur Acta autem omnium apostolorum
35 sub uno libro scripta sunt Lucas optimo Theophi-
lo comprehendit, quae sub praesentia eius singula
gerebantur sicut et remote passionem Petri
evidenter declarat sed et profectionem Pauli
ab ur-
be ad Spaniam proficiscentis epistolae autem
40 Pauli quae a quo loco uel qua ex causa directae
sint uolentibus intelligere ipsae declarant
primum omnium Corinthiis schisma haeresis interdicens deinceps Galatis circumcisionem
Romanis autem ordine scripturarum sed
et
45 principium earum esse Christum intimans
prolixius scripsit de quibus singulis neces-

se est a nobis desputari cum ipse beatus
apostolus Paulus sequens prodecessoris sui
Iohannis ordinem nonnisi nominatim septem
50 ecclesiis scribat ordine tali ad Corinthios
prima ad Ephesios secunda ad Philippenses ter-
tia ad Colossenses quarta ad Galatas quin-
ta ad Thessalonicensibus sexta ad Romanos
septima uerum Corinthiis et Thessalonicen-

55 sibus licet pro correptione iteretur una
tamen per omnem orbem terrae ecclesia
diffusa esse denoscitur et Iohannes enim in A-
pocalypsi licet septem ecclesiis scribat
tamen omnibus dicit uerum ad Philemonem unam

60 et ad Titum unam et ad Timotheum duas pro affec-
tu et dilectione in honore tamen ecclesiae ca-
tholicae in ordinatione ecclesiasticae
[folio 11r] disciplinae sanctificatae sunt fertur etiam ad

Laodicenses alia ad Alexandrinos Pauli no-
65 mine fictae ad haeresem Marcionis et alia plura quae in catholicam ecclesiam recipi non
potest fel enim cum melle misceri non congruit epistola san Iudae et superscriptio

Iohannis duas in catholica habentur et Sapi-
70 entia ab amicis Salomonis in honorem ipsius
scripta apocalypses etiam Iohannis et Petri tantum recipimus quam quidam ex nostris legi in ecclesia nolunt pastorem uero

nuperrime temporibus nostris in urbe
75 Roma Hermas conscripsit sedente cathe-
dra urbis Romae ecclesiae Pio Episcopo fratre
eius et ideo legi eum quidem oportet se pu-
blicare uero in ecclesia populo neque inter
prophetas completum numero neque inter
80 apostolos in finem temporum potest

Arsinoi autem seu Ualentini uel Mitiadis
nihil in totum recipimus qui etiam nouum
psalmorum librum Marcioni conscripserunt una cum Basilide Assianum Catafrygum
85 constitutorem. . . .

Appendix C:
English Translation of the Fragment

Metzger's English translations of the Fragment follows.[1] The author chose to use Metzger's as an exemplar for the reader due to the fact that, though Metzger leans toward the Early Hypothesis, he is not an active proponent of either of the two hypotheses and thus his work is less likely to betray bias. Words in bold are rubricated in the manuscript.

Metzger's English translation follows:

> [folio 10r] ... at which nevertheless he was present, and so he placed [them in his narrative].
> **The third book of the Gospel is that according to Luke.**
> Luke, the well-known physician, after the ascension of Christ,
> when Paul had taken with him as one zealous for the law,
> 5 composed it in his own name,
> according to [the general] belief. Yet he himself had not
> seen the Lord in the flesh; and therefore, as he was able to ascertain events,
> so indeed he begins to tell the story from the birth of John.
> **The fourth of the Gospels is that of John, [one] of the disciples.**
> 10 To his fellow disciples and bishops, who had been urging him [to write],
> he said, 'Fast with me from today for three days, and what will be revealed to each one
> let us tell it to one another.' In the same night it was revealed to Andrew, [one] of the apostles,
> 15 that John should write down all things in his own name
> while all of them should review it. And so, though various
> elements may be taught in the individual books of the Gospels,
> nevertheless this makes no difference to the faith
> of believers, since by the one sovereign Spirit all things
> 20 have been declared in all [the Gospels]: concerning the

---

[1] Metzger, *The Canon of the New Testament*, 305–7.

nativity, concerning the passion, concerning the resurrection,
concerning life with his disciples,
and concerning his twofold coming;
the first in lowliness when he was despised, which has taken place,
25 the second glorious in royal power,
which is still in the future. What
marvel is it then, if John so consistently
mentions these particular points also in his Epistles,
saying about himself, "What we have seen with our eyes
30 and heard with our ears and our hands
have handled, these things we have written to you"?
[folio 10v] For in this way he professes [himself] to be not only an eye-witness and hearer,
but also a writer of all the marvelous deeds of the Lord, in their order.
Moreover, the acts of all the apostles
35 were written in one book. For "most excellent Theophilus" Luke compiled
the individual events that took place in his presence—
as he plainly shows by omitting the martyrdom of Peter
as well as the departure of Paul from the city [of Rome]
when he journeyed to Spain. As for the Epistles of
40 Paul, they themselves make clear to those desiring to understand,
which ones [they are],
from what place, or for what reason they were sent.
First of all, to the Corinthians, prohibiting their heretical schisms;
next, to the Galatians, against circumcision;
then to the Romans he wrote at length, explaining
45 the order (or, plan) of the Scriptures, and also that Christ is their principle
(or, main theme). It is necessary
for us to discuss these one by one, since the blessed
apostle Paul himself, following the example of his predecessor
John, writes by name to only seven
50 churches in the following sequence: to the Corinthians
first, to the Ephesians second, to the Philippians third,
to the Colossians fourth, to the Galatians fifth,
to the Thessalonians sixth, to the Romans
seventh. It is true that he writes once more to the Corinthians and to
55 the Thessalonians for the sake of admonition,
yet it is clearly recognizable that there is one Church
spread throughout the whole extent of the earth. For John also in the
Apocalypse, though he writes to seven churches,

nevertheless speaks to all. [Paul also wrote] out of affection and love one to Philemon,
60 one to Titus, and two to Timothy; and these are held sacred
in the esteem of the Church catholic
for the regulation of ecclesiastical
[folio 11r] discipline. There is current also [an epistle] to
the Laodiceans, [and] another to the Alexandrians, [both] forged in Paul's
65 name to [further] the heresy of Marcion, and several others
which cannot be received into the catholic Church
—for it is not fitting that gall be mixed with honey.
Moreover, the epistle of Jude and two of the above-mentioned (or, bearing the name of)
John are counted (or, used) in the catholic [Church]; and [the book of] Wisdom,
70 written by the friends of Solomon in his honor.
We receive only the apocalypses of John and Peter,
though some of us are not willing that the latter be read in church.
But Hermas wrote the Shepherd
very recently, in our times, in the city of Rome,
75 while bishop Pius, his brother, was occupying the [episcopal] chair
of the church of the city of Rome.
And therefore it ought indeed to be read; but
it cannot be read publicly to the people in church either among
the prophets, whose number is complete, or among
80 the apostles, for it is after [their] time.
But we accept nothing whatever of Arsinous or Valentinus or Miltiades,
who also composed
a new book of psalms for Marcion,
together with Basilides, the Asian
85 founder of the Cataphrygians…

Bibliography

Aland, Kurt, et al., eds. *The Greek New Testament*. 3rd ed. New York: United Bible Societies, 1975.

Amelli, Ambrogio M, ed. *Miscellanea Cassinese, ossia nuovi contributi alia storia, alle scienze e arti religiose, raccolti e illustrati per cura dei PP, Benedettini di Montecassino*. Monte Cassino: Tipografia di Montecassino, 1897.

Armstrong, Jonathan J. "Victorinus Pettau as the Author of Canon Muratori." *Vigiliae Christianae* 62, no. 1 (2008): 1–34.

Barnes, E. "Inference to the Loveliest Explanation." *Synthese* 103, no. 2 (May 1995): 251–77.

Bartlet, Vernon. "Melito the Author of the Muratorian Canon." *The Expositor* 2 (1906): 214–24.

Barton, John. *The Spirit and the Letter: Studies in the Biblical Canon*. London: SPCK, 1997.

Bauer, Walter. *Rechtgläubigkeit und Ketzerei im ältesten Christentum*. Tübingen, 1934.

Brown, Raymond E. *The Epistles of John*. Garden City, NY: Doubleday, 1982.

Bruce, F. F. *The Canon of Scripture*. Downers Grover, IL: InterVarsity, 1988.

———. "Some Thoughts on the Beginning of the New Testament Canon." *Bulletin of the John Rylands Library* 65, no. 2 (1983): 37–60.

Buchler, Justus, ed. *The Philosophy of Peirce: Selected Writings*. London: Routledge, 2014.

Bunsen, C. *Analecta Ante-Nicaena*. London: Longman, Brown, Green, and Longmans, 1854.

Bynon, Theodora. *Historical Linguistics*. Cambridge: Cambridge University Press, 1977.

Campbell, Lyle. *Historical Linguistics: An Introduction*. Edinburgh: Edinburgh University Press, 1998.

Campenhausen, Hans von. *The Formation of the Christian Bible*. Philadelphia: Fortress Press, 1972.

Campos, Julio Ruiz. "Epoca del Fragmento Muratoriano." *Helmántica* 11, no. 34–36 (1960): 485–496.

Chapman, J. "Clement d'Alexandrie sur les fevangiles, et encore le Fragment de Muratori." *RBén* 21 (1904).

Childs, Brevard S. *The NT as Canon: An Introduction*. Philadelphia: Fortress, 1984.

Collins, Raymond F. *Introduction to the New Testament*. Garden City, NY: Doubleday, 1983.

Credner, Karl August. *Zur Geschichte des Kanons*. Halle: Verlag der Buchhandlung des Waisenhauses, 1847.

Dahl, Nils A. "Welche Ordnung der Paulusbriefe wird vom muratorischen Kanon vorausgesetzt?" *Zeitshrift für die neutestamentlische Wissenschaft* 52 (1961): 39–53.

———. "The Origin of the Earliest Prologues to the Pauline Letters." *Semeia* 12 (1978): 233–77.

Day, T. and H. Kincaid. "Putting Inference to the Best Explanation in its Place." *Synthese* 98, no. 2 (February 1994): 271–95.

Donaldson, James. *A Critical History of Christian Literature and Doctrine: From the Death of the Apostles to the Nicene Council*. Vol. 3, *The Apologists (Continued)*. London, Macmillan, 1866.

Dunelm, J. B. "The Muratorian Fragment." *The Academy* 36, no. 907 (September 21, 1889).

Ehrhardt, A. A. T. "The Gospels in the Muratorian Fragment." *Ostkirchliche Studien* 2 (1953): 121–38.

Erbes, Carl. "Die Zeit des Muratorischen Fragments." *Zeitschrift für Kirchengeschichte* 35 (1914): 331–62.

Farkasfalvy, Denis M. "The Ecclesial Setting of Pseudepigraphy in Second Peter and its Role in the Formation of the Canon." *The Second Century* 5, no. 1 (Spring, 1985–1986).

Farmer, William F. and Denis M. Farkasfalvy. *The Formation of the NT Canon: An Ecumenical Approach*. New York: Paulist, 1983.

Ferguson, Everett. "Canon Muratori: Date and Provenance." In *Studia Patristica*. Vol. 19, edited by Elizabeth A. Livingstone, 677–83. Oxford, UK: Pergamon, Press, 1982.

Gallagher, Edmon and John Meade. *The Biblical Canon Lists from Early Christianity: Texts and Analysis*. New York: Oxford University Press, 2017.

Gamble, Harry T. "Canon. NT," in *Anchor Bible Dictionary*. New York: Doubleday, 1992.

———. *The New Testament Canon: Its Making and Meaning*. Philadelphia: Fortress, 1985.

Guignard, Christophe. "The Muratorian Fragment as a Late Antique Fake? An Answer to C. K. Rothschild." *Revue Des Sciences Religieuses* 93, no. 1/2 (2019): 73–90

———. "The Original Language of the Muratorian Fragment." *Journal of Theological Studies* 66, no. 2 (October 2015): 596–624.

Hahneman, Geoffrey M. "More on Redating the Muratorian Fragment." In *Studia Patristica*. Vol. 19, edited by Elizabeth A. Livingstone, 359–65. Leuven, BE: Peeters Press, 1989.

———. "The Muratorian Fragment and the Development of the Canon." D.Phil. thesis, University of Oxford, 1987.

———. *The Muratorian Fragment and the Development of the Canon*. Oxford, UK: Clarendon Press, 1992.

Harman, Gilbert. "The Inference to the Best Explanation." *Philosophical Review* 74, no. 1 (January 1965): 88–95.

Harnack, Adolf von. "Das Muratorische Fragment." *Zeitschrift für Kirchengeschichte* 3 (1878).

———. "Über den Verfasser und den literarischen Charakter des Muratorischen Fragments." *Zeitschrift für die Neutestamentliche Wissenschaft* (1925).

Heckel, Theo K. *Vom Evangelium des Markus zum viergestaltigen Evangelium*. Tübingen: Mohr Siebeck, 1999.

Henne, Philippe. "La Datation du 'Canon' de Muratori." *Revue Biblique* 100, no. 1 (1993): 54–75.

Hesse, Friedrich Hermann. *Das Muratorische Fragment*. Giessen: J. Ricker'sche, 1873.

Hill, Charles E. "The Debate Over the Muratorian Fragment and the Development of the Canon." *Westminster Theological Journal* 57, no. 2 (Fall 1995): 437–52.

Horbury, William. "The *Wisdom of Solomon* in the Muratorian Fragment." *Journal of Theological Studies* 45, no. 1 (April 1994): 149–59.

Hug, Johann Leonhard. *Einleitung in die Schriften des Neuen Testaments*. 4th ed. Vol. 1. Stuttgart: Cotta, 1847.

Katz, Peter. "The Johannine Epistles in the Muratorian Canon." *Journal of Theological Studies* 8, no. 2 (October 1957): 273–74.

Kelly, J. N. D. *Early Christian Creeds*. 2nd ed. London: Longmans, Green and Co., 1960.

Koch, Hugo. "Zu A.v.Harnacks Beweis für den amtlichen römischen Ursprung des Muratorischen Fragments." *Zeitschrift für die Neutestamentliche Wissenschaft* 24 (1925): 154–63.

Koester, Helmut. *Ancient Christian Gospels: Their History and Development*. London: SCM, 1990.

Köstenberger, Andreas J. and Michael J. Kruger. *The Heresy of Orthodoxy: How Contemporary Culture's Fascination with Diversity Has Reshaped Our Understanding of Early Christianity.* Wheaton, IL: Crossway, 2010.

Kuhn, Gottfried. *Das muratorische Fragment über die Bücher des Neuen Testaments: Mit Einleitung und Erklärung.* Zurich: Höhr, 1892.

Kümmel, Werner Georg. *Einleitung in das Neue Testament.* 17th ed. Heidelberg: Quelle und Meyer, 1975.

Leipoldt, Johannes. *Geschichte des neutestamentlichen Kanons: Erster Teil, Die Entstehung.* Leipzig: Hinrichs, 1907.

Lightfoot, Joseph Barber. *The Apostolic Fathers: A Revised Text with Introduction, Notes, Dissertations, and Translations.* London: MacMillan, 1885.

Lipton, Peter. *Inference to the Best Explanation.* 2nd ed. London: Routledge, 2004.

Magistris, Simon de. *Daniel secundum septuaginta ex tetraplis Origenis nunc primum editus.* Rome: Typis Propagandae Fidei, 1772.

McCullagh, C. Behan. *Justifying Historical Descriptions.* Cambridge: Cambridge University Press, 1984.

———. *The Logic of History: Putting Postmodernism in Perspective.* London: Routledge, 2004.

McDonald, Lee Martin. *The Biblical Canon: Its Origin, Transmission, and Authority.* Grand Rapids: Baker Academic, 2007).

———. *The Formation of the Christian Bible.* 2nd ed. Peabody, MA: Hendrickson, 1995.

McDonald, Lee M., and James A. Sanders, eds. *The Canon Debate.* Grand Rapids: Baker Academic, 2002.

Metzger, Bruce M. *The Canon of the New Testament: Its Origin, Development, and Significance.* Oxford, UK: Clarendon Press, 1987.

Mohrmann, Christine. "Les Origines de La Latinite Chretienne À Rome." *Vigiliae Christianae* 3, no. 2 (April 1949): 67–106.

Moule, Charles F. D. *The Birth of the New Testament.* London: Continuum, 2002.

Muratori, Ludovico Antonio. Vol. 3, *Antiquitates italicæ mediiævi: sive dissertations de moribus, ritibus, religione, regimine, magistratibus, legibus, studiis literarum, artibus, lingua, militia, nummis, principibus, libertate, servitute, foederibus, aliisque faciem & mores italici populi referentibus post declinationem Rom. imp. ad annum usque MD*. Mediolanum, IT: Ex typographia Societatis palatinæ, 1740.

Osiek, Carolyn. *The Shepherd of Hermas: A Commentary*. Minneapolis: Fortress, 1999.

Psillos, S. "Simply the Best: A Case for Abduction." In *Computational Logic: Logic Programming and Beyond*, edited by A. C. Kakas and F. Sadri, 605–26. Berlin: Springer-Verlag, 2002.

Quasten, Johannes. *Patrology*. 4 vols. Westminster, MD: Christian Classics, 1950.

Quinn, Jerome D. "P46, The Pauline Canon?" *The Catholic Biblical Quarterly* 36, no. 3 (July 1974): 379–85.

Reicke, Bo. *Re-examining Paul's Letters: The History of the Pauline Correspondence*. Harrisburg, PA: Trinity, 2001.

Roberts, Alexander and James Donaldson, eds. *The Ante-Nicene Fathers (ANF)*. 10 vols. 1885–1887. Reprint, Peabody, MA: Hendrickson, 1995.

Robinson, John A. T. *Redating the New Testament*. London: SCM, 1976.

Rothschild, Clare K. "The Muratorian Fragment and Roman Fake." *Novum Testamentum* 60, no. 1 (2018): 55–82.

Schaff, Philip and Henry Wace, eds. *The Nicene and Post-Nicene Fathers (NPNF)*. 14 vols. 1890–1900. Reprint, Peabody, MA: Hendrickson, 1995.

Schnabel, Eckhard J. "The Muratorian Fragment: The State of Research." *Journal of the Evangelical Theological Society* 57, no. 2 (2014): 231–64.

Schneemelcher, Wilhelm, ed., and R. McL. Wilson, trans. *New Testament Apocrypha*. Vol. 1, *Gospels and Related Writings*. Rev. ed. Louisville, KY: Westminster John Knox Press, 1991.

Smith, William, and Henry Wace, eds*., Literature, Sects and Doctrines: Being a Continuation of "The Dictionary of the Bible., Volume 1."* 3 vols. London: Murray, 1882.

Sober, Elliot. *Ockham's Razors: A User's Manual*. Cambridge: Cambridge University Press, 2015.

Stanton, Graham N. "The Fourfold Gospel." *New Testament Studies* 43, no. 3 (July 1997): 317–46.

Strauss, D. F. *Die christliche Glaubenslehre in ihrer geschichtlichen Entwicklung und im Kampfe mit der modernen Wissenschaft*. Vol. 1. Tübingen: Osiander, 1840.

Streeter, B. H. *The Primitive Church*. London: Macmillan, 1929.

Strong, James. *Strong's Exhaustive Concordance of the Bible*. Peabody, MA: Hendrickson.

Sundberg, Jr., Albert C. "The Bible Canon and the Christian Doctrine of Inspiration." *Interpretation* 29, no. 4 (October 1975): 352–71.

———. "Canon Muratori: A Fourth-Century List." *Harvard Theological Review* 66, no. 1 (1973): 1–41.

———. "The Old Testament of the Early Church (A Study in Canon)." PhD diss., Harvard University, 1957.

———. "Towards a Revised History of the NT Canon." In *Studia Evangelica*. Vol. 3, *Papers Presented to the Third International Congress on NT Studies held at Christ Church, Oxford, 1965, Part 1, The NT Scriptures*. Edited by Frank Leslie Cross. Berlin: Akademie-Verlag, 1968.

Thagard, P. "The Best Explanation: Criteria for Theory Choice." *Journal of Philosophy* 75, no. 2 (February 1978): 76–92.

Theron, Daniel J. *Evidence of Tradition: Selected Source Material for the Study of the History of the Early Church, Introduction and Canon of the New Testament.* Grand Rapids: Baker Book House, 1957.

Thiersch, H. W. J. *Versuch zur Herstellung des historischen Standpuncts für die Kritik der neutestamentlichen Schriften.* Erlangen, DE: Carl Heyder, 1845.

Tomassi, Paul. *Logic.* London: Routledge, 1999.

Tregelles, Samuel Prideaux. *Canon Muratorianus: The Earliest Catalogue of the Books of the New Testament.* Oxford: Cambridge, 1867.

———. "On a Passage in the Muratorian Canon." *The Journal of Classical and Sacred Philology*, 2 (March 1855): 37–43.

Venerable Ambrosian Library. "Manuscript Publication: 676–750." Accessed December 21, 2018. ambrosiana.comperio.it/opac/detail/view/ambro:catalog:76502.

Verheyden, Joseph. "The Canon Muratori: A Matter of Dispute." In *The Biblical Canons*, edited by J.-M. Auwers and H. J. De Jonge, 487–556. Leuven: Leuven University Press, 2003.

Walton, Douglas. *Abductive Reasoning.* Tuscaloosa: University of Alabama Press, 2005.

Westcott, Brooke Foss. *A General Survey of the History of the Canon of the New Testament.* 7th ed. London: Macmillan, 1896.

Zahn, Theodor. *Geschichte des neutestamentlichen Kanons.* Vol. 1, *Das Neue Testament vor Origenes.* Erlangen, DE: Deichert, 1888–1889.

———. *Geschichte des neutestamentlichen Kanons.* Vol. 2, *Urkunden und Belege zum ersten und dritten Band.* Erlangen, DE: Deichert, 1890.

Zimmermann, Friedrich Gottlieb. *Dissertatio historico-critica scriptoris incerti de canone librorum sacrorum fragmentum a Muratorio repertum exhibens.* Jena: Göpferdt, 1805.

www.ingramcontent.com/pod-product-compliance
Lightning Source LLC
Chambersburg PA
CBHW070900080526
44589CB00013B/1152